First-Century Gospel Storytellers and Audiences

Biblical Performance Criticism Series
Orality, Memory, Translation, Rhetoric, Discourse

David Rhoads, Kelly R. Iverson, and Peter S. Perry Series Editors

The ancient societies of the Bible were overwhelmingly oral. People originally experienced the traditions now in the Bible as oral performances. Focusing on the ancient performance of biblical traditions enables us to shift academic work on the Bible from the mentality of a modern print culture to that of an oral/scribal culture. Conceived broadly, biblical performance criticism embraces many methods as means to reframe the biblical materials in the context of traditional oral cultures, construct scenarios of ancient performances, learn from contemporary performances of these materials, and reinterpret biblical writings accordingly. The result is a foundational paradigm shift that reconfigures traditional disciplines and employs fresh biblical methodologies such as theater studies, speech-act theory, and performance studies. The emerging research of many scholars in this field of study, the development of working groups in scholarly societies, and the appearance of conferences on orality and literacy make it timely to inaugurate this series. For further information on biblical performance criticism, go to www.biblicalperformancecriticism.org.

Books in the Series

Holly E. Hearon & Philip Ruge-Jones, editors
The Bible in Ancient and Modern Media

James A. Maxey
From Orality to Orality:
A New Paradigm for Contextual Translation of the Bible

Antoinette Clark Wire
The Case for Mark Composed in Performance

Robert D. Miller II, SFO
Oral Tradition in Ancient Israel

Pieter J. J. Botha
Orality and Literacy in Early Christianity

James A. Maxey & Ernst R. Wendland, editors
Translating Scripture for Sound and Performance

J. A. (Bobby) Loubser
Oral and Manuscript Culture in the Bible

Joanna Dewey
The Oral Ethos of the Early Church

Richard A. Horsley
Text and Tradition in Performance and Writing

Kelly R. Iverson, editor
From Text to Performance:
Narrative and Performance Criticisms in Dialogue and Debate

Annette Weissenrieder &
Robert B. Coote, editors
The Interface of Orality and Writing:
Speaking, Seeing, Writing in the Shaping of New Genres

Thomas E. Boomershine
The Messiah of Peace:
A Performance-Criticism Commentary on Mark's Passion-Resurrection Narrative

Terry Giles & William J. Doan
The Naomi Story—The Book of Ruth From Gender to Politics

Bernhard Oestreich
Performance Criticism of the Pauline Letters

Marcel Jousse
Edgard Sienaert, editor
Memory, Memorization, and Memorizers
The Galilean Oral-Style Tradition and Its Traditionists

Margaret E. Lee, editor
Sound Matters
New Testament Studies in Sound Mapping

First-Century Gospel Storytellers and Audiences

The Gospels as Performance Literature

THOMAS E. BOOMERSHINE

CASCADE *Books* · Eugene, Oregon

FIRST-CENTURY GOSPEL STORYTELLERS AND AUDIENCES
The Gospels as Performance Literature

Biblical Performance Criticism Series 17

Cascade Books
An Imprint of Wipf and Stock Publishers
199 W. 8th Ave., Suite 3
Eugene, OR 97401

www.wipfandstock.com

PAPERBACK ISBN: 978-1-6667-3382-2
HARDCOVER ISBN: 978-1-6667-2878-1
EBOOK ISBN: 978-1-6667-2879-8

Cataloguing-in-Publication data:

Names: Boomershine, Thomas E., author.

Title: First-century gospel storytellers and audiences : the gospels as performance literature / Thomas E. Boomershine.

Description: Eugene, OR: Cascade Books, 2022. | Biblical Performance Criticism Series 17. | Includes bibliographical references and index.

Identifiers: ISBN 978-1-6667-3382-2 (paperback). | ISBN 978-1-6667-2878-1 (hardcover). | ISBN 978-1-6667-2879-8 (ebook).

Subjects: LSCH: Bible.—Gospels—Criticism, interpretation, etc. | Bible.—Mark—Criticism, interpretation, etc. | Bible.—John—Criticism, interpretation, etc. | Storytelling—Religious aspects—Christianity. | Performance Criticism. | Oral tradition.

Classification: BS2555.55 B66 2022 (print). | BS2555.55 (ebook).

Contents

Acknowledgments

The author and the publisher gratefully acknowledge the permission to publish the following articles and essays in revised form.

"Jesus of Nazareth and the Watershed of Ancient Orality and Literacy." *Semeia* 65 (1994) 7–36.

"The Narrative Technique of Mark 16:8." *JBL* 100 (1981) 213–23.

"Mark 16:8 and the Apostolic Commission." *JBL* 100 (1981) 225–39.

"Peter's Denial as Polemic or Confession: The Implications of Media Criticism." *Semeia* 39 (1987) 47–68.

"The New Testament Soundscape and the Puzzle of Mark 16:8." In *Sound Matters: New Testament Studies in Sound Mapping*, edited by Margaret E. Lee, 215–44. BPCS 16. Eugene, OR: Cascade Books, 2018.

"Teaching Mark as Performance Literature: Early Literate and Post-Literate Pedagogies." In *Communication, Pedagogy and the Gospel of Mark*, edited by Elizabeth E. Shively and Geert van Oyen, 73–94. SBL Resources for Biblical Studies 83. Atlanta: SBL Press, 2016.

"Audience Address and Purpose in the Performance of Mark." In *Mark as Story: Retrospect and Prospect*, edited by Kelly R. Iverson and Christopher W. Skinner, 115–44. SBL Resources for Biblical Studies 65. Atlanta: SBL Press, 2011.

"Audience Asides and Mark's Audience: The Difference Performance Makes." In *From Text to Performance: Narrative and Performance Criticisms in Dialogue and Debate*, edited by Kelly R. Iverson, 80–96. BPCS 10. Eugene, OR: Cascade Books, 2014.

"The Medium and Message of John: Audience Address and Audience Identity in the Fourth Gospel." In *The Fourth Gospel in First-Century Media Culture*, edited by Anthony Le Donne and Tom Thatcher, 92–120. LNTS 426. London: T. & T. Clark, 2011.

Abbreviations

AB   Anchor Bible

ABD   *The Anchor Bible Dictionary*. Edited by David Noel Freedman.
            6 vols. New York: Doubleday, 1992

BAMM   The Bible in Ancient and Modern Media

BDAG   Walter Bauer, Frederick W. Danker, W. F. Arndt, and F. W. Gin-
            grich. *A Greek–English Lexicon of the New Testament and Other
            Early Christian Literature*. 3rd ed. Chicago: University of Chi-
            cago Press, 2000

BJS   Brown Judaic Studies

BDF   F. Blass, A. Debrunner, and Robert W. Funk, *Greek Grammar of
            the New Testament*. Chicago: University of Chicago Press, 1961

BPCS   Biblical Performance Criticism Series

CEV   Contemporary English Version

ET   English translation

JB   Jerusalem Bible

JBL   *Journal of Biblical Literature*

JTS   *Journal of Theological Studies*

LNTS   Library of New Testament Studies

NAB   New American Bible

NEB   New English Bible

NA28   *Novum Testamentum Graece* (Nestle–Aland). 28th ed. Edited by
            Holger Strutwolf. Stuttgart: Deutsche Bibelgesellschaft, 2012

NIV   New International Version

NRSV   New Revised Standard Version

NT	New Testament
NTS	*New Testament Studies*
RSV	Revised Standard Version
SBL	Society of Biblical Literature
TEV	Today's English Version
UBS5	*The Greek New Testament*. 5th rev. ed. Edited by Holger Strutwolf. Stuttgart: Deutsche Bibelgesellschaft, American Bible Society, United Bible Societies, 2014
WH	Westcott–Hort Greek New Testament
ZNW	*Zeitschrift für die neutestamentliche Wissenschaft und die Kunde des älteren Kirche*
ZTK	*Zeitschrift für Theologie und Kirche*

Introduction, Conclusions, and the Future

The purpose of the essays in this collection is to investigate the four canonical Gospels in their original historical context as compositions of sound that were performed by storytellers for audiences. This introduction will briefly tell the story of some of the influences and experiences that have shaped this body of work over some fifty years and the methodological evolution of what is now being called performance criticism. These chapters offer a critique: historical-critical study of the Bible has been based on a pervasive anachronism read back into the ancient world. That anachronism presupposes that the media culture of the seventeenth to nineteenth centuries was basically continuous with the media culture of the ancient world. The Bible has been seen as a library of texts that were read by individual readers generally in silence.

In contrast, the foundational proposal of performance criticism is that the Bible was a series of compositions of sound that were performed for audiences of predominantly illiterate persons by storytellers variously with or without a manuscript. These essays are initial experiments focused on Mark and John that seek to identify the implications of this new paradigm for the perception and interpretation of the Gospels in their original historical context. This collection explores the first-century origins of the Gospels in performance.

Early Engagement with Biblical Performance

My introduction to historical-critical study of the Bible was the first semester required "Introduction to the Old Testament" course with Dr. James Muilenburg (Union Theological Seminary, 1962). The specter in the student oral tradition of OT Intro was the dreaded "Pentateuch Paper," a thirty-five page source-critical analysis of the JEPD strands in a Genesis

1

story, on which the entire grade depended. It was a baptism by fire in the documentary hypothesis.

In retrospect the course was also my introduction to performance criticism. Dr. Muilenburg was the first person I remember telling a biblical story. He had a craggy face topped by a shock of slightly unkempt white hair, the embodiment of a Hebrew prophet. As an integral part of his lecture on Genesis 2–3, he told the story of the man and the woman in the garden of Eden. It was fantastic! I remember it vividly some nearly sixty years later: "The Lord God brought to the man all the beasts of the field and the birds of the air to see what he would call them. And whatever the man called them, that was its name. He brought this big red beast to the man. And the man looked it up and down and said, "Hippo . . . potamus." And the Lord God said, "That's its name!" I can hear his voice now. That was Muilenburg! As a dramatist-poet English major, I found Muilenburg's storytelling to be more interesting than source criticism but the combination made a provocative stew.

Muilenburg also introduced us to Sigmund Mowinkel's description of the covenant renewal festivals in Israel. In Mowinkel's description these were dramatic reenactments of the enthronement of the king. The cultic drama was an annual autumn festival of the New Year.[1] The idea of a religious drama in the tradition of Israel opened a fascinating possibility for my fieldwork with teenagers in East Harlem. The church ran a neighborhood dance club five nights a week. Lots of teenagers came to the dance club, but they had nothing to do with the "religious" stuff of the church. I proposed that I would write a play that would be a combination of "West Side Story" and Mark's passion narrative if they would do it. We did it on Good Friday and it was a big hit. I was hooked on drama as a biblical performance art.

For the next three years (1963–1966) of my MDiv work, I pursued religious drama. I did three months of summer stock at the Missionary Orientation Center in Stony Point, New York. I wrote several plays: a Christmas pageant, a review called "East Harlem Swings," that was performed by a Neighborhood Youth Corps drama troupe of teenagers, and a series of dramatic liturgies for worship. In search of a theory of Christian drama, I wrote my senior thesis on a comparison of the parables of Jesus and the theatrical parables of Bertolt Brecht.

During my first ministerial appointment at First Congregational Church of Chicago, I started a drama program and studied theater games with Viola Spolin, who inspired the improvisational drama troupe at Second City in Chicago that in turn launched the careers of actors such as John

---

1. Mowinkle, *He That Cometh*, 80–84.

Belushi, Gilda Radner, Bill Murray, and Stephen Colbert. It also became increasingly clear, however, that religious drama was not going to be a viable ministerial career. Local churches just were not that interested in drama. From both a theoretical and a practical perspective, drama was a dead-end for the discovery of the primary performance traditions of the religion of Israel.

Storytelling and Black Preaching

The more I studied the Bible, the more I became convinced that books such as the Gospel of Mark were the product of storytelling rather than drama. However, the classic form-critical studies of the oral traditions that preceded the written Gospels—Bultmann's *History of the Synoptic Tradition* and Dibelius' *From Tradition to Gospel*—concluded that the oral tradition consisted only of short stories and sayings that were later strung together in longer written documents. When I experimented with telling those stories and sayings, they only took two or three minutes.

I wondered what the longer forms of performance of the Gospel tradition might have been. I have a vivid memory of the day in Chicago when I decided to experiment with reading the whole book of Mark aloud, in effect performing it for myself. I didn't make it past the messianic confession before I fell asleep. My initial experiment convinced me that the medium of the Gospel was not a reader reading Mark aloud to himself.

A month or so later, however, I went to a black Baptist church down the street for worship. The preacher was a storytelling preacher and in good black church tradition the sermon was long—over an hour and fifteen minutes. And at the end people were cheering for more! It was electric. He wove together stories from the Bible with a wide range of personal and contemporary stories. I learned from that great preacher, whose name I do not know, that it was possible to hold an audience for two hours, but only if it was in a far more animated manner than my manuscript reading.

This experience raised a major question: What was the medium of Mark in its original historical context? I wondered about the style of the preacher as a window into the media world of Mark. I returned to Union (1967) to do a PhD in the storytelling traditions of early Christianity.

Narrative Criticism

A primary resource for my PhD study of early Christian storytelling was the narrative criticism of twentieth-century literary criticism I had learned at Earlham College. My introduction to narrative criticism was by Wayne Booth, who was my teacher and major advisor for four years as he was writing his major work, *The Rhetoric of Fiction*. The basic approach of Booth's work was to analyze the interactions between the narrator, the implied author, and the reader. This included detailed analysis of the interaction of various styles of narrative guidance, the control of distance in characterization, the establishment and appeals to norms of judgment and the engagement of the reader in the twists and turns of plot in literary storytelling. Booth devoted an entire chapter to an analysis of the control of distance in Jane Austen's *Emma* along with extensive commentary on Laurence Stern's *Tristram Shandy*.

Booth's approach to literary criticism eschewed the identification of extrinsic causes of a literary work such as an author's biography, historical setting, or literary sources and sought an intrinsic description of the internal dynamics of the work itself, a characteristic emphasis of the "new" criticism. At the core of this inquiry was his fascination with the complexities of the interactions between the author and the reader, a theme that he developed in a later book, *The Company We Keep*.

The application of Booth's narrative criticism to the study of biblical narrative in a doctoral dissertation was more controversial than I anticipated. My dissertation proposal to study Mark's Passion/Resurrection Narrative as a story had been approved. I got all of the books on Mark out of the library and started working through them. But the more I read the more discouraged I became. There was a lot of highly speculative source-critical work on a pre-Markan passion narrative, quest of the historical Jesus works on the historical probabilities of Mark's account, and redaction-criticism descriptions of Mark's theology. But I was learning nothing about the story as a story. Unfortunately, Hans Frei's book, *The Eclipse of Biblical Narrative*, that explains the Enlightenment hermeneutics of meaning as ostensive and ideal reference, was still being conceived and would not be published until 1974. I was paralyzed and could see no way forward.

One afternoon, as I was agonizing about this dilemma, I heard an interior voice say, "Put away the books, memorize the story in Greek and tell it with your guitar." Although it seemed like an irrational and even crazy thing to do, I did what this inner voice said. And this experiment was immensely revealing and energizing. My first performance of Mark's passion and resurrection narrative in Greek was for my colleague, Adam Bartholomew. I remember the somewhat quizzical look on his face. As part of my ongoing research, I began telling stories from Mark's Gospel for audiences: classes at Union, coffee houses in New York, churches, scripture lessons in James Chapel, and local church worship services. My storytelling experiments confirmed that Mark's story was a viable oral narrative that could be analyzed and experienced as a story rather than as a referential document for the identification of historical facts and theological ideas.

I submitted a dissertation that was a detailed analysis of Mark's Passion and Resurrection Narrative as an oral narrative. While the dissertation was framed in the methodological categories of "rhetorical criticism" as outlined by Muilenberg in his 1968 SBL presidential address, "Form Criticism and Beyond," it was actually narrative criticism in a rhetorical-criticism frame. The central chapters were two-hundred-fifty pages of description of the narrative characteristics of Mark's story, first in a diachronic verse by verse analysis of the story, and then in a synchronic analysis of the story's narrative point of view and commentary, dynamics of characterization, norms of judgment, and plot. A sixty-page chapter then outlined the conclusion that a narrative analysis revealed a radically different picture of the meaning and impact of Mark's stories of Peter's denial, the trial before Pilate, and the women's flight and silence than the picture drawn by earlier scholarship. I assumed that this product of three years of intensive research and writing would be accepted as a new venture in biblical criticism. You can imagine my shock when the dissertation was rejected and I was told to start over on some other topic.

After extensive negotiations with the committee, it was agreed that I could submit the dissertation with no conclusions about the meaning of Mark's story in its original context. The major conclusion was that it was possible to study and gather coherent data about Mark's story as a story. The theoretical frame for that conclusion was that the form and medium of Mark's story was an integral dimension of its meaning and impact rather than an instrumental means of communicating a theological message. An integral part of the dissertation was an audiotape in which I first read the story in a typical pulpit tone and then told Mark's story in English and in Greek. In spite of reservations about rhetorical/narrative criticism and the validity of such data, my committee approved the dissertation and granted the degree. The three articles in this volume on the ending of Mark at 16:8 and the chapter on Peter's denial are in each case a revision of the material from that 1974 dissertation. This experience seared into my brain the conviction that the development of narrative criticism and storytelling was a major change that I could only describe as a paradigm shift in biblical scholarship.

The Network of Biblical Storytellers and the SBL Literary Aspects of the Gospels and Acts Group

Another major influence in the research that has led to these essays took place almost exactly six months after the completion of the PhD. On Nov. 9, 1974, at about 8:30 on Saturday morning, I was driving to the Bedford-Stuyvesant neighborhood of New York to teach in a certificate program of New York Theological Seminary. My car overheated and I stopped at a filling station on the Bronx River Parkway to get help. I was standing in back of a car waiting to talk to the attendant when he yelled, "Watch out!" Another car came off the parkway too fast and hit me. My legs were severely fractured. I was in casts for six months and out of work for a year. During this time I found that telling myself the stories I had learned for my dissertation research, especially the healing of the paralytic, were a great source of energy and hope in the long process of recovery. I then began to wonder what would happen if I taught other people to learn and tell the stories so that they, too, would know some Jesus stories by heart in their times of crisis.

After returning to teaching that next fall I experimented with ways of enabling others to learn and tell biblical stories. I developed a biblical storytelling workshop in which students learned a biblical story and explored the connections of that story with their own experience. Telling the stories quickly emerged as a significant resource for local church ministry. Within a year, a number of Masters and DMin students at New York Theological Seminary were actively telling biblical stories as a dimension of their ministries and needed support.

The Network of Biblical Storytellers International (originally NOBS, now NBSI) was launched in 1977. Years of small meetings and ongoing teaching led to the first Festival of Biblical Storytelling in 1985 and annual Festival Gatherings since 1989. The Network has continued to grow through the years and is now an international organization with significant impact around the world. NBSI has prompted research on the biblical storytelling tradition both in its original historical context and in the global village of the twenty-first century. Storytelling performances of the Gospels have proved to be a highly generative process.

In that same time period (1976–1979), I discovered that I was not the only person who was exploring narrative study of the Gospels. The first realization was meeting David Rhoads who became my roommate at the annual meetings of the Society of Biblical Literature (SBL) for the next twenty years. David had read my dissertation and thought it was great. It was the first enthusiastic affirmation of the dissertation I had received. David has been a major influence in the generation of these essays over the years and now as an editor. I joined the Literary Aspects of the Gospels and Acts working group at SBL (1978) in which I found a community of persons who were utilizing narrative-critical methods. That group, to which I am deeply indebted, included David Rhoads, Joanna Dewey, Robert Tannehill, Robert Fowler, and Elizabeth Struthers Malbon.

In the discussions of that group, however, I was increasingly uneasy because of the underlying assumption that the Gospel of Mark was like contemporary narratives with implied authors and unreliable narrators. I had become convinced that Mark was a storyteller who composed and told the Gospel, hence the title of the dissertation, *Mark, the Storyteller*. The experience of telling the stories made it clear that there was a major difference between a text read in silence and a composition told to an audience. However, in the Literary Aspects group we were studying the Gospels as narratives like modern novels read by readers in silence. This was natural since narrative-critical methods were developed for the study of the novels of the printing press era. I found it difficult to persuade my colleagues of the importance of this difference for the study of ancient stories and to pursue its methodological implications. This dilemma led to the next major influence on the development of these essays: media criticism.

Media Criticism and
The Bible in Ancient and Modern Media Group

During a course in my MDiv senior year at Union Theological Seminary (1965–1966), we were required to read Marshall McLuhan's new book, *Understanding Media* (1964). His mantra, *"the medium is the message,"* supported my sense that the interaction between the historic oral culture and the increasingly dominant literate culture in the ancient world was of major importance. I had the opportunity to investigate the relationship between the history of communication technology and the interpretation of the Bible during a partial leave of absence while teaching at United Theological Seminary in Dayton, Ohio (1981). I discovered the works of Walter Ong S.J., in particular *The Presence of the Word* and *Orality and Literacy*. Ong had done his master's work with McLuhan and both continued and broadened the research on the intersection between cultural and psychological formation and the evolution of communications technology.

I was also impressed by Eric Havelock's argument in *Preface to Plato* that Plato had expelled the poets from the Republic in order to break the strangle hold of the rhapsodes who performed Homer's epic poems, *The Iliad* and *The Odyssey*. This research confirmed my hypothesis that there was a direct correlation between major changes in the dominant medium of communication and the systems of biblical interpretation. The most graphic of those correlations was the invention of the printing press and the formation of historical criticism of the Bible based on the study of the original Greek and Hebrew texts. This "new" criticism in turn sponsored the distribution of vernacular translations of the Bible and energized the Reformation's ecclesiastical and political challenges to the "tradition."

Clarifying the impact of media change on biblical interpretation was and is a larger framework within which the interaction of orality and literacy in the Gospels can be understood. However, the investigation of the media of the Bible was a much larger project than I could accomplish. This project needed a research group. It was in the context of this dilemma that I met Werner Kelber. I had read Kelber's work on Mark including his collection of redaction-critical studies of Mark's passion narrative, *The Passion in Mark*. While our conclusions about Mark's passion narrative were radically different (as is reflected in the chapter in this volume on Peter's denial), we had both read Walter Ong and shared a strong interest in media studies.

In a memorable conversation at the 1980 SBL annual meeting in Dallas, Werner and I agreed that a wider community was needed. We decided that he would pursue the publication of his major work and I would seek to organize an SBL research group. After an initial rejection of my proposal in 1981 by the SBL program committee, I enlisted the support of Krister Stendahl at the 1982 annual meeting in New York. He was president of SBL that year and he shepherded a revised proposal through the program committee entitled "The Bible in Ancient and Modern Media." As historical congruence would have it, the publication of Kelber's book, *The Oral and the Written Gospel*, and the first meeting of what came to be known as BAMM both happened in 1983.

Those initiatives have borne great fruit. BAMM continues to be a center for ongoing research and we now have a much clearer picture of the media world of antiquity. The essay in this volume on Peter's denial was presented at the second BAMM session in Chicago, 1984. To my knowledge, it was the first time in history that a biblical story was performed at an SBL meeting. The presenters at that session included Walter Ong and Werner Kelber. And to my great surprise and delight, Wayne Booth was also present at that session. I remember how graciously Werner responded to my strong critique of his work. For the record, our conversations then have become the foundation of a close friendship. The chapter entitled "Biblical Megatrends" in this volume was presented at the BAMM session in Chicago, 1988. When Bernard Brandon Scott, another key member of BAMM, came bounding up after my paper, I knew I was on to something significant.

Happily, several of the members of the Literary Aspects group became central participants in the ongoing work of the Bible in Ancient and Modern Media group. Joanna Dewey served as co-chair of the group for several years. As is reflected in her volume in the Biblical Performance Criticism Series, Joanna has made a major contribution to our understanding of Mark as performance literature produced in the complex interaction of orality and literacy in antiquity.[2] She also was the editor of the Semeia volume in which the chapter in this volume titled "Jesus of Nazareth and the Watershed of Ancient Orality and Literacy" was published.[3]

The systematic investigation of the media of the Bible in the subsequent two and a half decades by a growing number of scholars associated with BAMM has led to a foundational conclusion. The current assumption that the Bible was a series of ancient texts read by individual readers often reading in silence is historically improbable. Most people in the ancient world could not read. One highly influential estimate by William Harris in his book, *Ancient Literacy*, is that the highest rate of literacy in urban centers was between 10–15% with the rates in rural areas and in earlier periods being much lower. The first century CE had the highest rates of literacy in the period of the biblical literary tradition (approximately 1000 BCE-100 CE). However, the percentage of literate persons and the various meanings of literacy remain highly contested.[4]

Regardless of the specific percentages of different levels of literacy, most people in the ancient world heard the Bible performed. Furthermore, in the relatively few accounts of individual readings from that period, the readers normally read aloud, essentially performing it for themselves. We can, therefore, conclude that the Bible was a series of compositions of sound that were performed for audiences. While there was a relatively small coterie of readers who were able to acquire manuscripts for private reading, this was unusual and atypical of the majority of persons who experienced biblical compositions. Widespread silent reading of the Bible by individual readers only happened in the centuries after the invention of the printing press.

---

2. Dewey, *The Oral Ethos of the Early Church*.

3. Dewey, ed., *Semeia* 65: *Orality and Textuality in Early Christian Literature*.

4. See, for example, Hurtado, "Oral Fixation"; and Hurtado, *Destroyer of the Gods*, 105–42.

Performance Criticism

The recent transition in scholarship from narrative criticism to performance criticism has grown out of the recognition that there was a fundamental difference between, on the one hand, the study of the Gospels and the Bible as textual traditions read by readers and, on the other hand, as oral traditions that were performed for audiences.

My first conscious awareness of the differences between a text read in silence by a reader and a composition performed for audiences was a poetry reading group I started as a senior English major at Earlham (1961–1962). I observed that poetry had significantly declined in its cultural impact since the days of Frost, Eliot, Yeats, and Cummings—household names in an earlier generation. I wondered why.

During a foreign study term in England the previous spring, I had experienced several Shakespearean plays that I had read in an earlier Shakespeare class. The performances at the Old Vic in London and at the Royal Shakespeare Theatre in Stratford-upon-Avon were exhilarating, and the contrast between the impact of my silent reading of the plays (often boring and frequently sleep inducing) and the performances was stark. It would be a travesty to omit from memory the powerful oral readings that Warren Staebler performed for us during his course on Shakespeare. Nevertheless, in the context of the beauty of great English poetry and its virtual disappearance from the cultural scene of the late twentieth century, I wondered what difference the performance of poetry might make. I recruited a group of English majors and we mounted some poetry readings.

It would be a misstatement of fact to say that the poetry reading group was a smash hit on campus. Attendance at our readings was small, but it was significant, fifty or so. Impact was minimal, especially outside the English majors. Not even all the English professors came. But the readings were terrific. The audiences loved it. Performance of poetry made a big impact, much more than silent reading. One of our readings was T. S. Eliot's 1939 *Old Possum's Book of Practical Cats*. Andrew Lloyd Weber must have had a similar insight in the development of his magnificent 1981 musical, "Cats," the fourth-longest-running show on Broadway. I concluded that a reason for the cultural decline of poetry was that people had stopped performing poetry for audiences and were reading the poems alone in silence.

A driving force in the background of biblical performance criticism in the 1990s was the actual performance of a range of biblical traditions in a variety of contexts: seminary classes, local churches, and the annual meetings of SBL. I had begun telling Gospel stories in classes and churches in the late 1960s. Hearing Alec McCowen's dramatic performance of Mark in

1971 confirmed my intuition that Mark could be told in one evening. David Rhoads has been a performance-criticism pioneer—as a performer, as the author of the initial proposals for biblical performance criticism, and as the editor of the Biblical Performance Criticism Series. He began performing Mark in the late 1970s and performed several biblical compositions at SBL: Mark, Galatians, and the Revelation of John. These performances in the intimidating context of the international consortium of scholars established the viability of biblical compositions as performance literature.

A further major influence on the development of these essays has been the work of generations of students in classes at New York Theological Seminary and United Theological Seminary. I began requiring students to learn and tell biblical stories as an integral part of my courses in 1975. The development of the pedagogy of performance in academic biblical courses has generated a multifaceted exploration of the interaction of ancient and modern ways of introducing students to the richness of the biblical tradition. The chapter in this volume on teaching Mark as performance literature outlines processes that are equally applicable to the full range of biblical compositions.

The exploration of audience address in ancient biblical performance grew out of a student performance of the Gospel of John. We divided up the book among the twenty students so that each person told a full chapter. It was the culmination to a semester of intensive study and exploration of ways of presenting Jesus as a character. In the long discourses of the Gospel, each student made Jesus present in distinctive ways.

In this climactic epic telling of John, as I listened, I realized that Jesus was addressing me as, variously, Nicodemus, the Jews who were torn between believing in him and wanting to kill him (5–12), and the disciples (13–17). I found myself being addressed by Jesus in a highly intensive manner that drew me into the experience of these characters. It wasn't the students addressing an audience that included their professor. It was each of them embodying Jesus who was addressing me, first as one who was interested in him such as Nicodemus, then as one who was torn between believing in him and rejecting him, then as a beloved disciple. The chapter in this volume on audience address and audience identity in John is an analysis of this clearly marked structure of the fourth Gospel.

Direct address to the audience by characters embodied by a storyteller is one of the major differences between storytelling performance and reading. Comments to a reader in a written work are between the author/narrator and a reader. The interaction takes place in the imagination of the reader. In the works of Henry Fielding, for example, the narrator addresses the reader frequently. In Laurence Sterne's *Tristram Shandy*, the story is primarily told in first person by the main character. The reader, however, is not addressed as a character in the story but as an observer. In effect, in the performance of the Gospels, the audience is invited to listen to Jesus as the characters in the story: e.g., as the disciples in Mark 13 and John 14–17, as Nicodemus in John 3, as scribes and Pharisees in Matthew 23. The chapter in this volume about the difference between narrative comments in a novel and audience asides in a storytelling performance is an analysis of this difference.

Another way of describing this dynamic of storytelling is the difference between the performance arts of drama and storytelling. In drama, there is usually no narrator and the actors usually play only one character each. The primary action takes place between the characters on the stage. The actors are separated from the audience by a kind of imaginary wall. In storytelling, on the other hand, the storyteller presents all of the characters but is first and foremost him/herself. The other persona in the performed story is the audience that, like the storyteller, "becomes" a variety of characters in interaction with the characters presented by the storyteller. There is no wall in storytelling. There are only two personas, the storyteller and the audience, both of whom can change character in the course of the story. Each art form has distinctive ways of engaging the audience. The chapters in this book about audience address in Mark and John address different dimensions of storytelling performance.

Sound Mapping

The last influence that has shaped these articles is the investigation of the Bible as sound. As a lifelong pianist and organist, I have loved the sound of music. The analogies between music and the Bible have been a source of revelation to me. One of those analogies is the relationship between musical manuscripts and biblical texts. Printed musical manuscripts have been a primary means for the transmittal of music. Over the centuries composers have developed an elaborate and highly sophisticated way of sharing their musical compositions by writing them out on lined paper.

These manuscripts include indications of volume, tempo, and rests. The marking of phrases by the drawing of curved lines is a central element of musical manuscripts. Those lines are indications of breathing marks. For vocalists and the players of wind instruments those lines are actual signals about when to breathe. For keyboard players they are the marks of the beginnings and endings of the phrases in a melody or rhythmical sequence. The manuscripts make it possible to reproduce the sound of the music with a high degree of connection to the composer's original inspiration. The manuscripts are recordings of sound for performance.

The identification of sound as the medium of biblical compositions means that biblical texts were recordings of sound. The recording of sound by records and audiotapes was not possible in the ancient world. The only way of recording sound was by writing out a manuscript. We have known for centuries that the trope marks in the Masoretic texts of the Hebrew were indications of melodic phrases. But there has been uncertainty about the musical markings in the Greek texts.

The development of sound mapping by Bernard Brandon Scott and Margaret Ellen Lee has initiated a new method for the analysis of the Greek biblical texts. A reading of the writings of the grammarians and rhetoricians of ancient Greece has revealed that they had a highly sophisticated system of composition. They thought in breath units and considered composition to be a linking of breaths building to a climax. The fundamental unit of composition was the "colon." Two or more cola were linked to form a "period." An ideal of Greek rhetorical address was a periodic composition in which a series of cola build up to periodic climaxes. Sound mapping is a way of indicating the cola and periods of a Greek composition in a written manuscript. The final chapter of this collection applies the basic principles of sound mapping to the analysis of Mark 16:8 as the auditory climax to the Gospel.

Conclusions

It may be helpful for readers to have a sense of where this collection of essays might lead. What follows is a summary of some of the conclusions implicit in these essays.

1) If the Bible was originally a collection of compositions of sound, biblical scholarship based on a silent reading of the compositions as texts is an inaccurate perception and interpretation of the Bible in its original historical context. Conclusions about the Bible as texts perceived by sight are based on a different set of sense data than the original compositions of sound. A Bible of sound is different than a Bible of sight. The incredibly complex systems in the human brain for the perception and processing of visual and auditory data, while often interacting, are separate and distinct. From the thousands of vibrating hairs in the inner ear to the millions of cones and rods in the retina, sense data of sound and sight are processed by different mechanisms. In as far as the goal of biblical scholarship is the

interpretation of the biblical compositions in their original context, it is essential that they be heard and analyzed as sound.

2) A related conclusion is that the sounds of the Bible were primarily heard by audiences rather than read by individual readers. A dimension of our communal problem is that "readers" has two distinct meanings. Since the Enlightenment, "the reader" has referred primarily to an individual sitting with a text reading in silence. "The reader" in this sense is named as the receiver of biblical sense data in most contemporary biblical commentaries and monographs. Likewise contemporary "reader response criticism" is a description of the experiential world of silent readers in interaction with texts. But in the ancient world, a "reader" was a performer who read a composition aloud for audiences who were predominantly illiterate. Thus, what could be called "audience response criticism" is a description of the interactions between an audience and a performer.

3) A further conclusion about ancient biblical performance is that there were two different types of performance: a storyteller with no manuscript in hand and a reader who read a text aloud. A major difference between these two performers, the teller and the reader, is the role of memory. The reader may have been required to memorize some or all of the manuscript being read because of the character of ancient manuscripts, but the manuscript was present. The teller, on the other hand, is totally reliant on memory. The recital of long oral poems from memory was a common practice in the ancient world. For example, the memorization and recital of the epic poems of Homer and Virgil was widespread. Thus, both forms of performance were present in antiquity. Future research may help to clarify their prevalence and character in ancient performance culture. But the common ground is the performance of compositions of sound.

4) The three chapters exploring the dynamics of audience address in the Gospels lead to a surprising conclusion: the audiences of the Gospels are almost always addressed as Judeans/Jews. The audiences are addressed as a wide range of Judean groups: scribes, Pharisees, Sadducees, the crowd, the women at the tomb, and most frequently—especially in the later sections of the Gospels—the disciples. The major exception to this pattern is the address to the Markan audience as Gentiles who do not know the Israelite traditions of observance of the purity laws (Mark 7:3–4).

This conclusion is in contrast to the conclusions that the audiences of the Gospels were the network of Christian congregations (Bauckham, *The Gospel for All Christians*) or a single Christian group (Marcus, *Mark 1–8, 9–16*). This pattern of audience address raises the question of the relationship between the audiences addressed in the Gospels and the actual historical audiences. While this strikingly consistent pattern does not necessarily mean that there is a correspondence between the audiences addressed and the actual audiences in the post-70 CE world, it does indicate a strong probability that there was a correlation between the two. After all, it makes sense to shape a composition for performances with the actual audiences who will be present.

The highest degree of correlation between the structures of audience address in the Gospels and Acts and the possible historical audiences in the post-70 CE world is with the communities of Hellenistic Jews who spoke Greek and lived in the cities of the Diaspora.[5] If then the stories were composed for performances to audiences of Hellenistic Judeans/Jews, they were not anti-Jewish. They were rather compositions that were engaged in Jewish sectarian dialogue and conflict in the aftermath of the Jewish-Roman war. This does not mean that Hellenistic Gentiles were excluded from Gospel audiences. Full and appropriate interaction with the Gospels by Gentiles did require, however, that they identify with the communities and traditions of Israel and hear the stories as Israelites.

The further inference from this data is that the Gospels were originally performed in a variety of venues in the world of the last quarter of the first century. The most frequent location may have been performances in private homes as an evening of storytelling entertainment. But the most important may have been performances of the Gospels in the network of Hellenistic Jewish synagogues in the ancient world. The Acts 2 list of devout Jews from every nation under heaven may be indicative of the geographic compass of the Gospels: "Parthians, Medes, Elamites, residents of Mesopotamia, Judea and Cappadocia, Pontus and Asia, Phrygia and Pamphylia, Egypt and the parts of Libya belonging to Cyrene, visitors from Rome both Jews and proselytes, Cretans and Arabs" (Acts 2:9–11a). Thus, the picture of Paul going first to the synagogues of his various cities was clearly credible for the early audiences of Acts. These were the most probable locations for the performance origins of the Gospels.

5) The three chapters in this volume on Mark 16:8 collect and outline evidence that 16:8 was the original intended ending of the Gospel. The analysis of its narrative characteristics and of the patterns of its sound reveal that in 16:8 the composer of Mark used techniques of composition in a climactic manner that are also utilized throughout the earlier sections of the story and throughout the history of Israelite storytelling. It is not an anomaly nor is it inadequate. The ending is a series of climactic short cola in which highly sympathetic characters do something that is, in the norms of the story, wrong. The effect of this ending is to invite the listeners to reflect

---

5. See Stark, "The Mission to the Jews," in *The Rise of Christianity*, 49–71.

on the women's commission to tell. Like the flight of the disciples and Peter's denial, this ending focuses the audience's attention on the challenge and cost of discipleship.

6) Sound mapping matters. The present editing of biblical texts in sentences and paragraphs misrepresents the sound characteristics of the compositions. The reconception and reediting of the Bible in the original units of sound will both provide a more accurate manuscript of the original character of the compositions and will facilitate the exegesis and performance of the compositions now.

The Future of Performance Criticism

It may be helpful for future pioneers on the performance criticism trail to sketch some possible dimensions of the future of biblical performance criticism. While it is certain that many of the following proposals will be applicable to the Hebrew and Aramaic compositions in the biblical collection, I will focus on the particularities of the Greek testament. Much of this futuristic sketch is an extension of initiatives taken in the volumes of the Biblical Performance Criticism series.

A first step is the delineation of the sound units of the Greek compositions, the cola, periods and perhaps episodes. Presenting those units in a manuscript sound map will facilitate the internalization and appropriate performance of the compositions. The sound mapping of the compositions of the New Testament will itself be a major project that will involve a reexamination of the existing manuscripts and papyri as recordings of sound. This will hopefully include the identification of the mnemonic cues that are structural elements of the compositions. Furthermore, the reformulation of "text" criticism as the analysis of traditions of manuscript sounds will identify a different set of criteria for the evaluation of the amazing variety of the manuscript traditions.

A second dimension will be the tracing of the relationship of the sounds of the biblical compositions to the other compositions in the cultural past and present of the ancient world that shape the connotations of the sounds heard by the audiences. These auditory connections of the Greek testament that Richard Hays has appropriately named as "echoes" are most frequently resonances with the Septuagint translation of the Hebrew/Aramaic testament and the various Greek compositions in the Apocrypha and Pseudepigrapha. But there is also the possibility that there are echoes with the vast traditions of compositions in classical Greek: e.g., rhetoric, drama, philosophy, epic poetry. In the case of the Gospels, there is a strong possibility of multifaceted connections with the Homeric epics, as Dennis McDonald's initial explorations have identified.

There may also be connections between particular auditory threads and performance gestures associated with those sounds. Whitney Shiner's delineation of the gestures in the comedies of Terence and the speeches of Quintilian as examples of gestures implicit in the performance of Mark is a major breakthrough in imagining how Mark sounded and looked.[6] Because of our constricted performance traditions for the recital of the Scriptures, much more attention needs to be given to the richly differentiated cultures of verbal performance in the ancient world. Ancient audiences brought those associations with them when encountering the performances of biblical compositions.

A sign of the need for the reorientation to performance is that we call this comparative work "intertextuality." We need a new word and "interorality" is not satisfactory. There are two dimensions of this reorientation. The first is the delineation of the relationship between the various traditions as echoes and interactions of sound rather than text. The second is understanding the complex and evolving interrelationship between the cultures of orality and literacy in the ancient world. Major works such as "The Dictionary of the Bible in Ancient Media," the collected essays of Werner Kelber (*Imprints, Voiceprints, and Footprints of Memory*) and the Biblical Performance Criticism Series provide a greatly enriched context for this ongoing research.

The further development of performance criticism will generate a series of detailed exegetical studies of particular compositions that will in turn be the basis for a new generation of commentaries. My monograph, *The Messiah of Peace: A Performance Criticism Commentary on Mark's Passion-Resurrection Narrative* is a step in that development. Given the amount of detailed study that has already been done on the compositions of the Bible, initial indications are that a very different picture of the meaning and impact of these compositions for ancient audiences will emerge from performance criticism exegesis. The assumption that the Bible was a library of texts read by readers has been a pervasive and often distorting influence on the perception of the meanings of these compositions in their original historical context. Detailed comparison of the exegetical results of this new perspective with previous exegesis often yields surprisingly different as well as supplementary conclusions.

---

6. Shiner, "Gesture and Movement," in *Proclaiming the Gospel*, 127–42.

This new perspective also has significant implications for biblical translation. As James Maxey has outlined in his monograph,[7] oral translation seeks to communicate the impact of the sound of the compositions in their original performances as well as for performance in the various languages of our own time and place. A new generation of translations for performance is needed. The creation of this new series of biblical translations will reestablish the centrality of testing new translations by performance that was the practice of the King James translators. These new translations will be based on performance, intended for performance, and tested by performance.

A central feature of the future of performance criticism will be the full integration of performance in scholarly methodology. A new dimension of the investigation of these ancient compositions will be performances of major sections and whole books. Learning and performing larger compositions reveals distinctive dimensions of their original meaning and impact such as structures of memory and audience interaction. In Genesis, for example, the primeval epic (Gen 1–11), the Abraham stories (Gen 12–23), the Jacob stories (Gen 28–36), and the Joseph cycle (Gen 37, 39–50) are extended stories shaped by and for performance. In the Greek testament, each of the books including the Acts of the Apostles is a candidate for an epic telling. This will be a new invitation to scholars of biblical compositions at all levels of expertize to experience, analyze and perform these great works.

The length of these compositions was not an issue for ancient audiences. *The Iliad*, for example, requires a minimum of 18 hours to perform. They can be told over more than one evening of biblical entertainment with multiple tellers and musical interludes adding distinctive flavors to an extended story or series of prophetic discourses. A central feature of the annual Festival Gatherings of the Network of Biblical Storytellers International is a two-hour epic telling of an extended biblical composition by multiple storytellers. Learning the art of biblical storytelling is a requirement for serious engagement with performance criticism.

The reformation of biblical pedagogy is another dimension of the future of performance criticism. Students experience the Bible in a radically different and often more interesting way if they are required to listen to and perform the stories themselves. I can guarantee that hearing the stories of the biblical tradition is more interesting than an introduction to the Synoptic Problem. Admittedly, the "m" word is a formidable challenge for students who have had little or no introduction to the internalization and public presentation of great works of literature. The role of memory is one of the major differences between the cultures of ancient and modern

7. Maxey, *From Orality to Orality.*

education. In ancient education, memorization from the earliest years was a daily discipline and a person's degree of education was directly related to how many discourses and stories he knew by heart. But, while large scale internalization and performance may be unusual for twenty-first-century students, they are fully capable of mastering long and complex stories.

Performance Criticism as a New Paradigm

Performance criticism is a new paradigm for the study and interpretation of the Bible in its original historical context. The new paradigm is based on a perception of the Bible as sound that was experienced in the performance of the compositions for audiences: "Hear, O Israel." The advantage of performance criticism over text-based methods is that it is a more accurate perception of the compositions of the Bible in their original context. Furthermore, it is fully possible that performance criticism can be the basis for a more accurate description of the history of tradition. This volume is a contribution to the reformation of historical biblical criticism and its effort to interpret the Bible in its original historical context. The origins of the Gospels were in performance.

Performance criticism is also a new paradigm for the experience and interpretation of the Bible in the present day context of digital culture. In the history of biblical interpretation, there is a direct correlation between the emergence of a new medium of perception and communication of the Bible—writing, printing, silent reading—and the formation of a new paradigm for the interpretation of the Bible in that new communication culture. The development of electronic followed by digital communication technology is having a transformative impact on the human community and its religions. It is the most comprehensive change in communication technology since the development of literacy and writing. The interpretation of the Bible for that new culture is the most significant challenge facing the community of biblical scholarship. The proposal here is that performance criticism is a foundation for the new paradigm of biblical interpretation for the communication culture of the digital age.

PART I

Ancient Media Culture and
the History of Biblical Interpretation

1

Biblical Megatrends

Towards a Paradigm for the Interpretation of the Bible in Electronic Media

Prelude

This chapter was first composed in 1987 and was delivered to the Bible in Ancient and Modern Media research group at the Society of Biblical Literature meeting that year. The concept of "electronic media" at that time primarily referred to the predominant "mass media" of that period: television, film, and radio. The emergence of digital media as the means for the production and distribution of television and film was in its early stages. And the explosion of the digitalization of all things print was beginning to take place. This article reflects that period and its terminology. Since one of the purposes of this collection is to trace the history of this research, the article is included here in its original form rather than being recast for the media context some thirty-five years later. The basic thesis of the analysis remains valid and indeed has been fulfilled by subsequent developments.

Introduction

The purpose of this chapter is to offer some observations about megatrends in biblical interpretation and, in particular, the interpretation of the Bible in the electronic media culture of the late twentieth century. The generative question can be put in several ways: What is the shape of the paradigm of the electronic Bible, of the traditions of Israel's religion on the holy TV and the holy computer as well as in a holy book? What does an electronic hermeneutic look like or sound like? Would you know one if you met one in a vision or walking beside you on the street? And if you met one should you run away, kill it, or take it to your heart? We are not at a stage in which a fully documented theory can be formulated. The value of this type of reflection is in drawing some tentative observations together into a theory that can be tested by further explorations.

Paradigm Shifts and Scientific Revolutions

Thomas Kuhn's description of paradigm shifts in the history of science identifies processes involved in paradigm shifts that are appropriate here.[1] Paradigm shifts occur when there is a failure in normal problem solving, when the results yielded by the old methods no longer work. This leads to thought experiments and to a proliferation of various articulations and willingness to try new approaches. Out of this comes a new gestalt, a primary shift in the way in which the material is perceived. Two things happen: 1) the achievements based on a new theory and type of research attract an enduring group of adherents away from competing modes of scientific activity; 2) the theory is sufficiently open-ended to leave all sorts of problems for future practitioners to resolve.

I hear the symptoms of a crisis of paradigmatic proportions in current biblical scholarship. The primary reason is that the old paradigm no longer achieves its purpose. The promise of the historical-critical paradigm was that it would render the past alive and would result in illumination and vitality for the religious community. The religious communities that have accepted historical criticism since the nineteenth century are in decline and the educational enterprise of critical study of the Bible has been massively reduced in theological curriculums since the 1930s because it did not produce spiritual vitality and life.

The symptoms of the problem are also reflected in the Society of Biblical Literature (SBL). The basic paradigm of historical criticism that was generally accepted as late as the 1970s has been fractured. The multiplication of methodologies and research paradigms at an SBL meeting is incredible in comparison to meetings as recent as 1970. But, in spite of all our labor, the impact of historical-critical study of the Scriptures on religious communities and the culture in general is minimal in comparison to the beginning of this century. But normal science goes on as if the same formulas and

1. See Kuhn, *The Structure of Scientific Revolutions*.

patterns of research will have the same effect. We continue to undertake textual research projects and to publish books. But increasingly we only write for each other and the results of our research are ignored, even by the religious community. We write more and more with less and less effect. To put it simply, the existing paradigm is not producing the results it promised.

Theories have two primary functions: they make it possible to account for the data that can be presently observed and they make possible predictions that can be tested by normal scientific research. I want to suggest a theory that explains why this is happening and that generates a radically different paradigm for future research. Arthur Schlesinger made a clear statement of the primary principle of this theory on a recent PBS program about Marshall McLuhan: "Marx argued that the major movements in history are caused by changes in the modes of production and exchange. McLuhan said that the major movements in history are caused by changes in the modes of communication."[2] Stated in relation to the interpretation of the Bible, the thesis would be that the major movements or paradigm shifts in the history of biblical interpretation are related to changes in the dominant medium of communication.

Thus, the task of biblical interpretation is to render the primary traditions of the Bible meaningful and alive for persons and communities in later, radically different, cultural and historical contexts. The primary communications system of the culture provides the contexts within which biblical interpretation happens. It determines the values, attitudes, and overall hermeneutical options for the interpretation of the biblical tradition in that cultural context.

The Paradigms of Biblical Interpretation

If the theory is accurate, the expectation would be that the major changes in communications systems are followed by new paradigms of biblical interpretation. The theory appears to work and a discernible paradigm of biblical interpretation can be identified in each new media age.

The Bible in Oral Culture

In the oral age, the medium was exclusively sound and the sounds were transmitted by memory. The sounds were generally a kind of chant at least for the narrative and psalm traditions. In the narrative material this chant

2. Schlesinger, "Marshall McLuhan."

was improvised on known formulas as in oral poetry now. The way of connecting the present experience of the audience with the holy event of the past was by retelling or representing the material in light of later experience. Thus, the editors of the Pentateuch and the authors of the Gospels all used a common hermeneutical system. Interpreters of this oral tradition were accredited as disciples by the authority of a master of the tradition. Storytellers constituted the primary system of distribution.

The Bible in Manuscript Culture

The historical analysis of the appropriation of writing is more complex. But to make the complex simple, I would propose that writing was appropriated as a servant of oral hermeneutics until the late first century. At that time, a decision had to be made within Israel because of a combination of social, political, and cultural factors of which the prevalence of writing as the dominant communications system in the Hellenistic world was the most important sign of the growing dominance of Hellenistic culture.

The new paradigm was based on the distribution of the primary traditions of Israel in writing. Signs of this paradigm were: the collection and organization of oral traditions in manuscripts, the production of multiple biblical manuscripts, the formation of a canon, the performance of manuscripts in public worship, the formation of the synagogue and congregation as places for public readings, and the development of oral forms of commentary on the written manuscripts. Both rabbinic and Christian Judaism adopted the reading aloud of manuscripts as a primary form for the experience of the written tradition. The words were recited exactly as written and even the chants began to be regulated. This regulation developed until it was written down and fixed by the development of accent systems—in Hebrew the trope marks, and in Greek the accents. The accreditation of an interpreter of the tradition was accomplished by oral disputation. The movements shared all of these characteristics.

But Christian Judaism developed a new hermeneutic of biblical interpretation growing out of this communications system. The primary characteristic of this new hermeneutic was interpretation by ideas. It was essentially an appropriation of the philosophical methods of the Greeks for which Eric Havelock's description of the earlier transition in Athenian culture is instructive. In order to render the Scriptures meaningful in relation to this Neo-Platonic system, allegorical interpretation was developed and became the normative form of biblical interpretation in Christianity. Theology, the identification and development of doctrine, and the formation of a communications system based on writing in a catholic church are symptoms of this paradigm shift.

Rabbinic Judaism also adopted writing as an integral part of biblical interpretation. But in the rabbinic paradigm the oral law remained primary. The oral tradition that produced the Mishnah and the Talmud was organized around memorization of oral law, the interpretation of the written law in relation to the living of individual and communal life, and the maintenance of face-to-face community. The oral law was passed on for decades before being codified in writing. Rabbinic Judaism never developed a full-orbed theological tradition and it appropriated writing in strict subordination to orality. Thus, the paradigm shift associated with writing is evident in the divergent hermeneutics of Christianity and Judaism as each community sought to respond to Hellenistic culture in which writing was the most powerful medium of communication.

The Bible in Print Culture

The paradigm shift in biblical interpretation associated with printing is relatively easy to identify. The highly allegorical hermeneutics of medieval exegesis were gradually replaced by the combination of literal and figural hermeneutics in the Reformation. This major change was part of a new paradigm of biblical interpretation. Vernacular translations, the printing and distribution of the Bible, historical studies of Greek and Hebrew documents in relation to their original meaning, the priority of the sermon, the development of Lutheran hymns and Calvinist psalmody—these were all parts of the new paradigm of biblical interpretation that emerged in the aftermath of the printing press. The sounds of the Scriptures continued to be read aloud but increasingly in a normal voice without intonation. The availability of texts made it possible for private reading of the texts to become a normal context for study and interpretation. The accreditation of interpreters shifted from an oral disputation to the oral defense of a written thesis. A new distribution system emerged as printed texts of the Scriptures and interpretations of the Bible in printed books and tracts became highly marketable.

The Bible in the Culture of Silent Print/Documents

Historical criticism developed in the context of the age of silent reading. In the late seventeenth and eighteenth centuries in Europe and in the nineteenth and twentieth centuries in America, silent reading became the normal mode for perception of written texts. This is evident in the shift of audience address from "Listen, lordings" in the poems of the sixteenth century to "Dear reader" in the novels of Henry Fielding and Jane Austen. In this period, for the first time, biblical documents were normally studied in silence and the text became increasingly disassociated from sound. Sometimes the sounds continued to be imagined or even spoken by the readers. But private oral reading has declined in recent generations as speed reading has been more widely adopted as a necessity for survival with the multiplication of secondary literature.

Hans Frei's work, *The Eclipse of Biblical Narrative*, is an accurate description of the paradigm of biblical interpretation in the age of the Enlightenment. As Frei shows, both the radical historical critics and the conservative supernaturalists shared a new common presupposition that he calls "meaning as reference." The meaning of the texts was defined by their value as documentary sources for the establishment of either historical facticity—what Frei calls "ostensive reference"—or theological truths or ideas—what Frei calls "ideal reference." The system of distribution of both biblical texts and interpretations was and is a massive multiplication of books: reference sources, the biblical texts themselves in various arrangements and translations, and books about the Bible in ever increasing numbers. The paradigm of historical criticism has become the dominant frame for biblical interpretation in the Enlightenment culture of silent reading.

Thus, there appears to be a demonstrable correlation between media change and the emergence of paradigm shifts in the history of biblical interpretation. And certain characteristics can be identified when one examines each of these paradigms as a separate system. When seen as a whole history, sound, chant, and memorization decline and largely disappear in the dominant paradigm. But the old paradigms do not disappear totally. Instead, the old paradigms are reappropriated and used in new ways in the new paradigm. Thus, the chanting of the original oral medium persisted throughout the manuscript era and the allegorical/theological hermeneutic of the manuscript paradigm has been continued in new forms in each of the subsequent paradigms.

Furthermore, in each age, other paradigms including virtually all of the paradigms of previous ages have persisted in groups that have resisted earlier paradigm shifts. As a result, paradigm shifts happen at very different stages in the development of different religious and cultural groups. Thus, Raymond Brown in Roman Catholicism and Jacob Neusner in rabbinic Judaism have been leaders in the quite recent appropriation of the paradigm of historical criticism for the interpretation of the Scriptures in Catholic tradition and of the Mishnah and the Talmud in Jewish tradition. Perhaps not coincidentally, these scholars have generated a prodigious output of books not unlike the output of earlier generations of German Protestant scholars.

A Pattern of Response to Biblical Paradigm Shifts

There also appears to be a discernible correlation between the major schisms in the communities of the Judeo-Christian tradition and the development of new paradigms of biblical interpretation. In each period of adjustment to the culture generated by a new communications medium and a new paradigm of biblical interpretation there is a pattern of response that can be characterized as resistance, appropriation, and capitulation.

The conservative response in each age is to resist the new culture generated by the new medium, but to incorporate the new medium into the old culture and its hermeneutics. Thus, in the period of the adaptation of the tradition of Israel to the manuscript paradigm, Pharisaic Judaism resisted the Hellenistic culture associated with writing. It incorporated writing and the written law into Jewish culture and even formed a canon of the written law. But the written law was studied and appropriated in the context of orality and the characteristic cultural patterns of the oral age. The ongoing formation of the oral law in first the Mishnah and then the Talmud continued the primary oral hermeneutic of biblical interpretation. Interpreters of the tradition continued to be authorized by the oral processes of rabbinic education rather than in any sense by publication of written works.

Christian Judaism appropriated the new medium and its culture and formed a new synthesis that integrated the old medium and its culture into a new hermeneutical paradigm. The struggle between the Antiochene and Alexandrian schools of literal and allegorical interpretation was a primary sign of the tensions in this new paradigm. The Antiochene wing maintained a close relationship with rabbinic Judaism while the world of Hellenistic philosophy formed the primary cultural matrix of the Alexandrians. In the end, the new synthesis formed by Christianity adopted the allegorical methods of Hellenistic culture while maintaining essential continuity with the more literal methods of interpretation generated by the oral culture that gave birth to the Scriptures. The tension between Origen and Jerome resulted in a new hermeneutical synthesis.

Gnosticism in both its Jewish and Christian forms can be seen as a capitulation response in which the new medium and its culture became so dominant that the old medium and its culture were rejected. The highly individualistic culture of the world of writing with its consuming interest in speculative and creative ideas became the norm of biblical interpretation in the various forms of Gnosticism. The new culture and its values generated a hermeneutical system and institutions that actively sought to disassociate the sophisticated present from the primitive past. Thus, the division of the religion of Israel into rabbinic Judaism, Christianity, and Gnosticism is correlated with the distinctive systems of biblical interpretation that the communities formed in the adaptation of the religion to the communication culture of literacy.

In the period of adjustment to the paradigm of print and the culture with which it was associated, the initial Roman Catholic response was fierce resistance to the new culture of which the printing, distribution, and historical interpretation of the Scriptures was a part. In the aftermath of the Council of Trent, Catholics appropriated the essential patterns of the culture associated with printing such as the establishment of seminaries. But in relation to biblical interpretation, this adaptation maintained strict subordination to the cultural patterns and "fourfold" hermeneutical paradigms of the manuscript period. In no way was independent interpretation of the Scriptures allowed to compromise the tradition until the mid-twentieth century.

Protestantism adopted the new medium and its culture, and developed a new synthesis that maintained essential continuity with the tradition. Luther and Calvin were biblical scholars who generated a massive series of printed texts including vernacular translations, commentaries on the original Greek and Hebrew texts, and doctrinal systems that used the texts as the primary source. Their hermeneutical system was primarily theological and their doctrine was based on a "literal" interpretation of the Hebrew and Greek texts. This new hermeneutic generated the widespread distribution of biblical texts and doctrinal commentaries. Massive literary output was the foundation for communities of independent biblical interpreters who were held together by a common hermeneutical framework.

Protestant scholasticism capitulated to the culture of the university and rejected both the old culture and the old medium. The university rather than the church became the primary institutional matrix for this form of culture Christianity.

Once again, the division of Christianity into the panoply of Protestant churches, the Roman Catholic Church, and the institutions of Protestant and Catholic scholasticism is correlated with the distinctive systems of biblical interpretation that the communities developed in the communication culture of the printing press.

Finally, in the age of silent print, in various stages in Europe and America, the historical-critical study of the Bible as a document to be read in silence was resisted by Catholics, Protestant supernaturalists and fundamentalists, and orthodox Jews. In each instance, the new medium and the study of the Bible as a historical document has gradually been incorporated into the old culture. But the synthesis of a scientific interpretation of the Bible and the culture of the Enlightenment took place first within the mainstream of the Protestant churches. The Protestant churches adopted the new medium and its culture and created a new hermeneutical paradigm while maintaining continuity with the tradition. The formation of scientific societies for the study of the Bible—the Society of Biblical Literature (SBL), the Society for New Testament Studies (SNTS), and the Catholic Biblical Association (CBA)—are the institutional offspring of this paradigm shift. Werner Georg Kümmel's history of interpretation, *The New Testament: The History of the Investigation of Its Problems*, is a chronicle of this paradigm and its development. The radical liberal tradition capitulated to the culture of the university and eliminated the basic characteristics of the old medium such as, for example, the memorization and recital of the Scripture. Thus, the division between the mainstream Protestant churches and the fundamentalist churches is directly connected to the formation of alternative systems of biblical interpretation that were a response to the culture of silent print and the Enlightenment.

When seen in the context of the interactions between the major changes in the dominant medium of cultural communication and the systems of biblical interpretation, it is striking that all of the institutions generated by those changes are alive and well. All of these religious communities have been reformed in various ways over the centuries but they have maintained continuity with the legacy of their initial hermeneutical system. Those systems have continued to be taught at their educational institutions and to be practiced in their religious communities.

Furthermore, the theory that changes in the dominant communications medium of the culture are closely correlated with the megatrends of biblical interpretation also sheds light on the sources of reformation and schism in the history of religious communities. There is a close correlation in the history of the various forms of the religion of Israel between institutional divisions, paradigm shifts in biblical interpretation, and changes in the systems of cultural communication.

Biblical Scholarship Today in Light of Media Megatrends

The implications of this theory for the present context of biblical interpretation are interesting. In relation to communications technology, the twentieth century has witnessed the most extensive changes in the technological means of communication since the development of writing. The printing press was only a more efficient and uniform way of producing written materials, and silent reading was a change in the way in which writing was normally perceived. But the elements of continuity with the written manuscript were primary: marks on paper, bound together in books, read with the eyes, distributed by being moved from place to place, and requiring extensive training in order to be perceived and interpreted.

Electronic communications is a radically different means of communication: paper unnecessary, widely varied distribution systems, both audio and visual data, instant availability, and easily accessed without formal education. The only media change that compares in magnitude with the shift from literacy to electronics is the shift from orality to literacy. In light of the changes in biblical interpretation that took place in response to earlier media shifts, we live at a critical juncture in the history of biblical interpretation.

The most powerful interpreters of the Bible in electronic media are conservative evangelicals and Pentecostals, most of whom have minimal scholarly training. The Bible is talked about constantly but is rarely presented in electronic media. The religious communities in which this type of interpretation is done are growing at a rapid rate. In my judgment, the interpretation of the Bible in the present world of electronic media is a capitulation to American media culture and is profoundly flawed in ways that do not maintain essential continuity with the tradition. The new culture that has developed with electronic media has become the norm for biblical interpretation. What will sell on American TV has become the primary norm of exegetical validity. However, while this is in my opinion an accurate generalization, it needs to be tested by more detailed evaluation of the range of biblical interpretation that is being produced on records, TV, and film.

The community of biblical scholarship and the churches that it serves have generally resisted electronic media and its culture. The guild has generally resisted interpreting the Bible in the electronic world. Biblical scholarship has integrated elements of audio-visuals such as slides and some films into its paradigm to a minimal degree. Computers, which make possible the electronic processing of texts, have been enthusiastically integrated into the paradigm of historical-critical scholarship. But the world of audiotapes and records, TV, and films has been an alien culture for orthodox biblical interpretation. At this point in history, the best biblical interpreters of our culture have abandoned the defense and commendation of responsible interpretation of the biblical tradition in the most powerful communications medium of our age. That task has been given over to self-appointed religious entrepreneurs.

A projection on the basis of the megatrends of the past would suggest that this response will become increasingly retrogressive and will result in a withdrawal of the scholarly community from the dominant culture into a defensive posture. This response is not necessarily cataclysmic. Those parts of the tradition that have resisted earlier media changes—rabbinic Judaism, Roman Catholicism, conservative/fundamentalist Protestantism—have made important contributions to the interpretation of the Bible. But the culture that is being formed by electronic media will thereby be ignored. And the consequences of allowing this travesty of authentic biblical interpretation to go unchallenged in the present religious and political context will be great.

However, while biblical scholarship has not consciously addressed the issue of media change, the theory does explain the fracturing of the historical-critical consensus that has taken place in the last two decades. The collapse of biblical theology as a strong and viable hermeneutic, the emergence of narrative theology and literary-critical methods of exegesis, the impact of semiotics and deconstruction, the development of social-science methods of analysis—all are connected by a common epistemological thread that moves away from the distinction between the phenomenal and the noumenal to the phenomena of sense experience itself. In electronic media and its cultures, what is known is what is seen and heard. That is, the theory would suggest that the declining impact of historical-critical scholarship is a symptom of a change in the culture. These developments in biblical scholarship are responses to that new culture and its ways of knowing. This effort is more likely to succeed, however, if the need for a new paradigm of biblical interpretation is addressed directly.

A Paradigm for Biblical Interpretation in Electronic Culture

The transmission and interpretation of the Bible is a process of communication. The means or media of communication in any particular cultural setting directly influence the meaning of communication acts. This fact is particularly evident when new communications technologies emerge and gradually establish a new communications system. The meaning of the old system of interpretation changes and becomes associated with the past rather than the present. The old system can only be maintained by cutting the connection to the emerging new culture, generally by attacking the new medium and the culture with which it is associated. Inevitably, however, even the maintenance of the old system requires adjustments to the new communications situation and the old hermeneutic is modified.

The transmission and interpretation of the Bible in a new communications system and its various cultural matrices requires the development of a new paradigm. Some of the major elements in the paradigms of biblical interpretation are: the reformation of the biblical traditions themselves for transmission in the new medium, the development of systems of production and distribution, and the formation of a hermeneutic that will make possible meaningful connections between the traditions in the new medium and the original tradition.

The Bible in Electronic Culture

The first step is to put the biblical tradition into the new medium, what might be called the "transmediazation" of the tradition. In each new media age, this is the first task: e.g., the writing of the original manuscripts of the oral tradition, the translations into the Latin Vulgate, Codex Vaticanus and the Gutenberg Bible, Westcott and Hort and the spate of recent translations for silent reading. In each case, the Bible was put into the new medium of the age in a loving and responsible manner that preserved continuity with the traditions of the past. What is needed, therefore, is an electronic Bible that accomplishes the same purpose for this new media age.

The computer is making this possible in electronic text with relative ease and with much greater breadth than has ever before been possible: for example, Ibycus and the TLG CD-ROM system. But in the audio and video media the task remains to be done in ways that integrate the previous paradigms into the new paradigm. Audiotapes of the King James Version have been made by Elizabethan actors and videos of dramatized versions of central biblical narratives are being made in the New Media Bible. But they are anachronistic and often poorly conceived. To dramatize biblical narratives is to change their form from narrative to drama, from a single speaker to a company of actors. However, this is only one of a series of problems that need to be solved. Audio is easier than video in which the problem of images must be resolved. But, regardless of the problems, the task is clear. The biblical tradition itself needs to be made available in the medium of the age, electronic media.

A foundational step will be to reconceive the Bible as sounds rather than as documents. This in turn raises a new set of questions for historical research: how did the Bible sound in its original form? While it may be impossible for us to know precisely how Greek and Hebrew were pronounced in the ancient world and the exact melodies that were used for a particular text, historical research will at least get us in the ball park. The basic methodology for this study is to compare the extant traditions of Hebrew and Greek cantillation and to reconstruct by comparison the sounds of the original sources from which these extant traditions developed. The scholarship in this area has reached a high degree of agreement that cantillation has been an integral part of Christian and Jewish worship and education throughout the East and until as late as the medieval period in the West. That is, we know that the Scriptures were originally chanted in worship services of both synagogue and church. In view of recent research on oral poetry and narrative such as the studies of Lord and Parry, the probability is also high that this practice in the recital of the manuscripts continued and formalized a more spontaneous process of chanting that was characteristic of oral tradition.

Thus, we will need to know more about the sounds of the biblical tradition in order to accomplish an informed translation of the Bible into the sounds of our age. A major element in the paradigm shift is the recognition that the Bible is sounds that were recorded in manuscripts so that they could again be resounded, rather than texts to be studied in silence. We also need to know the basic units of sound in the history of the tradition. Rather than the units of the documentary tradition as an editing of words or ideas as we have tended to think, the tradition history of the Bible was a recomposition of sounds not unlike the transposition and development of American hymn tunes in the music of Ives or Copland. The entire paradigm on which the study of the Pentateuch and the Synoptic problem has been based is fundamentally flawed because of an anachronistic reading back of our media world of silent documents into the ancient world. We need, therefore, to reexamine the entire tradition history of the Scriptures historically as a tradition of sound.

Once this is known to a greater degree it will be possible to develop interpretations of the tradition using the melodies and harmonies that are more characteristic of modern civilization in electronic media. Thus, we need to develop a whole new translation of the Bible for performance rather than for study. New ways of printing the texts will indicate the units of sound in the tradition. Various types of recital of the tradition in experimental modes will make the Scriptures directly available in electronic media. Thus, just as a primary task of scholarship has been to produce the best documentary form of the tradition, a new task is to produce the best electronic form of the tradition, the electronic version of Codex Vaticanus, the Masoretic text, the King James Bible, and whatever modern translation you think is best. But a foundational element of that Bible will be the music and melody of the sounds of the tradition.

In relation to video, the question is: what are the appropriate visual components of biblical texts? Symbols, art (both icons and paintings), photographs and video montage, the sights of liturgy and worship, the faces of living persons, historical documentary footage, and dramatizations—all are possible visual elements of biblical texts. Answering this question will involve research into the history and theology of images and experimentation with a range of options.

The Production and Distribution of the Bible in Electronic Media Culture

As is evident from the book display at SBL, the community of biblical interpreters is presently organized to produce and distribute interpretations of the Bible in the medium of print, primarily print intended to be read in silence. The task before us is the development of systems of production and distribution for the Bible in electronic media. The religious communities will probably be the primary source for these systems, but biblical scholars may need to take their own initiatives. To my knowledge, there are no existing production houses or distribution agencies that have been persuaded of this need. The past sales record of the Bible itself and related materials may eventually provide the commercial motivation once viable projects are generated. But this is unlikely in the early stages. Biblical interpreters will have to fight to maintain integrity because of the complexity and cost of the electronic production and distribution systems needed to accomplish the task.

The Medium of Interpretation of the Bible in Electronic Media Culture

In the previous paradigms of biblical interpretation, the earlier media of interpretation were continued and reformed in relation to the new paradigm. The original oral medium of the storytellers, prophets, and psalmists was reformed in the paradigms of writing into oral interpretation of the written texts in preaching and teaching. In an electronic paradigm, oral and written interpretation will be continued and reformed. New forms may emerge. For example, storytelling has experienced a renaissance in the culture and in biblical interpretation in the last ten years. The development of narrative preaching and biblical storytelling is a post-literate orality that could only have happened in the context of the culture of the electronic age. The character of books is also changing: e.g., fewer tomes, more short books, multiplication of specialized publications and journals. The medium of interpretation of the Bible in electronic media will be a media-mix of oral, written, and electronic elements.

The Hermeneutics of the Bible in Electronic Media Culture

The most complex issue is the way in which meaningful connections will be made between the contemporary world and the world of the Bible in a paradigm for biblical interpretation in electronic culture. Media change is a major factor that has generally been unrecognized in the hermeneutical literature including that of the "new" hermeneutic. What will be the hermeneutics of the electronic age?

The medium of communication establishes certain constraints that operate in the formation of meaning in that medium. In *Preface to Plato*, Eric Havelock has shown the way in which the transition from orality to literacy necessitated an epistemological revolution of separating the knower from what is known through reflecting on the ideas implicit in sense experience. This primary revolution of the perception of sense experience as pointing beyond itself to transcendent ideas is an essential component of the world of literacy. I would suggest that, in the tradition of biblical interpretation, this epistemological revolution associated with literacy took place in the development of theology as the primary hermeneutical system for biblical interpretation within Christianity. In its various forms, theology has been the dominant way that connections have been made between the contemporary world and the world of the Bible in the Christian tradition, hence the network of "theological" seminaries. Theology as a hermeneutic has been based on the distinction between the phenomena of the Bible itself and the theological truths or noumena to which the Bible points.

The problem of biblical interpretation in an electronic paradigm is that theological modes of interpretation are not as effective in this medium. One sign of the problem can be observed when one contemplates the transmediazation of theological works. Imagine the grandeur of Paul Tillich's *Systematic Theology* or Karl Barth's *Church Dogmatics* on TV or audio tape; or the fascination of theologians and biblical scholars on TV having a theological or exegetical debate. This is death with no resurrection. Electronic media reinforce a thoroughly empirical epistemology. Sense experience is reality, not simply a shadow on a wall. Theology is based on the distinction between sense experience and reality; it relies on abstractions and argumentation. In audio and video, midrash, well done, is far more interesting than theology. The need then is for a post-theological hermeneutic for the interpretation of the Bible in an electronic paradigm.

Narrative hermeneutics, semiotics, phenomenology, and process hermeneutics may all be candidates for this primary role in the transposition of the Bible into this new context. But my inclination is to let the hermeneutic develop from the Bible itself. This has been the mainstream of the biblical interpretive tradition in which the hermeneutics have never been philosophically pure but have combined elements in unique ways that are finally generated by the biblical tradition itself. This does not mean that we can go back to prooftexting, pesher, or to simple repetition of the traditions themselves. But it does mean that various interpretive methods will need to be used over a period of time and evaluated in relation to their appropriateness and faithfulness to the spirit that formed the Bible. It is the doing of this evaluative task for which theology will be of indispensable assistance in the future.

The argument can be stated in a less abstract manner. When we have put the authoritative interpreters of the orthodox tradition, namely, scholars who have spent their lives writing books, on TV, they are a disaster. They come off as boring, above it all, irrelevant, wordy, and generally a drag. And because they know that, most of them have never even dreamed of trying. On the other hand, fundamentalist evangelists who have never been to seminary, who practice an utterly irresponsible form of biblical interpretation, and who couldn't write their way out of a paper bag, get on TV and they are terrific. They are engaging, sharp, and accessible. Their exegesis sheds light on the biblical text and helps people connect with it. As interpreters of the tradition, they are far more effective in the medium than scholars.

What are we to conclude? Their content is weak but it works in the medium; the content of the orthodox is strong but it does not work in the medium. Many scholars have concluded that the problem is the medium, that electronic media are demonic and that we should fight it by writing more and more books. This strategy is increasingly becoming like that of the generals of the Polish army who sent division after division of cavalry against Hitler's tanks.

But another analysis is possible. The tradition of the scholarly community has been definitively shaped by the mastery of writing. We all got our degrees by proving our competence in the medium of silent print. Our tradition has been determined by the hermeneutics of the world of writing. That hermeneutical system and its styles of communication have not worked well in electronic media.

The tradition of the evangelicals on TV and radio has been definitively shaped by resistance to historical criticism. Most of the people on TV either never went to seminary or, if they did, learned little about historical criticism. Most of them cut their eye teeth on the sawdust trail and are masters of oral communication. The oral hermeneutics of the revival and of pesher interpretation work well in electronic media.

We have concluded as scholars that our message is incompatible with electronic media. And theological discourse and scholarly analysis in its traditional forms appears to be. But must we equate our tradition with the Bible itself?

In the paradigm of the world of writing, the Bible has been defined as a set of reference sources for the historical events and theological ideas of the biblical period. To be faithful has meant, therefore, that one must be faithful to those traditions. In Christianity, authenticity has been defined by theological orthodoxy, by the recognizable presence of certain ideas and styles. But theology is not the Bible nor is it the primary language of the biblical tradition. It is a hermeneutical language, a secondary, reflective language. If we use the language and literature of theology as our norm for what is authentically biblical, our approach to electronic media will be as if we would put literary, music, and film critics on TV and never have story-tellers, musicians, or athletes. Imagine TV as a series of critical discussions about stories, music, and sports.

I would propose, therefore, that the problem of the Bible in electronic media is a new form of the old problem of the authority of the tradition and the Scriptures. If the tradition of the interpretive paradigm of silent print is the authority for the Bible in electronic media, authentic interpretation of the tradition is impossible. But if the Scriptures themselves are taken as the authority and the model, the world of electronic media is open to a new world of interpretive possibilities.

We have become confused about the character of the Bible. In the traditions of Israel of which the early Christian sect was an integral part, over half of both the Hebrew and Christian canon were stories. The traditions of prophecy and psalm were poetry. The wisdom tradition was proverbs not unlike contemporary advertising. Parables, proverbs, poetry, apocalyptic—those were the primary languages of the biblical tradition and they will work well in electronic media.

We have equated the Bible and its faithful interpretation with theology. Our entire paradigm is designed to yield information about the ideas of the tradition rather than the experiences. The shape of a new hermeneutic is the shape of experience, of the direct rendering of the revelation of God in story, song, proverb, and vision.

Just as the Church faced a new situation in the second and third centuries in which the leaders and thinkers of the Church finally had no choice but to develop allegorical and theological methods in order to interpret the traditions of Israel and the early Church in the Hellenistic world, so now we need to develop new methods in order to interpret those same traditions in this new cultural context. Thus, we might begin to produce the Bible as a series of audio and videotapes in which connections to the contemporary culture are explored in parabolic, symbolic, and storytelling styles. But the question is: how can we accurately communicate the meaning of the biblical tradition in its original historical context in the world of electronic media and its various cultures?

A Personal Paradigm Shift

It might be helpful to share a personal experience of what was for me a paradigm shift. When I was doing research for my dissertation on Mark's Passion Narrative, I wanted to know what his story meant as a story. So I read all the commentaries and was trying to identify the units of Mark's narrative. And all I could see were the seams between Mark's redaction and the pre-Markan tradition and the implications of those additions for Mark's theology. But I literally could not find anything analyzing the story as a story. And the harder I looked, the more frustrated I became. After weeks of frustration getting nowhere, I decided to start over. The conclusion of most scholars was that Mark's Passion Narrative had probably been passed on by memory for some years before it was written down. And I knew that narratives in the ancient world were generally chanted, often with a lyre.

I put all my books away, got my guitar, and sat down at my desk and began to memorize and chant Mark's narrative in Greek. At first I thought I was crazy, and then later, when I sang it for my friends and my advisor, I knew I was crazy. But I worked on it until I could do the whole thing. In the process, I went through a paradigm shift. I have never been able to experience the documents in the same way since that time. For me, the Bible is no longer a document to be studied in silence. It is sounds that were intended to be heard again.

Concluding Suggestions

Changes in the dominant medium of communication create radically new situations for the transmission and interpretation of the Bible. There is a direct correlation between the development of writing, printing, and silent reading and the major revolutions in biblical interpretation, namely, allegorical interpretation, literal/figural interpretation, and historical-critical interpretation. The development of electronic communications in the twentieth century is the most radical change in the primary means of communication since at least the printing press and probably since the development of writing.

This communications revolution has had a major effect on biblical criticism and has been a primary source of the fracturing of the historical-critical paradigm in the last fifty years. But the formative cause of this change has largely been unrecognized. Biblical scholarship has continued to operate within the communications world of silent print as if electronic communications has not happened. It may be time now to recognize that the transmission and interpretation of the Bible in the world of electronic communications is the most important shaping influence and constructive challenge for the future of biblical scholarship. The reason for the declining impact of historical-critical work may be that we are not interpreting the Bible in ways that are congruent with electronic media, specifically radio, film, and TV. But in order to do that, we will have to change our ways of perceiving and interpreting the tradition. If this theory is accurate, biblical scholarship is in the early stages of a paradigm shift of major proportions. And if previous media changes are at all indicative of the future, religious communities will experience some significant conflicts over the issues that will be generated.

The proposal here is that the new paradigm needs to be integrally related to the media origins of the biblical tradition. The culture of the digital age is deeply connected with the oral and early literate cultures in which the stories, prophecies, poetry and letters of the Bible were conceived. The foundation for the exploration of this intersection is the exegesis and interpretation of the traditions in their original media context. The rediscovery of the media origins of the Bible will open a world of new possibilities for biblical exegesis and interpretation in post-literate, digital culture. Elements of the origins of the Bible in its original media context are sound, performance, and the interaction of storytellers and audiences. The chapters of this volume will describe in detail the reconception of the Gospels as performance literature in which stories were performed as sounds in the interaction of storytellers and audiences.

2

Jesus of Nazareth
and the Watershed
of Ancient Orality and Literacy

Communications Research and Biblical Methodology

The field of communications research has emerged in the twentieth century in response to the need to understand the complex effects of electronic communications technology on contemporary culture.[1] Contemporary communications research has developed a more comprehensive and nuanced awareness of the complex interactions between communications systems and cultural formation. The foundational conclusion of this research has been that changes in communications systems are related to profound shifts in modes of perception and thought, patterns of cultural formation, and religious concepts and practices.

A metaphor for these changes in communication systems—oral to manuscript, manuscript to print, print to silent print, silent print to digital—is a watershed. A watershed is not a divide but a direction for the flow of water, and, therefore, of energy. The watershed of orality and literacy is not a divide because oral culture remains omnipresent. The watershed is that cultural energy and the formation of cultural institutions gradually flows in a new direction. A change in a watershed can take either centuries or, as in the case of the current change from literate to digital technologies,

---

1. Carey, *Communication as Culture*; Czitrom, *Media and the American Mind*; Delia, *Communication Research,* 20–98; Fiske, *Communications Studies*; Lowery and DeFleur, *Milestones.*

decades. But, however long it takes, a change in communications systems is a kind of tectonic shift in the cultural plates of history.

The most widely recognized figure in communications research has been Marshall McLuhan. From the foundations laid by Harold Innis,[2] McLuhan popularized communications research in his book *Understanding Media*, which contained the now famous cliché, "the medium is the message." McLuhan argued that communications media are, rather than neutral transmitters of meaning, the major factor in the formation of culture.[3] In the past three decades, the basic presuppositions of communications research have been applied to the history of orality and literacy, above all by Walter Ong. Building on the work of McLuhan, Milmann Perry, Albert Lord, and Eric Havelock, Ong has traced the impact of changes in communications technology throughout the history of human civilization.[4]

The methodological presuppositions of form criticism were based on the communications theories of the nineteenth century. The assumption was that oral and literary communications were relatively neutral means for the transmission of tradition. In light of Ong's work, Werner Kelber recognized the formative role of this presupposition in the work of Bultmann and Gerhardsson. Kelber accurately identifies Bultmann's underlying assumption:

> What strengthened Bultmann's model of an effortlessly evolutionary transition from the pre-gospel stream of tradition to the written gospel was his insistence on the irrelevance of a distinction between orality and literacy. In most cases it was considered "immaterial" (*nebensachlich*) whether the oral or the written tradition has been responsible; there exists no difference in principle.[5]

This nineteenth-century picture of the orality/literacy transition in antiquity was a basic presupposition of form criticism. The key to understanding the history of tradition was the identification of the earlier oral forms of the sayings and stories. This picture generated a relatively narrow focus in historical-critical study of the Gospels on the tradition history of individual pericopes. While form criticism theoretically included the critical analysis

---

2. Innis, *Empire*, 195.

3. While McLuhan's work has been appropriately criticized as media determinism, his descriptions of the pervasive influence of communications systems have been highly generative; see, for example, the reflections upon McLuhan's work by Umberto Eco, *Travels*, 135–44.

4. Farrell, *Overview*, 25–43.

5. Kelber, *Oral and Written Gospel*, 6

of the differences between oral and written tradition,[6] it primarily treated oral tradition as a causal factor in the formation of the written tradition and saw no need to interpret the Gospel tradition in the context of the shift from orality to literacy in the broader culture.[7] As a result of recent orality/ literacy research, however, we now know that changes in communications systems are complex, pervasive, and conflictual, rather than smooth and easy. Furthermore, if these inaccurate assumptions have shaped our picture of the New Testament tradition, they also have affected our picture of Jesus.

The Puzzle of Our Present Picture of Jesus

When seen from the perspective of communications systems, our present picture of Jesus is profoundly enigmatic. The problem is the apparent discontinuity between Jesus' life and the movement that developed from his life and work. The radical distinction between the so-called historical Jesus and the Christ of faith may have been discredited, but remnants of that distinction remain very much in place.[8] One of those remnants is our picture of Jesus' relationship to the watershed of oral and written communications systems in antiquity. While this picture of Jesus dominated the last century, it is largely absent from recent scholarship, though it still lingers in textbooks.

Jesus was largely seen as an oral communicator within a Palestinian Jewish environment that was significantly separated from the more literate Hellenistic world. His ministry was mainly to Jews.[9] The assumption is

---

6. The point was grasped by Overbeck in 1882 (see Overbeck, *Anfänge*). The systemic differences between oral and written communication were more fully appreciated in the school of form criticism that descends from Martin Dibelius (*From Tradition to Gospel*) to Philip Vielhauer (*Geschichte der urchristlichen Literatur*) and Gerd Theissen (*Miracle Stories*).

7. This criticism applies mainly to Bultmann's use of form criticism in his history of the synoptic tradition. A further problem in historical criticism has been the assumption that, once the tradition had been written down, the communications system of antiquity was virtually the same as that of the later periods of print culture. As a result, the role of the distinctive communications system of the Enlightenment in the formation of historical criticism has been largely unrecognized. Throughout this period, for example, scholars have continued to refer to "the reader" as if ancient receptors were generally readers reading manuscripts alone in silence rather than audiences listening to public performances (see Achtemeier, "*Omne verbum sonat*").

8. While Martin Kähler is the source of the classic articulation of the distinction, the ghost is still abroad in a work such as Burton L. Mack's highly influential book, *The Myth of Innocence*.

9. Sanders, *Jesus and Judaism*; Senior and Stuhlmueller, *Biblical Foundations*; Hahn, "Methodische Oberlegungen," 26–41.

that he spoke Aramaic,[10] though a few scholars suggest Greek as well.[11] The historical Jesus was then a relatively insignificant oral teacher who formed one of the several proto-messianic movements in first-century Judaism (so Horsley). According to this construction, Paul was the great innovator who formed the Hellenistic Gentile church as a distinctive development that went far beyond the intentions of Jesus.[12] In Bultmann's *Theology of the New Testament*, for example, Jesus is identified with the Jewish sources but the beginnings of New Testament theology are identified with Paul.[13] Paul formed a literate communications system that, in turn, established a new form of Judaism in the midst of Hellenistic culture.[14] Thus, Jesus operated in the communications world of orality while Paul moved aggressively into the communications world of literacy. In this process, Jesus became the Christ whose death and resurrection were the decisive events in the history of salvation but whose actual life and teaching were of relative insignificance.[15]

The movement Jesus established within Judaism had some impact for a time. The history of Jewish Christianity is a sign of this ongoing movement; the opposition of the rabbis of the post-70 CE period confirms its existence.[16] The Jewish mission was, nevertheless, only minimally successful.[17] It was within the urban, Greek-speaking world that Christianity flourished and became a religion that far exceeded its ethnic, oral roots. From this perspective, Paul was the central figure in the transformation of the movement of Jesus into a religion in which Jesus Christ was the central figure.

This understanding of Jesus' role is related to our picture of the communications situation in the first-century of the common era: Jesus was an oral communicator who wrote virtually nothing, the only recorded instance being whatever he wrote—a symbol, doodlings, a word, or a picture—to a woman accused of adultery (John 8:2–11). Early Christianity was significantly based on the composition and distribution of documents.[18] From a communications perspective, our present picture paints Jesus as the oral precursor for the more literary movement that rapidly developed around

---

10. Fitzmyer, *Wandering*, 6–10.

11. Argyle, "Did Jesus Speak Greek?"; Sevenster, "*Do You Know Greek?*"

12. Harnack, *Die Mission*.

13. Bultmann, *Theology*, 3–26; see also Braun, *Jesus of Nazareth*.

14. Hartman, "On Reading," 137–46.

15. Heitmüller, "Hellenistic Christianity"; Wrede, *Messianic Secret*, 53.

16. Simon, *Verus Israel*, 145–325; Daniélou, *Theology*; Schoeps, *Theologie und Geschichte*.

17. Strecker, "On the Problem," 241–85; Simon, *Verus Israel*, 37–54; Lüdemann, "Successors," 161–73, 245–54.

18. Harnack, *Die Mission*.

his memory. Furthermore, Kelber's picture of orality and literacy in early Christianity widens the chasm between the communicators of the oral gospel—Jesus and his nonliterate followers, particularly Peter—and the more literate authors of the written gospel, such as Mark.[19] Thus, the watershed between oral and written communications systems is presently located between Jesus and the traditions of the church.

Yet this conclusion is itself a puzzle. Is it probable that there would be such radical discontinuity between the founder of a movement and the movement itself?[20] Was Paul such a charismatic figure that he was able to turn the Jesus movement in a radically different direction from that initiated by Jesus himself?[21] Furthermore, if Jesus lived more or less exclusively on the oral side of the great divide between the systems of orality and literacy, is it likely that he would have founded a movement that was structurally related to the world of literacy?

A needed step in a reexamination of these questions is to clarify the roles of oral and written communications in the first century. Just as we used to assume that Judaism and Hellenism were radically distinct until it became clear that Hellenism had thoroughly permeated Palestine,[22] so also the interaction of oral and written communications systems may have been far more complex than we have previously assumed. The formation of early Christianity and the documents of the New Testament need to be seen in the context of the history of communications systems in antiquity and in the religion of Israel.

Orality and Literacy in Antiquity

A comprehensive picture of the transition from orality to literacy in antiquity can only be drawn in its broadest outlines here. The extension of literacy in the ancient world was a slow process. The earliest evidence now available

19. Kelber, *Oral and Written Gospel.*

20. The use of the criterion of dissimilarity, while methodologically necessary for purposes of historical verifiability, accentuates the disjunction between Jesus and Christianity. For a critique, R. S. Barbour, *Tradition-Historical Criticism*, 5–20. On the question in general, see Hahn, *Methodische Oberlegungen*, 11–77; Käsemann, *New Testament Questions*, 23–65.

21. This was the position of the "history of religions" school in general: see the critique by Schoeps, *Paul*, 53. This view of the radical disjunction between Jesus and Paul has recently been revived by Hyam Maccoby through the early centuries of the Roman empire (Maccoby, *The Myth-Maker*; also see MacMullen, *Roman Social Relations*, 1–56; Rostovtzeff, *Social and Economic History*, 255–78, 344–52).

22. Hengel, *Judaism and Hellenism*; Momigliano, *Alien Wisdom*, 74–122; Batey, *Forgotten City.*

places the invention of writing in both Mesopotamia and Egypt near the end of the fourth millennium BCE (ca. 3200–3000 BCE).[23] The extensive tablets discovered in Elbbla reflect the uses of writing that were dominant until the later centuries of the second millennium BCE: records of business transactions and military victories. Throughout the next two and a half millennia (3200–700 BCE), writing was the province of a professional group of scribes and was limited in its overall cultural impact. This is reflected in the political roles of the scribes: they were subordinates to illiterate kings who used scribes but exercised power by oral decree. Thus, the communications system of literacy was developed in service of oral communication.

The first period in which writing appears to become a dominant factor in the formation of culture begins around 500 BCE. Though the same processes may have been happening elsewhere in the ancient world, the most extensive evidence for the formation of an early literate culture is in Athens. There a critical mass of early philosophers, scientists, and historians developed the characteristic institutions and modes of thought of literate culture. The Hellenistic empire of Alexander and his successors was the preeminent promoter of literate culture in the ancient world.[24] In the Hellenistic empire, writing and its modes of communication were organized around the Greek language, and the disciplines of philosophy and rhetoric gradually became important factors in the shaping of communication and culture.[25] Particularly in urban centers, writing became the preeminent system of communication and culture as the literate minority controlled the instrumentalities of power.[26] This process continued through the early centuries of the Roman empire.[27]

The watershed between the relative cultural power of orality and literacy in antiquity is probably drawn most accurately in the Hellenistic era of the fourth to the third centuries BCE. It was in this period that the characteristic marks of literate culture were established and gained cultural power. The transition from archives to libraries is one sign of that watershed. The early archives of written tablets constitute a long and complex history of over two thousand years. As K. C. Hanson has observed in a private correspondence: "we have thousands of tablets from Ebla (c. 2400–2300 BCE), Nuzi (c. 2360–2180 BCE), Mari (c. 1800–1750 BCE), Amarna (c. 1346–1332

23. Baines, "Literacy (ANE)," 3–4.

24. Hadas, *Ancilla*, 3–5; Hengel, *Judaism and Hellenism*, 58–106.

25. Hengel, *Judaism and Hellenism*, 94–115, 126–43.

26. Jones, *The Greek City*, 285

27. MacMullen, *Roman Social Relations*, 1–56; Rostovtzeff, *Social and Economic History*, 255–78, 344–52.

BCE), the Hittites (c. 1700–1300 BCE), Ugarit (c. 1300–1200 BCE), and the Neo-Assyrians (c. 934–609 BCE). They include tax records, inventory lists, royal correspondence (with foreign kings, regional governors, and other underlings), royal annals, royal decrees, treaties, law collections, texts to teach students about the performance of rituals and extispicy, collections of prophecies, astrological prognostications, prayers, sayings of the sages, and epics, etc." The relatively late collection of Ashurbanipal (668–627 BCE), called The Library of Ashurbanipal, comprises some 30,000 tablets. The first libraries of manuscripts designed to facilitate reading and study appear in classical Athens during the fourth century. The most famous collection was founded by Aristotle and became the model for the great library at Alexandria, which was built by Ptolemy II Philadelphus in the third century (308–246 BCE).[28]

While the basic elements of the communications system of literacy were formed during the Hellenistic era, the ability to read and write remained relatively rare in the general population. Estimates of the levels of literacy in the ancient world are steadily being revised downwards as the documentary evidence is being assessed. Thus, William Harris, in a recent work, *Ancient Literacy*, concludes that the overall rate of literacy in Attica is not likely to have risen above ten to fifteen percent by the end of the fourth century.[29] Literacy was largely confined to the ruling classes, hoplites and above.[30] In the period of the Hellenistic empire, literacy levels in regions other than Greece gradually increased to levels closer to that of classical Athens.[31] Furthermore, Harris's conclusions are that the great majority of the populations of the Roman Empire, including Rome itself, remained nonliterate. He estimates that the combined literacy level in Rome in the period before 100 BCE is unlikely to have much exceeded ten percent.[32] Literacy was largely confined to free men, although at least some slaves and women in the Roman world became literate.[33] While the levels of literacy may have been relatively low, the cultures of the Hellenistic world were nevertheless dominated by the culture of literacy.[34] Power and prestige in every area of life were connected with literacy.

28. Francis, "Library," 856–57.

29. Harris, *Ancient Literacy*, 328.

30. Thomas, *Literacy and Orality*; Harvey, *Literacy*, 585–635; Harris, *Ancient Literacy*.

31. Hengel, *Judaism and Hellenism*, 58–59.

32. Harris, *Ancient Literacy*, 329.

33. See also Youtie, "Pétaus," 127–43; Youtie, "*Agrammatos*," 161–76; Youtie, "*Bradeos graphoth*," 239–61.

34. Jüthner, *Hellenen*: 25–26, 34; Marrou, *History of Education*, 95–100, 150;

However, while the literate culture became increasingly dominant, the marks of oral culture were always present and remained central for the majority of persons. Harris' conclusion about literacy in the world of antiquity is appropriately nuanced:

> . . . there occurred a transition away from oral culture. This was, however, a transition not to written culture (in the sense in which modern cultures are written cultures) but to an intermediate condition, neither primitive nor modern. In this world, after the archaic period, the entire elite relied heavily on writing, and the entirety of the rest of the population was affected by it. But some of the marks of an oral culture always remain visible, most notably a widespread reliance on, and cultivation of, the faculty of memory.[35]

Thus, the overall picture of communications in the ancient world is constituted by the new mix composed of the growing power of writing in the midst of a changing though always present oral culture. The communications systems of literacy were inextricably connected with the emergence and power of the great empires of the era. It is no coincidence that the centers of literacy—Assyria, Babylonia, Persia, Egypt, Greece, Rome—were also the centers of military, economic, and political power that successively subjugated Israel. As Claude Lévi-Strauss has provocatively observed about the role of literacy in human civilization, "The primary function of written communication is to facilitate slavery."[36]

Oral and Literate Communications Systems in Israel

The appropriation of literacy in ancient Israel was an extremely complex process. Three stages can be identified in this process: initial signs of writing, the formation of literate systems of communications, and the development of sustainable communication systems for the preservation and extension of the religion in the culture of literacy. The signs of formation of a literate communications system are the integration of reading and writing into the structural patterns of religious and political life. The integration of literacy

Hengel, *Judaism and Hellenism*, 106; Youtie, *Hypographeus*.

35. Harris, *Ancient Literacy*, 327.

36. Lévi-Strauss, *Tristes Tropique*, 299. In his discussion of slavery, Lévi-Strauss clearly is referring to political, cultural, and economic domination rather than chattel slavery. His discussion is of particular importance because of the tendency of scholars and other high literates to idealize literacy in comparison to both oral and electronic communications systems.

into the life of Israel was a response to the emergence of literate culture in the empires of the ancient Near East. Israel's experience of the culture of literacy was inextricably connected with political and economic domination by the literate centers of power: Assyria, Babylonia, Persia, Egypt, Greece, and finally, Rome. Israel was, however, also a distinctive participant in the development of the culture of literacy.

Initial Signs

The first references to writing in Israel are to Moses, who writes the covenant (Exod 24) and reads his song and the law (Deut 31). Descriptions of reading and writing without further editorial comment refer to Joshua (Josh 1:8; 24:26), Samuel (1 Sam 10:25), David (2 Sam 11:14), Jezebel (1 Kgs 21:8–9), Jehu (2 Kgs 10), and Hezekiah (2 Kgs 19).[37] The first accounts of the reading of major literary compositions with relatively specific historical dates in the history of Israelite religion are the reading of the Deuteronomy scroll (2 Kgs 22, approximately 621 BCE) and the reading of Jeremiah's scroll (Jer 36, approximately 605 BCE).

Epigraphic evidence, particularly from the seventh to the early sixth century BCE, corroborates the biblical signs of an emerging literate communications system in Israel.[38] Furthermore, the synagogue as a community where literacy was required for the reading of sacred writings was probably established during the exile.[39] And it was probably during the period of the exile that the Pentateuch and the classical prophets were codified. That is, the first substantial signs of more extensive literary activity, and the initial formation of a literate culture and institutions based on reading and writing, appear in the seventh and sixth centuries BCE.

Formation of a Literary Communications System

The first accounts in biblical literature in which the marks of a literary communications system appear are the descriptions of the restoration under Ezra and Nehemiah. In the accounts of the covenant renewal in 444 BCE, the authors of Ezra and Nehemiah fully integrated reading and writing into the narrative fabric of Israel's religious life. Ezra, as the leader of the religious community, is named as a scribe. He is presented as the first fully

37. Millard, "Literacy," 388.
38. Millard, "Literacy," 338.
39. Schürer, *History,* 447; Hengel, *Judaism and Hellenism,* 82–83.

literate person in the history of Israel to have significant political power. The introductions of Ezra emphasize his literate credentials: "He was a scribe skilled in the law of Moses that the Lord the God of Israel had given . . ." (Ezra 7:6); "For Ezra had set his heart to study the law of the Lord, and to do it, and to teach the statutes and ordinances in Israel" (Ezra 7:10); "This is a copy of the letter that King Artaxerxes gave to the priest Ezra, the scribe, a scholar of the text of the commandments of the Lord and his statutes for Israel . . ." (Ezra 7:11). This last reference suggests a connection between Ezra's literacy and his authorization by King Artaxerxes of Persia.

As described in Nehemiah 8, the foundational act in the covenant renewal ceremony is a new communications event: a combination of the written and the oral Torah. While Ezra read the book of the law of Moses, the Levites, thirteen of whom are listed (Neh 8:7), provided an oral interpretation of the Law, "so that the people understood the reading" (Neh 8:8). During the celebration of the Feast of Booths that followed, Ezra is described as reading from the book of the law of God each of the seven days (Neh 8:18), and on the twenty-fourth day the people made confession to God after hearing a reading from the book of the law for "a fourth part of the day" (Neh 9:1–3). This story is the first sign in the tradition of the characteristic pattern of the dual Torah: written texts combined with oral commentary on those texts. A further dimension of the integration of reading and writing into the account of the covenant renewal is the signing of the written covenant (Neh 10). Apparently the scribes wrote a new covenant and representatives of the people—officials, Levites, and priests—signed it. The names of those who signed the covenant are listed in Neh 10:1–27.

The composition of Ezra and Nehemiah is now dated between 400 and 300 BCE.[40] Thus, the first descriptions of the systematic integration of reading and writing into the religious life of Israel appear in the early second temple period. The identification of this time period as the watershed between orality and literacy in Israel is supported by additional literary records. It was during this period that the literature that formed the balance of the Scriptures was written. The later canonical writings, the Apocrypha, and the Pseudepigrapha are the records of extensive literary movements that developed in Israel during the Hellenistic and Roman eras. These movements were based on the composition of documents by authors who apparently wrote them for distribution to communities of literate Jews. This was also the period of the Septuagint translation (third century BCE to early first century BCE). Furthermore, the discovery of the literary legacy of the community at Qumran has given us a picture of a Jewish religious community in

40. Klein, "Books," 732.

the late second temple period that had thoroughly appropriated reading and writing into its internal life. And, not surprisingly, all of this literary activity took place in the same period as the emergence of literate systems in the wider Hellenistic culture. From the perspective of communications systems, therefore, these developments in the literature of Israel are further signs of the emergence of a full system of literary communications.

As the reform of Ezra and Nehemiah indicates, however, the political impetus in Israel for the development of a system of communications based on writing was the desire to protect Israel from corruption by the culture of Hellenism. This desire was, however, in tension with the inevitable need to adapt to the new cultural system and, in a variety of ways, to adopt Hellenistic ways. As Martin Hengel has shown in his richly nuanced studies, the adoption of Hellenistic civilization by ancient Judaism and the conflict that resulted was a highly complex development that involved many levels of extreme tension. The issue for Judaism throughout the second temple period was how to deal with the powerful cultural forces of Hellenism, an integral aspect of which was the power of reading and writing.

The Emergence of Sustainable Communications Systems

The next major development in communications systems in the history of ancient Judaism was, from the point of view of media history, in many ways the most remarkable. In the aftermath of the Jewish war and the destruction of the temple, two significantly different communications systems emerged, the systems that shaped the basic character of what have become Judaism and Christianity.

The formation of rabbinic Judaism was associated with the development of the communications system that produced the writings and symbolic system of the dual Torah. As a result of the historical-critical analysis of the canonical writings of rabbinic Judaism, most characteristically the Mishnah and the Talmud, we now have a much clearer picture of the distinctive character of this system. As Jacob Neusner has shown in his multi-faceted analyses and comparisons with other literatures, the Judaism of the dual Torah was a fully literate system based on the formation of textual communities.[41] The formation of the mind of rabbinic Judaism was based

---

41. Neusner, on the one hand, rejects the significance of the differences between orality and literacy as "vastly overstated, especially for the culture of the Jews in antiquity" (Neusner, *Formation*, 14). On the other hand, at other points in his work he utilizes, in a fully acknowledged manner, both the categories and concepts that have grown out of the investigation of orality and literacy (Neusner, *Making of the Mind*, 8–19).

on highly sophisticated textual logics that interpreted the written texts in relation to the realities of Jewish life in the new cultural setting created by the loss of the temple.

The distinctiveness of the Mishnah and Talmud was in part the result of the particular combination of oral composition and transmission in a fully textual environment. Thus, for example, the students of the Rabbis memorized their teachers' oral sayings,[42] thereby approximating the accuracy of written transmission in oral tradition. In the manner of oral tradition, nothing was written for decades or even centuries, but the modes of oral transmission were rigorous. The entire cultural communications system on which rabbinic Judaism was thereafter established had its foundations in the systematic oral interpretation of written Scripture.

The complexity and importance of the relationship between the development of Judaism and modes of communication can be seen in a fact that is initially surprising. The formation of rabbinic Judaism in the aftermath of the destruction of the temple was based on the more or less exclusive development of the communications system of the dual Torah.[43] Eventually the literary tradition of the second temple period virtually disappeared from the transmitted Jewish tradition. As Samuel Sandmel writes in his introduction to *The Old Testament Pseudepigrapha*, "Foreword for Jews":

> By the strangest quirk of fate respecting literature that I know of, large numbers of writings by Jews were completely lost from the transmitted Jewish heritage. These documents stem roughly from 200 B.C. to A.D. 200. Not only the so-called Pseudepigrapha, but even such important and extensive writings as those by Philo and Josephus have not been part of the Jewish inheritance from its past; these were preserved and transmitted by Christians.[44]

This disassociation of rabbinic Judaism from the literary traditions of the second temple period did not happen immediately. The contents of the two volumes of Charlesworth's Old Testament Pseudepigrapha provide clear evidence that Jews continued to write apocalyptic, testaments, wisdom, and even philosophy in the second to fourth centuries of the Common Era. Furthermore, these literary traditions may have been preserved in some rabbinic circles in the tannaitic and amoraic periods. Nevertheless, the new system that the rabbis established in the late first century CE eventually resulted in the characteristic patterns of Judaism that Sandmel has described.

42. See Neusner, *Invitation*, 28; and Neusner, *Memorized Torah*, 112.

43. Vermes, "Scripture and Oral Tradition," 79–95.

44. Sandmel, "Foreword," xi.

In light of the recognition of the radical character of shifts in communications systems, we can speculate that the exclusion of whole categories of Jewish writings was more or less intentional, analogous to Plato's exclusion of the poets from the Republic, rather than a quirk of fate or a puzzling forgetfulness. It may be that the rabbis recognized instinctively that the only way to maintain a community of purity in the midst of Gentile culture was to form a distinctive communications system and to cut the explicit links of the religion to Hellenistic literary culture. Regardless of the reasons for its formation, however, the system of the dual Torah was a highly creative and distinctive innovation in communications systems that sustained rabbinic Judaism throughout the ages of the dominance of literate communications systems in the West.

The other new development in communications systems among ancient Jews was the formation of the system of the Jewish sectarians who accepted Jesus of Nazareth as Messiah. The early Christian church developed a communications system that was another new synthesis of oral and written tradition. The composition of the New Testament writings in the first century CE established a tradition that generated the writings of first the Apologists and then the ante-Nicene fathers. The development of theology was, from the perspective of communications, a radically new post-biblical development within early Christianity. In the patristic period, Christian writers produced a veritable flood of new literary forms and traditions such as the rhetorical traditions of homiletics, liturgical writings, hymns, letters, dogmatic writings, and early canon law. They also continued to produce the more traditional literary forms—Gospels, Acts, Apocalypses, and Epistles—that are now collected in the New Testament Apocrypha.

Christians established a network of textual communities that produced and distributed a widely diversified literary tradition. Christians were aggressive in the appropriation of the communications technology of literacy. For example, among the earliest archeological discoveries of the codex rather than the scroll, as a means of producing and distributing written works, are fragments of Christian books from the second century CE. The development of a new communications system was foundational to the expansion of what began as a small Jewish sect into what became, in the fourth century, the dominant religion of the Roman Empire.

If there is a significant positive correlation between the emergence of new religious traditions and the development of new communications systems, then the split between Judaism and Christianity may have been, in addition to the various doctrinal, organizational, and ethnic differences, a consequence of different directions in their communications systems. The rabbis of the Mishnaic tradition maintained the role of texts as the recording of long-established oral traditions and poured their energy into the development of the oral Torah. This system defended the culture and religion of Israel from corruption by the culture of Hellenism and appropriated literacy as a communications system in strict subordination to orality.

In contrast, early Christians developed an extensive contemporary literary tradition in continuity with other aspects of the literary communications system that was formed in the period of the second temple.[45] This literature was either composed in writing, dictated to a secretary, or composed orally and written down after a relatively short period of oral transmission. It was then more or less immediately distributed in manuscripts for public and private reading. Christianity was then the Jewish sectarian group in the post-70 CE period that continued and further developed these characteristics of the literate communications system of the second temple period. In this context Christian preservation of the literary traditions of the Pseudepigrapha, and other writings of the second temple period was a natural and consistent development. In the internal struggle within Judaism about the uses of writing, the Christian sect continued the approach to literate communications developed by the more Hellenistic Jewish writers of the second temple period. In contrast to the communications system of rabbinic Judaism that preserved and defended the community's cultic purity, the communications system formed by early Christianity extended the knowledge of God in Hellenistic culture and transformed the impact of literacy on religious and political life.

When seen in relation to the transition from oral to literate communications systems in antiquity, however, both of these new systems were efforts to enable the religion of Israel to survive and to maintain faithfulness in a new cultural environment. Both rabbinic Judaism and Christianity formed new systems of literate communications that have continued to be viable in the literate cultures of the West. It is within these broad parameters that new light may be shed on the puzzle of the relationship between Jesus of Nazareth and the formation of Christianity.

Orality and Literacy in Jesus' Galilean Ministry

Clear evidence about the extent of literacy in Galilee is sparse, but the general situation can be discerned in broad outlines from the available data. It is generally assumed that there was a close association between the extension of literacy and the extension of Hellenism. The assumption may not be fully valid since there were persons who were literate in Hebrew who may not

45. Alexander, *Living Voice*, 221–47; Roberts, *Manuscript, Society and Belief.*

have known Greek. Nevertheless, it is probable that in the overall cultural world of the first centuries BCE/CE, there was a general correlation between Hellenistic culture and literacy. Wherever there is evidence of Hellenistic culture and the use of Greek, there are also signs of the extension of literacy.

One of the more surprising results of recent archeological work has been the evidence of the wide use of Greek in Galilee.[46] There is an overall consensus in the current discussion that Aramaic was the primary language of Palestine. Evidence, however, continues to grow that Greek was also an important language of social intercourse and perhaps even family life. The most striking signs of the use of Greek that have surfaced are the ossuary inscriptions. More than two-thirds of those discovered in Palestine are in Greek. As Meyers and Strange summarize the data, "From a corpus of 194 inscribed ossuaries, 26 percent are inscribed in Hebrew or Aramaic, 9 percent are in Greek and a Semitic language, and 64 percent are inscribed in Greek alone."[47] In the excavation of Beth Shearim, a second-century town in Galilee, thirty-three of the thirty-seven inscriptions discovered in catacombs twelve and thirteen were in Greek and only four in Hebrew and Aramaic, with an additional four Hebrew inscriptions in catacomb fourteen.[48] This evidence indicates that Greek was widely used even in the highly private context of family burials.

A further surprising indication of the prevalence of Greek is the third letter of the Bar-Kokhba correspondence. This letter, written from within the fortress in the last year of the revolt (135 CE), asks for palm branches and citrons for "the camp of the Jews" and then states, "the letter is written in Greek as we have no one who knows Hebrew [or Aramaic]."[49] This is, if anything, even more striking as a sign of the prevalence of Greek since speaking Greek was regarded by many conservative Jews as a sign of defection to the Hellenists. The explanation is clearly in response to conservative sensibilities.

These archeological data are the most striking instances of the widespread attestations of Greek material in Palestine in the time of Jesus. Furthermore, the evidence in regard to Galilee indicates that Greek was used more widely in "Galilee of the Gentiles" than elsewhere in Palestine. This makes sense since Galilee was on the boundary between Palestine and the northern and eastern countries dominated by Greek culture. Finally, the

46. Batey, *Forgotten City,* 56, 80.

47. Meyers and Strange, *Archeology,* 65.

48. Schwabe, "Greek Inscriptions," 249.

49. Yadin, *Bar-Kokhba,* 130.

extensive use of Greek is a sign of the degree to which Hellenistic culture had permeated Galilee in this period.[50]

Jesus' Language

Both this general evidence and specific episodes in the records of Jesus' life indicate that he may have spoken Greek as a second or third language after Aramaic and Hebrew. There are reports of Jesus' conversations with Gentiles in the Gospels:

- The centurion and his representatives (Matt 8:5–13; Luke 7:6–10);

- The Syro-Phoenician woman, whom Mark calls "a Greek" (Mark 7:24–30; Matt 15:21–28); and

- Pilate (Matt 27:1–14; Mark 15:2–5; Luke 23:3; John 18:33–19:11).

It is highly unlikely that any of these persons would have known Aramaic or Hebrew. In the absence of any translators, these conversations were only possible if Jesus spoke Greek. There are, however, significant historical questions in relation to these reports. In Luke's version of the centurion story, Jesus never speaks with the centurion directly but only through mediators who could have also been translators. Whether the version of Luke or Matthew, in which Jesus speaks directly to the centurion, is more historically accurate is difficult to determine. In the Pilate trial narratives, only in John does Jesus say more than two words in Greek to Pilate. There are two possible explanations of this conversation. Pilate may have used a court translator to carry on business, trials, edicts etc. with the local Aramaic-speaking population, or Jesus may have understood and spoken Greek. The Syro-Phoenician woman episode is only recorded in Mark and Matthew and may have been generated by Mark's interest in including Gentiles in his account of Jesus' mission.

Thus, while the evidence from the Gospels at most indicates a possibility that Jesus spoke some Greek, the emerging picture of language use in Galilee increases this possibility. John Meier's conclusion seems accurate: "Jesus regularly and perhaps exclusively taught in Aramaic, his Greek being of a practical, business type, and perhaps rudimentary to boot."[51] In light of the growing evidence of the prevalence of Greek in Palestine among Jews,

---

50. See also Downing, *Threat of Freedom*; Mack, *Myth of Innocence*, 65–66; Kee, "Early Christianity," 15.

51. Meier, *Marginal Jew*, 268.

however, it is possible to suggest that he did teach in Greek as well as in Aramaic to some Greek-speaking groups of Jews.

This multilingual situation in Galilee is also reflected in the names of Jesus' disciples. Andrew, Philip, and Bartholomew are familiar Greek names; Simon can be derived from the Hebrew Simeon, but was also a widely attested Greek name; likewise Thomas can be derived from the Aramaic for "twin," but was also a widely attested Greek name. Thus, Jesus' disciples reflected a wide range of definitions of what it meant to be Jewish, including having a Greek name.

The question of Jesus' ability to read is in some ways more difficult. The rates of literacy in Galilee during this period can only be inferred on the basis of comparative data. On the basis of Harris's data, it would be difficult to think of literacy rates as high as ten percent in Galilee. Meier rightly observes that Judaism in this period had generated written Scriptures, which fostered high respect for literacy. And while it was fully possible to be a Jew who was unable to read, the practice of the religion was increasingly organized around reading and discussing sacred texts.[52] That is, there was a growing Jewish literate culture in the first century.

The only credible evidence in the Gospels that Jesus may have been literate is his conversations with scribes and Pharisees about the interpretation of the Scriptures. The specific stories in the Gospels that present Jesus as literate are historically ambiguous. Luke's story of Jesus reading in the Nazareth synagogue, not present in Matthew and Mark, is the most explicit account of Jesus' literacy. The distinctiveness of Luke's version, the composite character of the Isaiah text, and the presence of Lukan motifs are, however, signs of Lukan composition.[53] The Lukan narrative is, therefore, an uncertain source of historical information since it is an integral part of the editor's portrayal of Jesus as a literate teacher. The story in John 8:6 of Jesus drawing on the ground proves nothing about his ability to write, even if it is a historically reliable tradition, since nothing is specified about what he drew. However, the question of the Jerusalem skeptics in John 7: 15—"How does this fellow know his letters [know how to read: γράμματα οἶδεν] when he has not studied?"—has no obvious redactional motive. It reflects the overall picture of Jesus in the Gospels as a person with a solid knowledge of Scripture and skill in interpretation that was frequently tested. In the absence of other figures in Judaism in this period who had this reputation and were illiterate, the most probable explanation is that this text reflects a tradition of Jesus as literate.

52. Meier, *Marginal Jew*, 258–59.
53. See Fitzmyer, *Luke*, 526–28.

John Meier has investigated the question of Jesus' literacy, first in relation to these texts and then in relation to the broader context of Jewish education in the period. While the state of Jewish education in the first century is unclear, there is no doubt that there was an extensive community of scriptural debate in Palestinian Judaism in which virtually all streams of Gospel tradition show Jesus as a skilled participant. While it was possible to know the Scriptures from hearing them read in the synagogue, the range of knowledge and distinctiveness of interpretation reflected in the conflict stories is most naturally explained by Jesus having the ability to read the texts himself. Meier concludes as follows: "general considerations about first-century Palestinian Judaism, plus the consistent witness of many different streams of Gospel tradition about Jesus' teaching activity, plus the indirect evidence from John 7:15 make it likely that Jesus could both read the Hebrew Scriptures and engage in disputes about their meaning."[54]

Thus, it is probable that Jesus was literate. The literacy of the disciples is doubtful. In Acts 4, Peter and John are described as ἀγράμματοί, which characterizes them as at least unable to write but probably as illiterate. There are no explicit signs that any of the disciples were literate, although the possibility is that Levi, the tax collector, was at least able to handle written records. It is highly unlikely, however, that literacy was a requirement for discipleship. Unlike the rabbinic schools of the post-70 period, which were located in a place and could have books, Jesus taught his disciples on the move; there are no indications that they carried scrolls with them.

Finally, John Dominic Crossan's recent study of the historical Jesus pursues a radically different methodology for the quest, which has yielded surprising results. When the available data about Jesus of Nazareth is compared with the various movements in the world of the period, the highest degree of congruence both in lifestyle and modes of thought is with the Cynics. Crossan distinguishes between upper-class, urban, literate Cynics and the lower-class, peasant variety whose literacy is improbable,[55] in which class Jesus presumably falls. It is not necessarily valid, however, to extend these broad generalizations about Cynic lifestyles to a particular Jewish teacher. In my view, the overall picture is that Jesus adopted aspects of the ways of the Cynics in a highly distinctive Jewish way that in no way excludes literacy. This congruence between Jesus and a broad philosophical movement in the Greco-Roman world is another indication of the degree to which Jesus of Nazareth can be seen within the overall framework of the Galilean Hellenistic literate culture.

54. Meier, *Marginal Jew*, 278.
55. Crossan, *The Historical Jesus*, 84–88.

Thus, Jesus' ministry was far more complex than that of a simple Galilean peasant who taught Aramaic parables to other Jewish peasants. The world of Jesus' day was going through a major shift in communications and culture. There is abundant evidence that this shift was happening in Galilee, as well as elsewhere in the Hellenistic world. In that cultural world, Jesus was a teacher who was probably literate, who spoke Aramaic, some Greek, and perhaps also Hebrew. His level of literacy was probably relatively low and did not include the ability to write. His ability to read was probably largely centered on reading the already familiar oral Scriptures. For example, he probably did not read Greek philosophical literature of the period. Whether he had read Jewish works written in Greek, such as Enoch, appears initially unlikely, but the influence of apocalyptic on Jesus' teaching leaves open the possibility.

Jesus as Teacher

The Socratic Analogy

Even if Jesus was literate to some degree, spoke Greek, and was in dialogue with Hellenistic culture, how could he have been the seminal figure in the establishment of a movement that participated so rapidly and thoroughly in the culture of literacy when he himself wrote nothing? The search for a clue to the puzzle of Jesus' role in relation to orality and literacy leads to Socrates. Socrates' role in the formation of the literate culture of Athens was seminal. He accomplished the essential task of enabling his students to think constructively in the patterns and forms of the emerging culture of literacy. In order to do this, he did not need to write but rather used oral speech in a new way.

The similarities between these two pivotal figures in antiquity are striking. Socrates, like Jesus, was an oral teacher who did not write but who trained followers who did write. In the writings of Plato, Socrates is the main character of the dialogues, just as Jesus is the main character of, for example, Matthew's Gospel. Socrates anticipated a radically new age for which he prepared his students by forming their minds to think about ideas objectively in the manner of the age of literacy. And, like Jesus of Nazareth, Socrates was martyred for his role in initiating radical cultural and religious change.

Socrates' dialogues laid the foundations for the ways of knowing associated with literacy. In *Preface to Plato*, Eric Havelock argued that Plato banished the poets from the Republic because he wanted to break the ways of knowing that were characteristic of oral culture. Plato identifies Socrates as the person who established a new way of knowing. In Plato's writings, Socrates is steadily seeking to needle his dialogue partners into reflection on ideas, instead of continuing to identify uncritically with the heroes of the great poetic epics. Socrates' questions were a steady invitation to step back from the immediacy of experience and to reflect critically on the presuppositions and ideas that were implicit in the conversation. What Havelock calls the "separation of the knower from the known," in which the known can be examined as an object, is the essential turn of mind that makes it possible to participate in the world of literacy.[56] Socrates and his student, Plato, invited persons to stand back from immediate experience and to think objectively about ideas.

Furthermore, Plato's theory of forms shifts the definition of reality from the world of sense experience to the world of a priori ideas present in the mind. For Plato, the enemy was the centuries long practice of self-identification with oral tradition. As Havelock writes, "The net effect . . . of the theory of forms is to dramatize the split between the image-thinking of poetry and the abstract thinking of philosophy."[57] This Platonic move established the foundations for the communications culture of literacy over against the culture of orality.[58]

Thus, prior to Jesus, at an earlier stage in the extension of literacy in Hellenistic culture, Socrates was another seminal figure who was literate but did not write. In a radically different context, Socrates established the foundations for the development of literate culture and its ways of knowing.

The Parabolic Teaching of Jesus

Did Jesus in any analogous manner develop a way of knowing that was seminal in the establishment of a movement within Judaism that became rapidly literate? As with Socrates, there is no evidence that Jesus wrote. Furthermore, the teachings of both men were composed for oral transmission. The form of Socrates' oral teaching, the dialogue, is the most visible sign of the new epistemology of the culture of literacy. The characteristic form of Jesus' teaching was the parable.

Bernard Brandon Scott's recent comprehensive study of the parables has clarified the distinctiveness of Jesus' parables. Against the background of the Hebrew Bible, the parables are related to the *mashal*, any saying that

56. Havelock, *Preface to Plato*, 197–233.

57. Havelock, *Plato*, 266.

58. Szlezák, *Platon*.

is "proverblike." The *mashal* utilizes connotative language, is memorable through the use of metaphors and vivid images, and is typical and representative rather than context-specific.[59] In Jesus' usage, however, the parable is, to use Scott's definition, "a *mashal* that employs a short narrative fiction."[60] While Nathan's warning to David and Ezekiel's tale of the eagle are developments toward parable, Scott rightly concludes: "no *mashal* in the Hebrew Bible directly parallels parable as a short narrative."[61]

Furthermore, Jesus' use of the form of parable is distinctive when compared with the traditions that can be reasonably identified with the Pharisees of the pre-70 CE period. Jacob Neusner's survey of pre-70 Pharisaic traditions finds wisdom sentences in the tradition, but not parables: "As to other sorts of Wisdom literature, such as riddles, parables, fables of animals or trees, and allegories, we find nothing comparable in the materials before us."[62] The parable is used extensively as a form of scriptural exegesis in the Palestinian (400 CE) and Babylonian (600 CE) Talmuds, and occurs in the Tosephta (twelve instances) and the Mishnah (one parable). This use of parable is both later than and distinct from that found in the Jesus tradition.[63] Thus, when seen as a whole, the traditions of Jesus are distinctive in the centrality and uniqueness of the form of parable.

Recent literary-critical research on the parables from a variety of perspectives has come to a surprisingly wide consensus about the overall effect of Jesus' characteristic form of teaching. From Jeremias' tradition history reconstruction to Scott's recent literary-critical study, a common theme is that the parables are shocking and profoundly paradoxical. The question is whether this shock can be seen as a new epistemology that is in any way structural to Jesus' parables.

Two characteristic elements in the structure of Jesus' parables that have emerged in recent study are the reversal of expectations and hyperbole. Sometimes only one of these elements occurs, as in the hyperbolic celebration of the shepherd in the parable of the lost sheep or the reversal of expectations in the parable of the Pharisee and the publican. Frequently, however, both reversal and hyperbole are present, as in the celebration of the younger son's return in the parable of the prodigal son (Luke 15:11–32) or in the punishment of the "one-talent" servant (Matt 25:14–30). What,

59. Scott, *Hear Then*, 13.

60. Scott, *Hear Then*, 8.

61. Scott, *Hear Then*, 13.

62. Neusner, "Types and Forms," 360.

63. Scott, *Hear Then*, 13–18.

then, is the epistemological effect of these two characteristic elements in Jesus' parables?

An analysis of the parable of the rich fool (Luke 12:16–21) reveals a dynamic structure that is characterized by what can be called epistemological shock. The parable begins by leading the audience into the rich man's dilemma—"What am I going to do?"—and decision—"I know what I'll do."[64] The function of an extensive inside view is to invite involvement:

> What will I do, since I have nowhere to store my crops? I know
> what I'll do: I will pull down my barns, and build larger ones;
> and there I will store all my grain and my goods. And I will say
> to my soul, "Soul, you have ample goods laid up for many years;
> take your ease, eat, drink, and be merry!" (Luke 12:17–19)

Jesus' listeners were invited to enter into the rich man's problem and his joyful anticipation of being free from any anxiety about the necessities of life. In its oral performance, this section of the parable probably moved from the rich man's quiet meditation on his problem to the boisterous celebration of his plan. The structure of the internal dialogue inside the rich man's mind—question, answer, and address to his soul—is an appeal to the listener to enter into the mind of the rich man and to experience his dilemma, his solution, and his celebration of freedom from anxiety. It is from this place inside the rich man's mind that the listener hears God's judgment: "But God said to him, 'Fool! This night your soul is required of you; and the things you have prepared, whose will they be?'" (Luke 12:20). In the oral reading or telling of the parable, God's speech is experienced as being addressed directly to each listener.

The parable is structured as a highly-charged shock to the listeners. The combination of hyperbolic judgment in the sentence of death and the reversal of expectations from a long life of ease to sudden death is psychologically wrenching. Insofar as Jesus' listeners identified with the rich man, they experienced the possibility of instant and total reversal of fortune in the moment of hearing the word of God: "Fool!" The impact of this parable is far more than a point such as: "It is not wise to build up money as a strategy for abundant life in the future Kingdom of God" or "It is not wise to mismanage the miracle of God's abundant harvest by appropriating it

---

64. The inside views of the shrewd steward's dilemma (Luke 16:4) and the prodigal son's meditation (Luke 15:17–19) have introductory formulas similar to the inside view of the rich man. Furthermore, the structure of the rich man's speech (Luke 12:17–18) is the same as the shrewd steward's (Luke 16:3–4): "What am I going to do . . . I know what I'll do . . ." These verbal and structural similarities in each case invite listener involvement with the character's dilemma.

for one's own self-interest." The parable shocks the listeners into reflection on their relationship to God and their attitudes about wealth. The reversal forces the listeners to stand back suddenly from preoccupation with the "real world" and to think from a radically different perspective.

The effect of the parable, then, is what could be called an alienation effect: it creates a high degree of separation or mental distance between the listener and everyday experience. The ones who are seeking knowledge about the Reign of God are suddenly distanced from the object seeking to be known and are forced to think and reflect about their own assumptions. I would propose that this effect, this sudden shock, is the same epistemological move that Socrates made in asking questions of his interlocutors. In place of sympathetic identification with the people of Israel escaping from Egypt and entering the promised land as a way of knowing the Reign of God, the experience of hearing Jesus' parables was a sudden reversal of expectations that created psychological distance and demanded reflection. Jesus' parables make the same basic epistemological move in knowing the Reign of God as Socrates' dialogues in knowing the world of the forms. It is the foundational epistemological move of the literate culture of Hellenism: the turn of mind away from the experiential ways of knowing associated with oral culture to the reflective ways of knowing associated with literacy.

Is this alienation effect characteristic of Jesus' parables? A similar dynamic structure can be found in a number of parables in which there is an appeal for identification with characters who are sympathetic or gifted at the beginning and who are radically criticized or condemned at the end:

- The parable of the vineyard/wicked tenants (Mark 12:1–11/ Matt 21:33–44/Luke 20:9–18/Thomas 65)

- The unmerciful servant (Matt 18:23–35)

- The workers in the vineyard (Matt 20:1–16)

- The great banquet and the guest without a wedding garment (Matt 22:1–14/Luke 14:16–24/Thomas 64)

- The faithful/unfaithful servant (Matt 24:45–51/Luke 12:42–46)

- The ten virgins (Matt 25:1–13)

- The talents (Matt 25:14–30/Luke 19:12–27)

- The last judgment (Matt 25:31–46)

- The prodigal son, in which the climactic emphasis is on the elder son (Luke 15:11–32)

- The rich man and Lazarus (Luke 16:19–31).

Variations on this structure occur in the parable of the dishonest steward (Luke 16:1–9), in which a character with whom the listener is invited to identify is first condemned and then surprisingly praised, and the parable of the good Samaritan (Luke 10:30–35), in which there is a primary reversal of audience expectations in the actions of the priest/Levite and the Samaritan.

The effect or impact of these parables is the same as that of the parable of the rich fool. The parable invites the listeners to enter into a situation in which a character is initially presented positively but is condemned in the parable's final turn. The distinctiveness of these short narrative fictions is that the puzzle or paradox of the reversal is necessarily connected with the audience's understanding of the Reign of God. Jesus' parables have the same effect as Socrates' questions: they require the audience to reflect and think from a position of psychological distance.

The question then is whether the new epistemology implicit in the parables can be traced back to Jesus. Undoubtedly, many of the parables have been shaped by subsequent redactors. The dynamic structure is, however, so pervasive in the parables that it is highly improbable that the redactors created it. The higher probability is that this was a pattern of oral teaching that Jesus established and that the redactors preserved to varying degrees. Thus, what can be identified here is the deep structure of a distinctive way of teaching about God.

In a seminal essay, Ernst Käsemann proposed that the origins of theology are to be found in apocalyptic: "Apocalyptic was the mother of all Christian theology—since we cannot really class the preaching of Jesus as theology."[65] What Käsemann calls "apocalyptic" is essentially cosmic, holistic thinking. In apocalyptic the key question is: "to whom does the sovereignty of the world belong?" Thus, one might rephrase Käsemann: reflection on cosmic questions was the beginning of Christian theology.

As a result of his rejection of the authenticity of the third person Son of Man sayings, and indeed all of the apocalyptic sayings of Jesus, as creations of the early church, Käsemann sees the beginnings of theology only in the writings of Paul. The primary evidence of apocalyptic modes of thought in the teachings of Jesus is not, however, in the apocalyptic sayings, but in the parables. The structure of epistemological shock identified above is directly related to the cosmic modes of apocalyptic thought. The essential characteristic of the parables is thinking back from the end of time into the present. The parable of the last judgment is the most explicit in its cosmic, apocalyptic content, but each of the parables listed above has this holistic perspective.

65. Käsemann, *New Testament Questions,* 102.

The shocking reversals of the parables communicate a new understanding of the character of God's sovereignty in cosmic time.

Jesus' development of the dynamic structures of the parable was, therefore, directly related to the epistemological sources of theology. Just as Socrates developed styles of argumentation in his dialogues that led to the full emergence of philosophy, so Jesus developed a style of oral discourse in his parables that led to the development of theology. Jesus' oral discourse was characterized by a dynamic structure that shocked listeners into reflection and an implicit demand for thought that was cosmic in scale. Jesus developed a way of interpreting the tradition of Israel's religion that was both congruent with the tradition and viable in the emerging literate culture. The clearest sign of its viability in literate culture is the impact of Jesus' parables in the two millennia of subsequent literate civilization.

Directions

When seen against the background of the communications systems of the Hellenistic world and the religion of Israel in the second temple period, the teachings of Jesus of Nazareth can be interpreted as moving toward a literate religious culture. Obviously, this inquiry is only an initial exploration of a certain direction in research. The initial results suggest that a clearer picture of the broad developments of the communications systems of orality and literacy in the ancient world may modify our understanding of Jesus' relationship to the formation of Christianity. If, for example, Jesus established the epistemological foundations for a form of the religion of Israel that was viable in the literate communications system of Hellenistic culture, there may be deeper lines of continuity between Jesus and Paul than were previously recognized. From this perspective, Paul simply developed what Jesus had already initiated.

Furthermore, a clearer picture of the history of religious communications systems may help to clarify the conflicts between Jesus and the Pharisees as the predecessors of the nascent movements that became rabbinic Judaism and Christianity in the post-70 CE period. Both of the Jewish sectarian movements that survived the war developed new and viable ways of maintaining faithfulness to the God of Israel in the midst of literate Hellenistic culture. The study of communications systems may shed new light on the common problem they faced and the different approaches they developed. Thus, the decision of the rabbis to disassociate rabbinic Judaism from most of the literary heritage of the second temple period made sense as an effort to control the impact of the new habits of mind and the patterns of communication associated with Hellenistic literate culture that were changing Israel's tradition. Likewise, the decision of early Christian Jews to develop further the literary traditions of the second temple period in a manner that would invite the Hellenistic literate world to participate in the monotheism of the religion of Israel also makes sense.

When the interaction of oral and written communications in antiquity is seen as the interaction of communications systems instead of simply as a neutral stage in the formation, transmission, and meaning of individual literary works, the outline of a different picture of Jesus of Nazareth emerges. The image is somewhat more literate and is set against a more thoroughly Greek background. The picture also reveals more lines of Jesus' connection with Paul and the early church than have appeared in the past. These lines appear because the basic transition from orality and literacy in the culture of antiquity happened before rather than between them. The Jewish sects that survived in the literate culture of the future did so because they formed new systems of thought and communication. In this picture, Jesus and Paul were both working on the same task. Furthermore, when this image of Jesus is seen against the background of the watershed of orality and literacy in antiquity, it can be seen that he established a distinctive style of communication that made a form of Judaism viable in the emerging culture of literacy.

PART II

Mark as Performance Literature

3

The Narrative Technique of Mark 16:8

Thomas E. Boomershine
and Gilbert L. Bartholomew

The bearing of Mark's narrative technique on the problem of whether Mark 16:8 was the original and intended ending of the gospel has been definitively stated by W. L. Knox.[1] He argued that the canons of narrative technique in ancient literature required that an author round off the incidents of his narrative fully, leaving nothing to the imagination. He then surveyed the endings of the major literary units in Mark as well as the conclusions of the major works of ancient popular narrative, both Jewish and Gentile, and found this canon at work in virtually every instance.[2] In the light of this evidence, Knox concluded in a delightfully hyperbolic manner:

> To suppose that Mark originally intended to end his Gospel in this way implies that he was totally indifferent to the canons of popular story-telling, and that by pure accident he happened to

1. Knox, "Ending," 13–23.

2. It should be noted that for Knox the few exceptions to this rule, such as the end of Jonah and a few dramatic endings in John's Gospel (13:30; 18:27, 40; 19:22), are further proof of the improbability that Mark 16:8 was the intended ending. Jonah is a parable and, therefore, a different literary genre than Mark. And while John ends a few incidents dramatically in his gospel, he does not dare employ such a technique as the conclusion of his total composition. See Knox, "Ending," 16–18, 22.

71

hit on a conclusion which suits the technique of a highly sophisticated type of modern literature. The odds against such a coincidence (even if we could for a moment entertain the idea that
Mark was indifferent to canons which he observes scrupulously
elsewhere in his Gospel) seem to me to be so enormous as not
to be worth considering. In any case the supposition credits him
with a degree of originality which would invalidate the whole
method of form-criticism.[3] The problem presented by Mark
16:8 is that the absence of any parallels to other endings either
within or outside of the gospel makes it probable that the ending
was unintentional and, therefore, accidental.[4]

The approach to this problem here will be to identify and compare
the specific narrative techniques of 16:8 with those of the endings of stories
earlier in the gospel. To the degree that there is continuity in the narrative
style of the endings in Mark, the probability that 16:8 was the intended and
original ending increases. Three major narrative techniques can be identified in 16:8: (1) the use of narrative commentary; (2) the use of intensive
inside views; and (3) the use of short sentences.

Narrative Commentary

Narrative commentary is one of the major means by which a narrator var-
ies the manner of address to audiences.[5] In the biblical narrative tradition,

---

3. Knox, "Ending," 22–23.

4. The argument, on the basis of the absence of parallels in other ancient literature,
that it is impossible that a gospel ended with γαρ has clearly yielded to an argument
favoring the possibility. The early evidence for final uses of γαρ was primarily endings of sentences or of brief papyri; see C. H. Kraeling's discussion of POxy. 1223 in
"A Philological Note," 357–58; also see Cadbury, "Mark 16.8," 344–45. R. R. Ottley
listed sentences ending with γαρ in Homer, Aeschylus, Euripides, and the Septuagint
(in "εφοβουντο γαρ Mark 16:8," 407–9). R. H. Lightfoot further expanded this list (in
Locality and Doctrine, 10–11). W. Bauer et al. (in *A Greek–English Lexicon*, 151) noted
additional sentences composed of only a verb with γαρ and cited a letter of Pseudo-
Demetrius, a story in the *Vita Aesopi*, and the end of the preface of Polyaenus's *Stratege-
mata* as instances of documents concluding in a sentence composed of a verb plus γαρ.
P. W. Van der Horst has most recently called attention to the ending of the 32nd treatise
of Plotinus (*Ennead* 5.5). Van der Horst concludes that these treatises were created by
Plotinus's student, Porphyry, who separated them by a caesura which indicates "at least
a large breathing space." Both Porphyry and Plotinus, therefore, thought that it was
appropriate for a treatise to end with a two word sentence with γαρ; see Van der Horst,
"Book End with γαρ?," 121–24.

5. The analytical categories for the detailed analysis of narrative technique have been
developed most fully in twentieth-century criticism of fiction. The most comprehensive

narrative commentary is relatively uncomplicated in its basic techniques. Biblical narrators generally interrupt the reporting of the events of their stories in order to give brief notes of additional information, to translate a foreign word, or, most frequently, to explain something surprising or confusing.

Mark uses each of these types of narrative commentary. Most of the functions of his comments are correlated with three distinctive grammatical forms: (1) comments in the form of appositives; (2) comments introduced by ἦν (ἦσαν) δὲ; (3) comments with γαρ. Appositive comments are brief interruptions within a sentence, often the first sentence of a story, which are used to give additional information about a character, a date, a place (e.g., 14:3, 10, 12, 43; 15:21, 40, 41, 42), or to introduce translations of Aramaic (e.g., 15:22, 34). Comments introduced by the formula ἦν (ἦσαν) δὲ are sometimes used to set an overall scene (e.g., 14:1; 15:7) but more frequently provide more extensive information about a theme introduced earlier in the story (e.g., 15:25, 40). Narrative comments introduced by γαρ are almost always used to explain confusing or surprising events that have been reported in the previous sentence (e.g., 1:16, 22; 2:15; 3:21; 5:8, 28, 42; 6:17, 18, 20, 31, 48; 9:6, 34; 10:22; 11:13; 14:2, 40, 56; 15:10; 16:4, 8). These comments are, therefore, an answer to the anticipated questions of the audience. Since their function is to explain a previous statement, these comments usually occur in the middle or at the end of literary units within a story and not at the beginning.

In the context of Mark's use of narrative comments in the gospel as a whole, the concentration of narrative commentary in Mark 16:8 is striking.[6] The comments are introduced by γαρ and therefore have the characteristic grammatical form of comments whose function is to explain puzzling elements in the previous sentence. The comments in 16:8 do clarify the reasons for the actions of the women in first fleeing from the tomb and then remaining silent. However, while these comments explain the women's flight and silence, the ending leaves many questions unanswered, such as: did the

---

analysis of the various techniques of narration is still Wayne Booth's now classic work, *The Rhetoric of Fiction*. Narrative commentary in modern fiction has been a major area of technical experimentation and it has, as a result, become extremely diverse in its forms and styles. Booth discusses, for example, reliable and unreliable narrative commentary, ornamental commentary, commentary that is part of the dramatic structure of the story, and the various types of indirect narrative commentary in impersonal narration (e.g., 169–209, 271–309). Biblical narrators are invariably reliable and the types of commentary vary in a much narrower range.

6. Concentrations of narrative commentary also occur in the stories of the death of John the Baptist (6:14–29; comments in 6:17, 18, 20) and the transfiguration (9:2–8; comments in 9:6).

women ever tell the disciples and did Jesus appear to them in Galilee? Furthermore, the explanations themselves raise a question that the story does not go on to answer: why were the women afraid? The explanation of puzzling elements in the narrative is combined, therefore, with the introduction of additional enigmatic elements.

The ending of Mark, then, raises as many questions as it answers. These observations lead us to ask whether there are other explanatory comments in Mark which come at the end of a story and which raise new questions as well as answer old ones.[7]

The narrative comments with γαρ earlier in Mark's Gospel generally occur in the midst of stories and provide relatively straightforward explanations of confusing or surprising elements in the narrative. However, there are two instances in which an explanatory narrative comment is the ending. Those are the stories of the walking on the sea (6:45–52)[8] and the plot of the authorities (14:1–2). In both cases the comment does raise new questions as well as answer old ones.

Walking on the Sea (6:45–52)

The ending of the story is as follows:

καὶ λίαν ἐκ περισσοῦ ἐν ἑαυτοῖς ἐξίσταντο, οὐ γὰρ συνῆκαν ἐπὶ τοῖς ἄρτοις, ἀλλ᾽ ἦν αὐτῶν ἡ καρδία πεπωρωμένη.

And they were utterly astounded, for they did not understand about the loaves, but their hearts were hardened.

This narrative comment, like 16:8, is a nexus of exegetical difficulties.[9] It explains the disciples' amazement in two ways: first, because they failed to understand the significance of the loaves, and then because their hearts were hardened.

The first part of the comment naturally refers back to the preceding story of the feeding of the five thousand (6:30–44). But since there has been

7. We will examine the endings of the literary units identified in The Greek New Testament published by the United Bible Societies.

8. As K. C. Hanson has observed in private correspondence, "Treading/standing/being enthroned upon/splitting the sea (Heb. *yam*) has its roots in the Ugaritic mythology of Baal subduing chaos in the form of 'Prince Sea' (*Yamm*) aka 'Judge River' (*Nahar*), and also "Rahab" (see, e.g., Isa 51:9–11; Ps 65:5–7; 89:9–10; 93:4–5). Note, for example, how the temple included a large bronze sea, mounted on the backs of twelve bulls. Mark 6 is very clear about what Jesus was doing."

9. For a comprehensive survey of the critical literature on Mark 6:52, see Quesnell, *Mind of Mark*, 1–28.

no discussion of the meaning of the loaves, or of the disciples' response to the feeding, the comment raises a question as well as answering one: what is the meaning of the loaves? This question cannot be answered with the information previously given.

The second part of the comment only increases the confusion. The reference to the hardening of the hearts brings to mind the Old Testament motif of the responses of Pharaoh and other Gentile kings to the Israelites. The negativity of this motif implies that the disciples' amazement was some-how wrong. The explanation has the effect of increasing the enigma of both the response of the disciples and the meaning of the loaves. Why were their hearts hardened? How can disciples of Jesus be like someone as villainous as the Egyptian pharaoh?

The analysis of this comment's narrative function leads to the same conclusion as Quesnell's redactional analysis,[10] namely, that the comment heightens the mystery surrounding the loaves. The questions raised at the end of this story are then illuminated in the rest of the narrative.

Thus, the narrative comment at the end of this story has the ambiguous impact of explaining a surprising response on the part of the disciples with a comment which in turn raises further questions. It is directly parallel in its form and function to the comments in 16:8.

The Plot to Kill Jesus (14:1–2)

The narrative comment that ends this brief story and the preceding statement that it explains are:

> καὶ ἐζήτουν οἱ ἀρχιερεῖς καὶ οἱ γραμματεῖς πῶς αὐτὸν ἐν δόλῳ κρατήσαντες ἀποκτείνωσιν. ἔλεγον γάρ, Μὴ ἐν τῇ ἑορτῇ, μήποτε ἔσται θόρυβος τοῦ λαοῦ.

> And the chief priests and the scribes were seeking how to arrest him by stealth and kill him; for they said, "Not during the feast, lest there be a tumult of the people."

The narrator's report that the chief priests and scribes were now seeking to use treachery (δόλος) in their plot against Jesus is a surprising development. Prior to this (11:18; 12:12), they have sought to arrest and

---

10. Quesnell concludes that 6:52 is clearly a redactional addition by which Mark sought to heighten the theological significance of the loaves (see, e.g., 66–67, 176, 257–68). Furthermore, as Quesnell demonstrates, 8:14–21 deepens the enigma of the loaves even further prior to its illumination in the second half of the narrative (see, e.g., 103–24, 152–74).

destroy him, but they never have resorted to actions that, in the context of the narrative's norms of judgment, make them unclean. Jesus' list of those things that defile a person (7:20–23) includes δόλος (7:22). By implication, therefore, the chief priests and scribes defile themselves by this action. This new and radical development in their plot invites explanation.

Mark's explanation refers back to his notice at the beginning of the story of the imminence of the feast (14:1—μετὰ δύο ἡμέρας = "on the second day" = "the next day")[11] and to his earlier description of the authorities' fear of the crowd (11:18; 12:12). The implication of the comment is, therefore, that the authorities have resorted to treachery because of the imminence of the feast and their fear of a riot by the people. But this implication raises a tantalizing question: will they give up their efforts to arrest and kill Jesus if they cannot arrest him before the feast? This in turn implies the possibility that Jesus may be able to escape his passion and death. Thus, the comment invites reflection on earlier elements of the narrative and raises questions about what is going to happen.

Both narrative comments with γαρ that end stories earlier in Mark's Gospel are, therefore, directly parallel in their narrative function to the comments in 16:8. In contrast to the usual clarifying function of most narrative comments with γαρ, none of these three comments wraps up the story in a tidy little parcel, but rather each leaves several strings hanging out which invite the audience to do some work. All three comments are enigmatic and encourage reflection back to earlier elements in the story as well as forward to the possibilities of what may happen in the future. But, as the history of criticism shows, the final comment in 16:8 is a supremely enigmatic and provocative narrative comment.

Therefore, Knox's generalization that, apart from 16:8, Mark always rounds off the sections of his narrative without leaving anything to the imagination of his audience is inaccurate. In both of the earlier narratives that end with narrative comments, the comments have the same form and function as the comments in 16:8.

Inside Views

The inside view is a variation in narrative point of view in which the narrator describes the perceptions, thoughts, or feelings of a character. The most typical narrative point of view is that of an observer or reporter. When

---

11. Mark almost certainly meant the time to be calculated in the same way as the resurrection prophecy (μετὰ τρεῖς ἡμέρας in 8:31 = "on the third day"); see Taylor, *Mark*, 528.

telling a story from this perspective, the narrator describes the events objectively. An inside view takes the audience "inside" a character and describes internal events which would not be known to an observer. The inside views in Mark can be classified into two types: perceptions of the characters and descriptions of emotions.[12] In Mark 16:8 there are two inside views which describe emotions:[13] εἶχεν γὰρ αὐτὰς τρόμος καὶ ἔκστασις, "for trembling and astonishment had come upon them," and ἐφοβοῦντο γάρ, "for they were afraid." Mark explains the women's flight and silence in response to the astonishing announcement of Jesus' resurrection by describing their feelings. The combination of these two inside views in a single verse focuses intense attention on the emotions of the women.

Let us look again at earlier stories in the gospel in order to see whether another possible characteristic of Mark's narrative style is to end a story with a climax of insight into the feelings of the characters. Three earlier stories in Mark end with an inside view: the walking on the sea (6:45–52), the second passion prophecy (9:30–32), and the conflict about paying taxes to Caesar (12:13–17).[14] We shall discuss each of these, taking them up in reverse order.

The Conflict about Paying Taxes to Caesar (12:13–17)

The climax of this conflict narrative is an inside view of the emotional response of the Pharisees and Herodians who had sought to trap Jesus: καὶ ἐξεθαύμαζον ἐπ'αὐτῷ, "And they were amazed at him." Its function is the

---

12. The exploration of variations in narrative point of view has been one of the primary features of the development of modern fiction. "Stream-of-consciousness" narration, for example, is a sustained inside view. For the classic discussion of point of view in the modern novel, see Lubbock, *Craft of Fiction*; also see Booth, *Rhetoric*, 163–65, 245–48.

13. Representative instances of the two types of inside views in Mark are as follows: (1) Perceptions: 1:10; 2:16; 3:2, 21; 5:6, 15, 32, 36; 6:48–49; 7:25; 8:33; 9:8, 25; 11:13 12:28, 34; 14:67, 69; 15:10, 35, 39; 16:5; (2) Thoughts/feelings: 2:6; 3:5; 4:41; 5:29, 30, 33, 42; 6:2, 6, 19–20, 26, 34, 50–52; 7:37; 8:11; 9:6, 10, 32; 10:14, 22, 24, 26, 32, 41, 11:18, 21; 12:15, 17; 14:4, 19, 33; 15:5, 43, 44; 16:5, 8.

14. Two other stories in Mark end with an inside view followed by a statement in which the feeling is expressed in direct discourse: the calming of the storm (4:35–41) and the healing of the deaf and dumb man (7:31–37). While these endings are similar in their effect, since they also end with a concluding description of the emotional responses of persons to actions by Jesus, they are not strictly concluding inside views. They are, however, similar in terms of narrative technique and should be noted as further examples of similar tendencies in Mark's methods of composition.

same as that of the inside views in 16:8. It describes emotional reactions to a surprising word or action of Jesus.

The Second Passion Prophecy (9:30–32)

Again, at the end of this story the narrator gives the listeners an inside view into an emotional response of the disciples to a surprising word of Jesus, namely, his reiteration of the prophecy of his passion: οἱ δὲ ἠγνόουν τὸ ῥῆμα, καὶ ἐφοβοῦντο αὐτὸν ἐπερωτῆσαι, "But they did not understand the saying, and they were afraid to ask him." In this case the content as well as the function of the inside view is the same as in 16:8. In both instances Mark describes a response of silence by Jesus' followers, a silence brought on by fear.

Walking on the Sea (6:45–52)

We saw in the section on narrative commentary above that the last sentence in this story is a narrative comment. It is also an extensive inside view. And once again it is an inside view into the disciples' emotional response to a surprising action of Jesus. Furthermore, the inside view is compounded. Both the description of the disciples' amazement, which needs to be explained, and the explanation, that the disciples did not understand about the loaves because of their hardened hearts, are inside views. As a result, this is one of the most intensive insights into the characters of the gospel prior to 16:8.[15] There is also another similarity between the inside views in 6:51–52 and those in 16:8. Both inside views report responses by Jesus' followers that are to some degree wrong.

Thus, Mark is consistent in the way he uses inside views to end stories. In all four cases they describe emotional reactions to Jesus' surprising words or actions. Sometimes the consistency extends to an identity or similarity of content. This suggests that ending a story with a climactic insight into the feelings of his characters is for Mark a deliberate narrative technique. The double use of this device would certainly be appropriate at the climax of the gospel.

---

15. For other intensive inside views in Mark, see the following stories: the woman with a flow of blood (5:27–30), the transfiguration (9:6, 8) and Gethsemane (14:33–35).

Short Sentences

A survey of the endings of narrative units in the UBS Greek text of all four gospels shows that on several occasions in each gospel a story ends with a simple and relatively brief sentence. There are three times as many instances of this in Mark as in the other three gospels. This fact is even more striking in light of the Gospel of Mark's comparative shortness.[16]

It is unlikely that this way of ending a story is an accident. Bultmann and others have called attention to the emphasis placed upon those elements of a story that are left until the end.[17] Furthermore, one recent work on oral communication points out the emphatic effect of a short sentence that follows a longer one.[18] The ending of a story with a simple, relatively short sentence is probably, therefore, a deliberate[19] stylistic technique at work in the composition of Mark's Gospel, a combining of the effect of brevity and final position in order to bring about maximum stress.

Are the words ἐφοβοῦντο γάρ in Mark 16:8 an independent, simple and brief period ending the gospel? If so, Mark 16:8 exhibits yet a third technique of narrative style which, along with narrative comments and inside views, is present in earlier parts of the gospel.

The difficulty here is that neither the UBS nor the Nestle-Aland text punctuates ἐφοβοῦντο γάρ as an independent sentence. The Nestle-Aland text precedes these words with a semicolon; the UBS with a comma. Nor do translators treat these words as a separate sentence. The NRSV, NEB and Jerusalem Bible all precede them by a comma. If we are to argue, then, that the ending of Mark's story of the resurrection exhibits yet a third narrative characteristic of the ending of other stories in the gospel, we are going to have to show that the last two words really should be taken as an independent sentence and not as simply a new clause in a compound sentence.[20]

---

16. Matthew 16:4; 17:23; 26:35. Luke 1:66; 9:9; 14:6. John 10:42; 18:40. Mark 6:6a; 11:14; 12:12; 17, 34, 37; 14:11, 31.

17. Bultmann, *Synoptic Tradition*, 191. See also Klatzky, *Human Memory*, 9 for experiments on the function of human memory that help to explain why attention to position is a good principle of style.

18. Davis, *Preaching*, 277–79.

19. See Freedman, "Pottery, Poetry and Prophecy," 12 regarding the validity of contemporary observations about poetic style regardless of whether the stylistic device was conscious or unconscious for the poet.

20. The punctuation of NT texts is largely a modern editorial creation. This statement of J. H. Moulton is, therefore, worthy of quotation: "When . . . we use an extremely careful edition like that of WH, where punctuations in text and in margin are constantly determining the meaning for us, we must always be careful to realize our freedom to take our own line on sufficient reason." In Moulton and Howard, *Grammar*, 2.48.

Two considerations lead us to regard ἐφοβοῦντο γάρ as a separate sentence. We shall take them up in turn.

The first is a grammatical consideration that at least allows the possibility of a separate sentence. One modern discussion of grammar defines a sentence as "any locution (word, phrase, clause, or sentence) spoken or punctuated as an independent unit of discourse."[21] It may be "complete" or "incomplete." A complete sentence is one that includes a subject and predicate and makes sense on its own as an independent assertion.[22] In addition, a sentence may be related to what has gone before it either asyndetically or by means of a more or less ambiguous particle or conjunction. Blass–Debrunner–Funk cites ουν, δε, and και as such particles,[23] but γαρ must be added to the list, since both the Nestle-Aland and the UBS text often precede a γαρ clause with a period.[24] The presence of a particle or conjunction is often the source of our difficulty in knowing whether or not we should regard the clause that contains it as a new sentence or as a continuation of the sentence that has gone before. Its relationship to what goes before must be sufficiently loose as to make it at least appropriate, if not necessary, to come to a full stop before it. The presence of the conjunction or particle by no means guarantees that it is a continuation of the sentence that has gone before. In the case of both the γαρ clauses in 16:8, it is just as possible to precede each with a full stop as with a relatively minor pause (either a semicolon or comma). These two narrative comments serve to explain the preceding statements that the women fled and that they remained silent, but they do not by any means have to be a part of the preceding sentences.

Secondly, we must consider the fact that the Gospel of Mark was surely composed to be heard rather than to be read in silence.[25] It may even have been composed and delivered orally before it was written down.[26] The

21. Birk, *Understanding and Using English*, 550.

22. Birk, *Understanding and Using English*, 551.

23. BDF, 241.

24. In both editions of the Greek text we find a period before a γαρ clause in these passages in Mark: 4:25; 5:8; 6:17, 31; 7:10; 8:35, 36; 9:6, 41; 13:8; 14:7.

25. In the ancient world even when a person read to himself, he read aloud rather than in silence. This is clear from such passages as the story in Acts 8:26–40 about the Ethiopian eunuch who was reading alone in his chariot when Philip came up to him and heard him reading, and also from Augustine's discussion in Confessions 6.3 of Ambrose's curious practice of reading silently (*vox autem et lingua quiescebant . . . eum legentem vidimus ta ite et aliter numquam*).

26. See Hengel, "Mc 7, 3 πυγμη," 50: "Vermutlich ist gerade das Mkevg. nicht rein als literarisches Werk zu betrachten, sondern wurde bereits vor seiner schriftlichen Fixierung im Gottesdienst der Gemeinde vorgetragen. Seine stilistischen Züge weisen nicht nur auf einen literarisch ungeübten Vf., sondern zu gleicher Zeit auf einen sehr

problem in relation to the punctuation of 16:8 is, therefore, to determine the probable character of the pause that Mark and those who told or read his gospel aloud made prior to the last two words of 16:8. Was it only a hesitation, or was it a major pause marked by a full breath?

In the earlier discussion of narrative comments above, we observed that the function of comments with γαρ is to answer questions that have been raised by the previous statement. Prior to each γαρ clause in 16:8, Mark reports an extremely surprising and puzzling action by the women. He first says that, in response to the young man's command to go and tell the news to the disciples, the women "fled" (ἔφυγον). This word reverberates with the connotations of its previous use in the report of the reactions of the disciples and the young man at Jesus' arrest. The report is a surprise and raises the question, "Why did they flee?" The explanation answers this question. If the function of this report of the women's flight and its explanation was first to raise a question and then to answer it, the narrator necessarily paused long enough to give his listeners a chance to feel surprise and wonder at the women's response. In view of its function, the probability is that the narrator made a full stop prior to the explanation. Since a full stop is permitted by the grammar, the first γαρ clause should be read as a separate sentence.

The same factors are present to an even greater degree in the report and explanation of the women's silence. The report evokes the questions, "Why were they silent? Why didn't they obey the young man and announce this wonderful news?!" The γαρ clause, ἐφοβοῦντο γάρ, is an answer to that question. The force of the narrator's answer to the question depended upon the narrator allowing his listeners enough time to ask the question themselves. In order to allow that time, he needed to come to a full stop. It is probable, therefore, that Mark's final two-word answer was also a separate sentence.

If Mark did intend that 16:8 be presented orally in this manner there is a climactic concentration of increasingly shorter sentences in this verse. The four sentences have consecutively six, six, four, and two words. The final two-word sentence is a climactic use of a narrative technique that is present throughout the gospel.

---

versierten volkstümlichen Erzähler hin." [ET: "Presumably, the Gospel of Mark is not to be regarded as a purely literary work but was presented to the community in a worship service before it was written down. Its stylistic traits point not only to a literarily inexperienced writer but at the same time to a very accomplished traditional storyteller" (K. C. Hanson, trans.)].

Conclusion

Mark employs the same narrative techniques that he uses in 16:8 to end earlier stories in his gospel. Furthermore, in 16:8 he uses these techniques in a concentrated and climactic manner. Combinations of these techniques do occur at the conclusion of earlier stories. Mark 6:5 is both an inside view and a narrative comment, while 12:17 is both an inside view and a short final sentence. But in 16:8 there is a combination of all three techniques as well as a multiple use of two of them. This concentration seems particularly appropriate for the ending of a story that brings to a close the gospel narrative as a whole. Consequently, purely from the point of view of the possibilities of narrative style, it is probable that Mark did indeed intend to end his gospel at 16:8.

In view of this, Knox's argument that Mark could not possibly have hit upon a narrative style that anticipated by some 1500 years the development of modern narrative techniques is not persuasive. Mark used this narrative style throughout the story. A relatively safe prediction would be, however, that further instances of similar techniques for ending a narrative will be discovered both in the biblical narrative tradition and in ancient popular narratives. In that case inheritance as well as inspiration may prove to have contributed to the unique enigma of the ending of Mark.

4

Mark 16:8 and the Apostolic Commission

The conclusion that Mark intended to end his gospel at 16:8 will remain in doubt until it is shown that 16:8 is a meaningful ending. In view of the continuity between the narrative techniques of 16:8 and earlier endings in Mark,[1] this discussion will concentrate on the interpretations of 16:8 as the intended ending.[2] The thesis presented here will be that 16:8 is the climactic reversal in the motif of the messianic secret and that it emphasizes, in Mark's characteristic style, the same theme as the endings of the other gospels, namely, the apostolic commission to proclaim the gospel. The process will be, first, to identify the conclusions about Mark's use of techniques of narration implicit in the major interpretations of 16:8 as the ending, and

1. Boomershine and Bartholomew, "Narrative Technique," which is presumed as a foundation for this study.

2. The history of interpretation of Mark's ending has two major streams: (1) those who have sought to interpret 16:8 as the intended ending and (2) those who have found 16:8 a meaningless and impossible ending and have tried to explain how it happened and/or to reconstruct the original ending. This second stream has developed an extremely wide spectrum of explanations and reconstructions ranging from sheer speculation to responsible critical analysis. Among those to be seriously considered are: (1) text-critical arguments for the authenticity of the shorter and longer ending (e.g., in favor of the shorter ending, Aland, "Bemerkungen zum Schluss"; and Aland, "Der wiedergefundene Markusschluss"; in favor of the longer ending, Farmer, *The Last Twelve Verses*; against Farmer's thesis, see the review by Birdsall; and against originality of both the longer and shorter endings, Elliott, "Text and Language of the Endings"); (2) efforts at construction of the hypothesized original ending (e.g., Bartsch, "Der Schluss Markusevangeliums"; Linnemann, "Markusschluss"; Trompf, "Resurrection Appearance and the Ending"); (3) explanations of how the ending at 16:8 came to be (Schmithals, "Der Markusschluss"). For a survey of recent research on the Markan ending, see Trompf, "Markusschluss in Recent Research."

then to evaluate those conclusions by an examination of Mark's use of those particular tools of the narrator's craft.[3] Because of the uncertainty of the resurrection narrative's tradition history, only the final form of the narrative will be studied.[4] I shall examine in turn the interpretations of 16:8 as a recommendation of holy awe, as a theological polemic, and as the conclusion to the motif of the messianic secret.[5]

The method of this study is most accurately seen as a development of form criticism. Form criticism sought to identify the elements of narrative technique that shaped the formation of the gospel narrative tradition.[6]

3. The problem of inconsistency between the shockingly negative character of Mark's ending and the endings of the other gospels has been stated by Taylor, *St. Mark,* 609: "To the later Evangelists this ending was intolerable: Matthew says that, with fear and great joy, they ran to tell His disciples; Luke said that they told all these things to the Eleven and the rest . . . it is incredible that Mark intended such a conclusion."

4. For an excellent summary of some analyses of the pre-Markan resurrection tradition, see Bode, *First Easter,* 25. The conclusions of critical efforts to reconstruct the tradition history of the pre-Markan resurrection narrative have been extremely varied. Since the early conclusion that Mark added 16:7 to an existing narrative (e.g., Bousset, Bultmann, Marxsen), redaction-critical studies have come to a wide range of conclusions. Thus L. Schenke's pre-Markan narrative is 16:2, 5, 6, 8a, *Auferstehungsverkündigung und leeres Grab*; Dormeyer's pre-Markan resurrection narrative is itself a secondary redaction of a primitive Christian martyrology and consists of 16:1, 2b, 4a, 5–8a, with 8b being a gloss; see Dormeyer, *Die Passion Jesu.* Crossan's conclusion that there was no pre-Markan tradition, which in turn "renders its reconstruction quite problematic," is justified by the absence of unambiguous signs of the narrative's developmental history; see Crossan, "Empty Tomb and Absent Lord," 145. The conclusion here is that the history of the pre-Markan resurrection tradition, if there was one, is shrouded in mystery and cannot provide a sound foundation for interpretation of the narrative in its final form.

5. A major interpretation of the ending at 16:8 which is excluded from consideration is the position widely held early in this century that, in the context of early belief in the resurrection on the basis of the appearances, Mark's ending explained why the testimony to the fact of the empty tomb remained unknown for so long and was of such recent origin. See, e.g., Bultmann, *Synoptic Tradition,* 285, who cites Bousset with approval Bousset; also Creed, "Conclusion of the Gospel," 175–80. For critiques of this interpretation, see Taylor, *St. Mark,* 609 and Fuller, *Resurrection Narratives,* 53.

6. Rhetorical criticism and its interests are outlined in Muilenburg's proposal ("Form Criticism") to go beyond form criticism's preoccupation with literary types and genres to a systematic consideration of the techniques of narrative and poetic composition. However, some aspects of these concerns have been addressed in form criticism; see, e.g., Bultmann, *History,* esp. 307–17. Bultmann, while primarily regarding oral tradition as an unconscious and virtually sociological process of composition, recognized that techniques of narrative composition were a major factor in determining the history of the synoptic tradition. In view of the danger of the confusing multiplication of "criticisms," it is better to reform and develop earlier methods in a more comprehensive direction than to sponsor new ones. Furthermore, we cannot know to what degree the use of these techniques of composition was conscious. The argument here is only that

The categories of narrative analysis that have been developed by twentieth-century criticism of fiction are adapted here in order to expand the resources for form-critical study and to make possible a more precise analysis of Mark's narrative techniques.[7]

The primary categories of narrative technique can be defined briefly.[8] *Narrative point of view* refers to the vantage point or perspective from which the narrator presents the actions of the story. Mark generally reports the action of his narrative from the perspective of an observer. A major variation in point of view is the *inside view* in which the narrator reports the internal thoughts or feelings of a character.[9] *Norms of judgment* are the ethical norms for the narrator's implicit evaluations of the actions of the characters that he invites his audience to share.[10] *Distance in characterization* describes the dynamics of sympathy and alienation, involvement or detachment that take place in the relationships between the narrator, the characters of the narrative, and the audience.[11] Among the factors that influence distance are: shifts in narrative point of view, positive or negative norms of judgment, patterns of behavior, and the connotations of the words that are used to describe the character. Finally, plot is the interrelationship of the actions of the narrative. The establishment and subsequent reversal of expectations is often a major element in a plot. All of these factors in narrative rhetoric combine to form the network of appeals made by the narrator to his audience. The clarification of the rhetorical characteristics of Mark 16:8 provides a new perspective from which to examine the anomalies of this ending.

The Positive Interpretation of 16:8: Holy Awe

R. H. Lightfoot suggested an interpretation of the ending that has commanded attention, if not assent, since its appearance in his collection of essays on Mark so distinguished by grace as well as insight. Lightfoot proposed

---

factors of narrative technique were at work as well as factors of literary types.

7. For the most comprehensive treatment and bibliography of the analysis of narrative technique in twentieth-century literary criticism of fiction, see Booth, *Rhetoric of Fiction*; see also Corbett, *Rhetorical Analyses*.

8. For a discussion of some aspects of narrative technique in Mark 16:8, see above Boomershine and Bartholomew, "Narrative Technique."

9. For a comprehensive discussion of inside views, see Booth, *Rhetoric of Fiction*, 163–65, 245–49.

10. Booth, *Rhetoric of Fiction*, 177–95, 249–64.

11. For a discussion of the control of distance in characterization, see Booth, "Control of Distance in Jane Austen's *Emma*," in *Rhetoric of Fiction*, 243–66. For a discussion of possible problems in the control of distance, *Rhetoric of Fiction*, 311–36.

that Mark's purpose in the ending was to emphasize the appropriateness, in response to God's revelation in the resurrection, of "awe or dread or holy fear of God." The key statement in his argument is as follows: "I desire to suggest . . . that it may be exceptionally difficult for the present generation to sympathize with St. Mark's insistence on fear and amazement as the first and inevitable and, up a point, right result of revelation."[12] Translated into the categories of narrative rhetoric, Lightfoot concludes that Mark appeals to a positive norm of judgment that he assumed his audience shared. According to this norm, a response of holy awe was right. The problem for our involvement with Mark's audience is that we no longer share Mark's norm of judgment and thereby make inappropriate judgments of the women's response.

Lightfoot's conclusion will now be tested by a detailed analysis of the norms of judgment which are operative in 16:8 as they appear earlier in the gospel narrative. Norms of judgment are the result both of the cultural and religious values that are shared by the narrator and the audience and of the cumulative impact of specific evaluations made in the course of the narrative itself. Therefore, the earlier parts of the narrative provide a comparative basis for clarifying the ethical appeals that are implicit in 16:8.

Three emotional responses of the women are reported in 16:8: φόβος (fear), ἔκστασις (astonishment), and τρόμος (trembling). An analysis of the ethical connotations of these three words and their relative verbs (φοβέομαι/ φόβος, ἐξίστημι/ἔκστασις, τρέμω/τρόμος) shows that there are many positive aspects to Mark's use of these words. For example, Mark uses ἐξίστημι (to be astonished) to describe the reaction of the crowd to the healing of the paralytic (2:12) and the response of Jairus and his wife to the raising of their daughter (5:42). Amazement at these deliverances from the power of evil is unambiguously right.

Mark also, at least twice, uses φοβέομαι/φόβος (fear) as a sympathetic response to describe awe in the presence of supernatural events: the stilling of the storm (4:41) and the transfiguration (9:6). In several other instances, awe is at least a significant element in the meaning of the word: the Gerasenes' response to the healing of the demoniac (5:15), the woman's reaction to her healing (5:33), Herod's reaction to John the Baptist (6:19–20), and the disciples' response to the third passion prophecy (10:32). Among these instances, the closest verbal parallel to 16:8 is the highly sympathetic response of the woman with the flow of blood who comes to Jesus φοβηθεῖσα καὶ τρέμουσα (with fear and trembling). Thus the words that Mark uses to describe the women's feelings in 16:8 do have positive ethical connotations

---

12. Lightfoot, *Gospel Message*, 97. See also Allen, "Mark 16:8"; and Allen, "Fear."

earlier in the narrative.[13] To this degree, Lightfoot has accurately described the norms of judgment that are operative in 16:8.

The descriptions in 16:8, however, must be seen in the light of their function as narrative comments. These inside views of the women's feelings are explanations of the women's flight and silence. As has been shown above,[14] comments introduced by γαρ explain surprising or puzzling actions. Mark's choice of this form shows that he assumed his listeners would be surprised by the women's flight and silence.[15] Therefore, in addition to clarifying the norms of judgment which are associated with the women's feelings, it is also necessary to specify the ethical norms associated with the women's actions of flight and silence.

The connotations of the women's flight are determined by the earlier narration of the flight of the disciples and the young man where the same verb, ἔφυγον, is used (14:50–52). The disciples' flight is presented as a scandalous act and is associated with the shame of the young man's running away naked. Since this turning point in the narrative includes the only prior use of the word, the women's flight is unavoidably associated with the disciples' action. It is set, therefore, in a strongly negative context.

The women's silence is even more inappropriate. The angelic young man commanded them to go and tell the disciples. The news of Jesus' resurrection is incomparably good news and the possibility of the disciples' seeing Jesus in Galilee is associated with joy. The women's silence is, therefore, the exact opposite of the angel's command and dashes the expectations of joyful reunion that Mark has established. It is the most blatant form of disobedience to a divine commission. Therefore, since the norms associated with the command of an angel are positive, the women's silence is unequivocally and unambiguously wrong. It is a shocking reversal of expectations.

Thus, the norms associated with the women's flight and silence are totally negative. Mark appeals to his audience to condemn the women's actions. But their actions are an equally total reversal of expectations. The shocking and unexpected character of the women's actions is, therefore, what Mark seeks to explain in his narrative comments.

The function of the positive connotations associated with the women's feelings of fear and trembling can now be seen. In his narrative comments, Mark explains in a sympathetic manner why the women ran away and

13. See also Fuller, *Resurrection*, 53, who observes that these emotions are a frequent biblical reaction to an angelophany (cf. Luke 1:12, 39).

14. See above, Boomershine and Bartholomew, "Narrative Technique."

15. I am here indebted to the critiques by Bultmann and Taylor of this interpretation; see Bultmann, *History*, 285; also Taylor, *St. Mark*, 609.

remained silent. His comments provide understandable reasons for their actions. The function of the comments is, therefore, to appeal for the maintenance of sympathetic distance in relation to the women. But, while appealing for understanding of their motives, Mark in no way minimizes the wrongness of their actions.

Lightfoot bases his positive interpretation of the ending on the positive connotations of the women's responses, particularly their response of fear. While he is right that fear has positive connotations, he fails to keep in clear focus the central scandal of the ending. The women's fear is not reported as a response to seeing the empty tomb or to hearing the angel's announcement of Jesus' resurrection.[16] Their fear is introduced in a narrative comment that explains their scandalous response to the commission to go and tell the disciples and Peter that Jesus is going before them into Galilee. The women's fear is, therefore, associated with their response to the divine commission to announce the resurrection rather than to the fact of the resurrection itself. The positive connotations of the women's fear do not give to Mark's resurrection narrative the character of a satisfactory and happy ending. While their fear is understandable and to a degree sympathetic, the dominant tone of the ending is negative.

The Negative Interpretation of the Ending: Theological Polemic

J. D. Crossan has suggested with characteristic clarity an interpretation of Mark's ending that draws together the implications of a series of recent redaction-critical studies of Mark. These studies share the common hypothesis that Mark developed his gospel as a polemic against early Christian theological opponents who were interested in miracles, *theios anēr* (divine man) Christology, and mission to Jews rather than Gentiles.[17] Crossan has proposed that as relatives of Jesus the women represent the Jerusalem church for Mark. The meaning of the women's failure to communicate the message grows out of their representative function: "the Jerusalem community led by

---

16. Against Balz, "φοβέω," 211: "What the women are afraid of in Mark 16:8 is the empty tomb and the incomprehensible message of the angel." This confusion about the specific character of what Mark says in the ending is a major source of the difficulties in arriving at a comprehensive interpretation of its meaning.

17. The history of the development of this interpretation of Mark within the framework of early intra-Christian polemic can be traced in: Kuby, "Zur Konzeption"; Tyson, "Blindness"; Schreiber, "Die Christologie"; Schreiber, *Theologie des Vertrauens*; Linnemann, "Die Verleugnung"; Weeden, *Mark*; Crossan, "Mark and the Relatives"; Kelber, *The Kingdom in Mark*.

the disciples and especially Peter, have never accepted the call of the exalted Lord communicated to it from the Markan community. The Gospel ends in juxtaposition of Markan faith in 16:6–7 and of Jerusalem failure in 16:7–8."[18] Crossan's interpretation accounts for the negativity of the ending, therefore, as the climax of a theological polemic.

In order to translate Crossan's suggestion into an analysis of Mark's use of narrative technique, it is necessary to go beyond what Crossan says explicitly and to deal with the implications of his interpretation. The risk of misrepresenting his view that is involved in this procedure is somewhat reduced by the fact that he sees the characterization of the women as analogous to the characterization of the disciples which has been developed more explicitly.[19] Crossan's interpretation leads to the conclusion that the characterization of the women, like the disciples, is a polemical characterization. The characterization is designed to create maximum negative distance and thereby to alienate the audience from the women.

The polemical interpretation of the characterization of the women can be evaluated by an analysis of the dynamics of distance in the characterization. As was noted above, the factors that influence distance are extremely varied and include shifts in narrative point view, positive or negative norms of judgment, patterns of behavior, and the connotations of the words that are used to describe the character. By identifying these factors, it is possible to clarify the overall structure of the dynamics of distance in the characterization.[20]

The characterization of the women as a group outside 16:1–8 occurs in two notices that conclude the stories of Jesus' death and burial (15:40–41, 47).[21] As was maintained above in comments on Mark's narrative

---

18. Crossan, "Mark and the Relatives," 149.

19. The polemical interpretation of the characterization of the disciples has been fully developed by Weeden; see *Mark*, esp. 26–51.

20. Crossan's evidence for a polemic against the women is based on a redaction-critical analysis of Markan shaping of the Beelzebub controversy (3:32–35), the rejection in Nazareth (6:1–6), and the notices of the women (15:40–41, 47). The connections between the women in 15:40–41 and the relatives of Jesus earlier in the narrative are very oblique. With the possible exception of Mary, the mother, the names do not occur earlier in the gospel. Thus, while Crossan's evidence in relation to a possible connection between the women at the end of the gospel and the earlier allusions to Jesus' mother is important, the characterization of the women as a group only begins in 15:40. Only two of the women are reported as witnesses of the burial (15:47). Furthermore, in the light of recent studies of Mary in the NT, a Markan polemic against the mother of Jesus seems improbable.

21. See, for example, Taylor, *St. Mark*, 598; also Nineham, *St. Mark*, 431, 435.

techniques,[22] endings are points of primary emphasis. Since it is generally agreed that these notices of the women witnesses are Markan redactional additions, Mark's positioning of these notices is an indication that they are important. The importance of these notices of the women is heightened because the women are the first followers of Jesus to be mentioned since the report of Peter's denial.

The descriptions of the women are extremely sympathetic. In both instances, they are the only followers of Jesus who witness these tragic events. Both notices are inside views that describe what they saw. While Mark does not say explicitly that they mourned for Jesus, the overall atmosphere of both stories implies their grief. Thus, the women are presented as the only followers of Jesus who risked being witnesses and mourners at his death and burial. Furthermore, the references to their relationship with him in Galilee are warm. The verb "to follow" is the key word for discipleship and is always a good action in the narrative (e.g., Peter's following into the courtyard, 14:54). The verb "to serve" has equally sympathetic overtones, having been used earlier to describe the angels (1:13), Peter's mother-in-law (1:31), and the Son of Man (10:45). These descriptions of the women, therefore, are characterized by elements that create a reduction of distance and a high degree of sympathetic identification.

The resurrection narrative itself begins with the names of the three women who were witnesses at Jesus' death (15:40–41). The repetition of their names and the report of their purchasing spices in order to anoint Jesus' body sustain the atmosphere of mourning. The announcement of the resurrection is preceded by two inside views that describe first the women's discovery of the open entrance to the tomb (16:4) and then what they saw inside the tomb (16:5). This extended description from the point of view of the women is the most highly developed inside view since Jesus' prayer in Gethsemane. The climax of this inside view is a description of their feelings: ἐξεθαμβήθησαν (they were alarmed). This word was last used to describe Jesus' agony in Gethsemane (14:33). In this series of inside views, Mark gives a degree of insight into the sympathetic perceptions and feelings of the women that is exceeded only in the characterizations of Peter and Jesus.

Thus, in the death and resurrection narrative prior to the angel's speech, all aspects of the characterization of the women—the extended inside views, the positive norms of judgment in relation to their actions, the overall atmosphere and mood—create a steady intensification of appeals for identification with the women. The implicit purpose in the structure of the characterization is to invite an intensive identification with the women prior

22. See Boomershine and Bartholomew, "Narrative Technique" (chap. 3 above).

to the resurrection announcement. The function of this invitation to identify with the women is to involve the audience in the experience of hearing the announcement of the resurrection from the perspective of the women.

The factors of distance in the final episode are, therefore, complex. The flight and silence are associated with negative norms of judgment. The negative judgment that is thereby solicited tends to create critique and increase distance. However, as we have also seen, the narrator's comments that explain their shocking actions are inside views of the women's feelings. These comments combine the most powerful narrative techniques for creating sympathetic distance. As a result, the distance factors in this episode create contradictory dynamics that pull in opposite directions. The actions must be judged as wrong but a high degree of identification is maintained. As in the story of Peter's denial, Mark combines strongly negative judgments with a high degree of sympathetic distance.

The implications of Crossan's interpretation for the characterization of the women can now be assessed. The polemical interpretation of the ending carries with it the correlate conclusion that the characterization of the women earlier in the gospel is highly negative. The analysis of the factors of distance in the characterization leads to almost exactly the opposite conclusion. The characterization of the women is in no sense a polemical characterization, in contrast to, for example, the characterizations of Judas, the chief priests, or the Roman soldiers. Thus, while the negative interpretation of the ending accounts for the wrongness of the women's flight and silence, the implication that Mark seeks to alienate his audience from the women is inaccurate. Mark's negative norms are directed against the women's *response* of flight and silence rather than against the women themselves. A valid interpretation of the ending, therefore, must account for the predominantly sympathetic characterization of the women.

The Ending and the Messianic Secret

Willi Marxsen has proposed that a primary motif in the ending is the tension between speech and silence. According to Marxsen, Mark added the angel's commission to the women (16:7) in order to complete the motif of Jesus going before them into Galilee (14:28). The women's response of silence is a reversal of the earlier theme of Jesus' injunctions to silence being transgressed in energetic spreading of the news (e.g., 1:44–45). This tension between disclosure and concealment is part of the messianic secret.[23] The messianic secret is revealed in the resurrection and the angel's commission,

23. Marxsen, *Mark the Evangelist*, 91, 111–16.

only to be complicated again by the reversal of expectations of the women's silence. Thus, for Marxsen, the plot motif of the messianic secret is centered on the issue of proclamation and is developed in the tension between disclosure and concealment, proclamation and silence.

Reginald Fuller's account of the history of the resurrection tradition builds upon Marxsen's foundation. While agreeing that Mark added 16:7, Fuller proposes that Mark's purpose was to allude to the first two appearances in an appearance list such as 1 Cor. 15:5 rather than to stories of resurrection appearances or to the Parousia.[24] These appearance lists were related in early Christian tradition to the inauguration of the apostolic mission. Fuller reasons as follows:

> Mark 9:9 has pointed forward to the resurrection as *terminus ad quem* for the preservation of the messianic secret. Mark must indicate that this *terminus ad quem* has now been reached. He could not narrate the final unveiling of the secret if no appearance narratives were as yet available for the purpose. So the angel simply points forward to the unveiling. In the light of Mark 9:9, Mark 16:7 points forward not only to the appearances to the disciples (and especially to Peter) but also to the publication of the messianic secret and the inauguration of the mission. Mark thus achieves in an oblique manner what the later Evangelists achieve more directly through the missionary charges which they put into the mouth of the Risen One.[25]

Thus, Mark's purpose in the allusion to the appearance list in 16:7 was to introduce the issue of the church's mission. The reason for this emphasis was Mark's concern about the importance of the extension of the church through the apostolic mission that he shared with the other evangelists.

Both Marxsen and Fuller have developed this interpretation of the ending primarily from a redaction history analysis of 16:7 and its function in the overall structure of Mark's Gospel. Neither has provided a detailed account of the meaning of 16:8.[26] Their proposal can be tested, therefore, by an analysis of the narrative structure of the ending and of the meaning of 16:8 within that structure.

The narrative structure of the ending is directly related to the structure of the passion narrative which is, in turn, built upon the framework of Jesus' passion-resurrection prophecies. A chart of the major sections of the passion-resurrection narrative after the last supper story alongside the

24. Fuller, *Resurrection*, 66–67.

25. Fuller, *Resurrection*, 67.

26. See Marxsen, *Mark*, 111–116 and Fuller, *Resurrection*, 61–64, 66–67.

elements of the third passion-resurrection prophecy shows this structural connection:

The Prophecy Mark 10:33–34	The Passion–Resurrection Narrative Mark 14–16
The Son of Man will be:	
(1) handed over to the priests and scribes	(1) The arrest (14:26–52)
(2) and they will condemn him to death	(2) The Sanhedrin trial (14:53–72)
(3) and turn him over to the Gentiles who will mock him, spit on him, flog him	(3) The Pilate trial and mocking by the soldiers (15:1–20)
(4) and kill him	(4) The crucifixion, death, and burial (15:21–47)
(5) and after three days he will be raised.	(5) The resurrection (16:1–8)

Thus, after the supper narrative, the passion-resurrection narrative is structured as a step-by-step fulfillment of Jesus' prophecy.

In view of the centrality of this prophecy-fulfillment motif, one might expect that the fulfillment of the prophecies would receive the greatest emphasis in the individual sections. But, with the exception of the Pilate trial, Mark ends the sections with, and thereby gives climactic emphasis to, the responses of Jesus' followers to the fulfillment of the prophecies. Thus, the arrest section ends with the flight of the disciples (14:50–52), the Sanhedrin trial with Peter's denial (14:66–72), the death and burial with the women witnesses (15:47), and the resurrection with the women's silence (16:8). Only the Pilate trial ends with climactic emphasis on the fulfillment of Jesus' prophecy in the mockery by the Roman soldiers. All the other sections end with the responses of Jesus' followers.

The character of the responses by Jesus' followers is negative in three out of four instances. Like the women's flight and silence, the flight of the disciples and Peter's denial are radically wrong. Among these climactic endings, only the description of the women witnesses of Jesus' death and burial relates a positive and appropriate response. Therefore, three of the five sections of Mark's passion-resurrection narrative end with, and thereby give climactic emphasis to, scandalous responses by Jesus' followers to the fulfillment of his prophecies.

An analysis of the endings of the arrest and of the Sanhedrin trial provides, therefore, a comparative framework that may further clarify the factors of meaning in the ending of the resurrection narrative. The two stories have a pattern of narrative characteristics that is remarkably similar to the pattern of 16:1–8. In each case, the narrator reports responses of Jesus' followers that call for negative judgments while at the same time appealing for the maintenance of sympathetic distance in relation to the characters. The purpose of this analysis will be limited to a demonstration of these parallels in narrative technique.

The norms of judgment for both of these stories are established in the prophecy of scandalization and denial (14:26–31). The conflict between Jesus and Peter of prophecy and counter-prophecy establishes that scandalization and denial are unequivocally wrong.[27] The right alternative to denial is stated by Peter: to die with Jesus. The alternative to being scandalized, on the other hand, is left ambiguous.

In the arrest narrative, Jesus' prophecy that he would be handed over to the chief priests and scribes is fulfilled when the crowd from the chief priests and scribes, led by Judas, lays hands on him. The first response to this fulfillment is the striking of the slave of the high priest. While the precise identity of the fighter is not made clear, the only persons present are the disciples and the crowd. Mark implies, therefore, that it is one of the disciples who strikes the slave. In view of Mark's portrayal of the crowd as armed and hostile and in the absence of any statements by Jesus forbidding violence either before or after the arrest, it appears that Mark presents this attack as a righteous action. The implicit appeal to the audience is to rejoice and to hope that others will join in the fight to set Jesus free. This event, therefore, heightens the sympathetic character of the disciples in the narrative and invites a higher degree of identification with them.

As a result, the flight of the disciples is a reversal of expectation and is in scandalous contrast to the righteousness of defending Jesus. The climax of the story is the flight of the young man. This brief account recapitulates the reversal and intensifies the surprise and the shame of the flight. The attempt of the young man to follow Jesus is a heroic action. His seizure is also sympathetic since he thereby begins to share Jesus' fate. His naked flight, therefore, is both unexpected and scandalous. Apart from Genesis 2:25, nakedness in the OT is almost always associated with some form of humiliation.[28] This naked flight is the climactic symbol of the shame and

27. The verb σκανδαλίζω has been used earlier in Mark to describe seeds that take root and die as a result of persecution (4:17), the response of the people of Nazareth to Jesus (6:3), the cause of doom for anyone who leads a believer to be "scandalized" or is "scandalized" himself (9:42–7).

28. There are three major uses of nakedness in the OT: (1) as a description of the poor (Job 24:7, 10; 31:19; Eccl 5:14; Ezek 18:16); (2) as a sign of shame or guilt (Gen 3:7, 10, 11; 2 Chr 28:15; Job 26:6; Hos 2:3; Amos 2:16; 4:5; Mic 1:8; Ezek 16:22, 39; 23:29);

humiliation of the disciples' response to Jesus' arrest. Thus, Mark's narration of the flight of both the disciples and the young man combines an appeal for a high degree of sympathy with norms that require a decisively negative judgment. The effect of the story is to involve the audience in an experience of shame associated with being scandalized and running away from Jesus at the time of his arrest.

The second story that ends with a scandalous response, the Sanhedrin trial, opens with the report that Peter followed Jesus into the courtyard of the high priest. In the light of this fulfillment of Peter's counter prophecy (14:31), the question implicit in the story is whether Peter will deny Jesus or die with him. When the trial ends with Jesus' condemnation, the alternatives of death or denial are even more firmly established. Peter's courage in entering the threatening atmosphere of the courtyard invites identification with him and awakens the hope that Peter will die with Jesus rather than deny him.

The three denials build to a climax of prophecy fulfillment. Mark explicitly identifies each denial so that his audience can count them. The explicit fulfillment of Jesus' prophecy in the second crowing of the cock immediately follows the final, vehement denial. The norms that have been established earlier require condemnation of Peter's action.

At this point in the story, Mark suddenly shifts his narrative point of view and gives an inside view of Peter's mind as he remembers Jesus' prophecy. Since inside views almost inevitably create sympathy for a character, this shift in narrative perspective reverses the distance relationship to Peter. Mark then reports that Peter wept, an action that implies his grief. This intimate description of Peter's response to his realization of what he has done is a poignant appeal for sympathy. This ending is also the shortest narrative statement in the Gospel prior to 16:8.

The stories of the arrest, the Sanhedrin trial, and the resurrection have, therefore, a similar narrative structure. The elements that recur in varying sequences in these three stories are:

(1) The fulfillment of an element of Jesus' passion–resurrection prophecies;

(2) The establishment of norms of judgment in relation to right and wrong responses to the fulfillment of the prophecies;

(3) The appeal for identification with one of Jesus' followers;

(4) The narration of that follower's wrong response.

---

and (3) in reference to birth (Job 1:21; Eccl 5:15).

The function of this structure is to invite the audience to identify with a sympathetic character who makes a radically wrong response to the fulfillment of the passion and resurrection prophecies. The experience of hearing the narrative sympathetically is, therefore, the experience of living through the motivations and results of the wrong responses to the specific events of Jesus' passion and resurrection through identification with the characters. The effect of this narrative structure is to appeal for repentance from the wrong response and for reinforcement of the right response.

What is then the intended meaning of the end of the resurrection narrative? The women's alternatives for response to the fulfillment of the resurrection prophecy are either to announce the resurrection or to be silent. Their choice of flight and silence is presented as utterly wrong but equally understandable and sympathetic. The ending concretizes, therefore, the powerful conflict between responsibility and fear that is implicit in the commission to announce the resurrection.

The intended meaning of the ending is, therefore, the total effect of the ending. The ending is designed to be an experience of conflict between the scandal of silence and the fear of proclamation. In response to the shock of realization that the response of silence is utterly wrong, the story appeals for the proclamation of the resurrection regardless of fear. In the silences surrounding the climactic short statements of 16:8 and the surprising ending, Mark invites his audience to reflect on their own response to the dilemma that the women faced.

We can now see more clearly the connection between the ending at 16:8 and the motif of the messianic secret as it has been interpreted by Marxsen and Fuller. As Marxsen has shown, the women's silence is the reversal of an earlier pattern in the gospel of inappropriate disclosure in response to commands of silence. The tension between disclosure and concealment to which this motif contributes is the central tension of the messianic secret and is present throughout Mark's narrative. The impact of the ending, therefore, is to appeal for repentance from silence in response to the commission to announce Jesus' messiahship. The effect of the ending could be called a purging of the fear associated with the apostolic commission. Thus, the ending is a climactic reversal of expectations in the central Markan motif of the messianic secret.

Furthermore, the accuracy of Fuller's conclusion that Mark is developing the same theme as the later evangelists with their missionary charges by the Risen One is also confirmed. One of the underlying difficulties in understanding Mark's ending has been its discontinuity with the endings of the other gospels. But, as the prophets of Israel knew well, there are two major ways of appealing for righteous behavior: positive sanctions for right actions and negative sanctions for wrong actions. Stated in rhetorical terms, the options are a rhetoric of threat or curse in which the purpose is to appeal for repentance from sinful actions and a rhetoric of promise or reward in which the purpose is to attract the audience to the blessings that will accompany righteous actions. Mark, therefore, seeks to eliminate the negative response of silence and to appeal for repentance from that response.

Matthew and Luke accentuate the positive response and report the apostolic commission in an atmosphere of promise and blessing. The ending of John, however, is more closely parallel to Mark's ending. Jesus' conversation with Peter (John 21:15–22) combines a high degree of sympathetic distance in relation to Peter with negative judgments about Peter's earlier actions. The theme of the conversation is Peter's apostolic commission. And the effect of the story could equally be called a purging of the fear associated with the apostolic commission. Thus, all four evangelists end with the theme of the apostolic commission. Each in his distinctive way deals with the problems and promises associated with that commission.

The character of Mark's ending would suggest that his listeners faced a situation in which proclamation of the gospel carried extreme risks and was associated with fear. The ending indicates, however, that for Mark the flight into silence was the supreme danger as well as the ultimate irony.

Thus, while there are areas of remaining ambiguity, the continuity between the meaning of 16:8 that emerges from an analysis of its narrative rhetoric and the meaning of the endings of the other gospels increases the probability that 16:8 was the intended ending. Furthermore, this interpretation of 16:8 in relation to the apostolic commission accounts for the combination of negative action and sympathetic characterization that occurs in Mark's narration of the women's flight and silence.

Conclusion

The re-creation in imagination of how Mark would have told the story to an audience of listeners provides one way of formulating interpretations of 16:8. I propose that Mark reported the women's actions of flight and silence in a tone of judgment. After each report, he explained with sympathy in his voice why the women had run away and remained silent. As a result, his listeners could both sympathetically understand the women's actions and recognize how wrong they were. Thus, Mark's final comment, the shortest and most enigmatic of his concluding comments, provoked his listeners to reflect on the future response of Jesus' followers, including themselves, to the commission to proclaim the Gospel.

5

Peter's Denial as Polemic or Confession

The Implications of Media Criticism for Biblical Hermeneutics

Werner Kelber's ground-breaking book, *The Oral and the Written Gospel*, explores the implications of contemporary media research for the interpretation of the Gospel tradition. Investigations of existing oral cultures[1] and the patterns associated with media transitions[2] have shown that a change in the dominant mode of communication within a culture, particularly the transition from oral speech to writing, invariably involves a major transformation of communication styles, patterns of community organization, and ways of thinking. In classical form criticism, the relationship between the oral and the written Gospel was understood as a linear relationship of substantial continuity. Kelber argues that, in the light of this more recent research, a more appropriate picture of the gospel tradition would emphasize the chasm that separates the gospel in the world of writing from the gospel in its original oral matrix. Kelber's central thesis, "that the written gospel is ill accounted for, and in fact misunderstood, as the sum total of oral rules and drives,"[3] generates a radically new picture of the history of the gospel tradition.

A component of Kelber's thesis is that Mark was carrying out a polemic against Peter and the disciples as representatives of the oral gospel. In

1. See, for example, Lord, *Singer of Tales;* Finnegan, *Oral Poetry.*
2. See McLuhan, *Understanding Media;* Ong, *Presence of the Word.*
3. Kelber, *Oral and Written Gospel*, 214.

his earlier works, especially *The Kingdom in Mark*, Prof. Kelber developed the now widely held position in Markan scholarship that Mark portrayed the disciples and Peter in a highly negative light in order to discredit them as representatives of a form of Jewish Christianity centered in Jerusalem to which Mark was opposed.[4] Kelber's argument is an extension and further development of that proposal. In light of the chasm separating the media worlds of oral speech and writing, Kelber sees Mark as criticizing the disciples and particularly Peter as representatives of not only the Jerusalem church but also of the entire tradition of the oral gospel.[5]

A formative analogy underlying Kelber's study is Eric Havelock's conclusion in his *Preface to Plato* that Plato banished the poets (*rhapsodes*) from his republic as part of his polemic against the oral culture formed around the recitation of Homeric poetry. Just as Plato attacked the poets as representatives of the Homeric oral world and its educational system, so also Mark disassociated the gospel from the disciples who represented the heterodox world of the oral gospel.[6] As Kelber writes:

> Mark's writing is fueled with a passion to disown the voices of his oral precursors. One is struck by this gospel's repudiation of the disciples, the prophets, and the family of Jesus. In sociological terms, Mark undermines the very structures that facilitate and legitimize oral transmission: the legitimately appointed authorities, the charismatic authorities, and the hereditary authorities. The very representatives of Jesus, those who can and must be expected to function as official, inspired, and traditional transmitters of his words, are dislodged. The guarantors of the tradition have been evicted.[7]

Stated in terms of narrative analysis, Mark's project was intended to create maximum distance between the Jesus tradition and the oral gospel represented by Peter and the disciples.

Kelber's analysis constitutes a hermeneutical circle. His picture of Mark as operating on the other side of the chasm between the oral and the written gospel is based on the exegesis of Mark's characterization of Peter and the disciples. This exegesis is in turn generated by a redaction-critical methodology in which the tradition is analyzed from a highly distanced perspective. This picture is thoroughly congruent with the primary orientation of contemporary biblical criticism and the media world within which

4. Kelber, *The Kingdom in Mark*, 146–47.
5. Kelber, *Oral and Written Gospel*, 97, 130.
6. Kelber, *Oral and Written Gospel*, 95–97, 194–95.
7. Kelber, *Oral and Written Gospel*, 104.

it has operated. However, the very basis of Kelber's analysis, the impact of media change, raises questions about the methodological paradigm of contemporary historical criticism.

The Basis for Media Criticism

A major contribution of contemporary media research is to call attention to the distance that exists between the epistemological worlds of modern and ancient experience of texts. The results of recent research into the impact of media change have made it clear, as Ong and Kelber have shown in their work, that media changes constitute a revolution in consciousness. A differentiated treatment of texts that were intended for being heard and those intended for silent reading is a necessary implication of this recognition. If the medium does significantly influence the perceived meaning of a biblical tradition, historical interpretation requires an effort to experience the tradition in its intended medium.

The reason for this necessity is clarified by Aristotle's analysis of the causes of meaning in poetry. Aristotle identifies three causes of the overall effect or meaning of poetry: the object, manner, and means of poetic imitation. Thus, Aristotle's opening methodological paragraph in *The Poetics*:

> Now epic poetry, tragedy, comedy, dithyrambic poetry, and most forms of flute and lyre playing all happen to be, in general, imitations, but they differ from each other in three ways: either because the imitation is carried on by different means or because it is concerned with different kinds of objects or because it is present, not in the same, but in a different manner.[8]

The object and manner of imitation are approximate correlates of our understanding of form and content. The object of imitation refers to the subject matter or characteristic content of different types of poetry: for example, tragedy imitates noble men and comedy baser types. In relation to the manner of poetry, Aristotle's basic distinction is between narration and dramatization.[9] He further refines the distinctions between different forms of verse in the genres of tragedy, comedy, and epic.[10]

The means or medium of imitation describes the materials from which poetry is made. The medium of poetry is, first of all, sound. Aristotle includes flute and lyre playing as a medium of poetry in which there is harmony and

8. Aristotle, *The Poetics*, 5.
9. Aristotle, *The Poetics*, 11.
10. Aristotle, *The Poetics*, 19–20.

rhythm but no words. In dramatic narrative poetry, therefore, language as spoken words is the medium. These spoken words are further distinguished by the employment of rhythm, melody, or harmony. The longer discussions of diction (sections XX–XXII) and the various meters of tragedy and epic (XXIII–XXIV) develop additional aspects of the medium of poetry.

For Aristotle, these elements of poetry are causes that control the over-all effect of poetry. This corresponds to Aristotle's understanding of the causes that produce all phenomena, natural or artificial. The relationship of the elements of poetry and the causes can be seen in the following table:

Cause	In Art Generally	In Poetry
Material:	Means or medium	Sound, language, rhythm, harmony
Formal:	Object or content	Actions with agents
Efficient:	Manner or form	Narrative, epic, dramatic

Contemporary media research has made clear the foundational accuracy of Aristotle's analysis. McLuhan's characteristically exaggerated statement of his basic conclusion is "the medium is the message."[11] While less comprehensive than Aristotle's more diversified analysis of the causal structure of poetry, McLuhan's phrase identifies an important fact: the medium has a determinative effect on the meaning of poetry. Media criticism is based on the recognition of the causal relationship between medium and meaning. Thus, Aristotle's analysis of the causes of the meaning of poetry and the particular development of Aristotle's insight in contemporary media criticism invites us to explore the original medium of the gospel tradition.

When applied to contemporary study of ancient texts, the implication of media criticism is that a change in the medium in which we study and experience an ancient text will inevitably change its meaning. Therefore, to the degree that our goal is to understand the meaning of the biblical documents in their original historical context, it is essential to know the medium in which they were originally experienced.

The Original Medium of Mark's Gospel

What was the intended medium of the oral and the written gospel? While Prof. Kelber acknowledges the evidence of oral reading in the ancient world,[12] the dominant description of Mark's textuality throughout the book is the silencing of the tradition. He writes, for example:

11. McLuhan, *Understanding Media*, 7.
12. Kelber, *Oral and Written Gospel*, 41–42.

> Mark's writing project is an act of daring and rife with conse-
> quences. To the extent that the gospel draws on oral voices, it
> has rendered them voiceless. The voiceprints of once-spoken
> words have been muted . . . For the moment, language has fallen
> silent.[13]

Kelber's analysis is in direct continuity with the basic assumption of form criticism that the writing of the tradition constitutes a more or less immediate transition to the media world of silent reading. This is a crucial assumption because it determines the modern scholar's medium of perceiving the narrative. That is, Kelber assumes a more or less immediate transition from the medium of orality to the modern world of textual experience as silent reading.

This assumption is not unusual. Contemporary biblical scholarship has consistently assumed that the original receivers of biblical literature were readers of texts. Discussions about "the reader" and "the text" abound in twentieth-century historical-critical exegesis. While there are often some qualifications of this paradigm with phrases such as "readers or hearers" and "audience," the general assumption is that biblical books such as the Gospel of Mark were read as documents by a single reader who read the document in silence. Thus, literary criticism of biblical texts has appropriated the paradigms of works such as Wolfgang Iser's *The Implied Reader* with the apparent assumption that a modern and an ancient reader's relationship to the text is the same.[14] The question is then: what did Mark assume about the manner in which his written Gospel would be experienced? Did Mark write a text that he assumed would be read in public or in private, aloud or in silence?

The evidence from the ancient world in regard to this issue is unambiguous. Manuscripts in the ancient world were virtually always read aloud. An ancient writer composed a text with the assumption that the composition would be read aloud. Throughout most of ancient history, the readings were public readings. As Moses Hadas has summarized:

> Among the Greeks the regular method of publication was by
> public recitation, at first, significantly, by the author himself,

13. Kelber, *Oral and Written Gospel*, 91.

14. The contemporary paradigm of the audience of biblical traditions as a "reader" who reads texts alone in silence is clearly rejected in a recent issue of *Semeia* titled "Reader Response Approaches to Biblical and Secular Texts." Robert Fowler's introductory essay, "Who is the Reader'?" is an excellent survey of recent developments in this area. Literary critics of Mark such as Robert Tannehill and Robert Fowler have appropriated the basic models of reader/text interaction as developed in the work of Wolfgang Iser.

and then by professional readers or actors, and public recitation continued to be the regular method of publication even after books and the art of reading had become common.[15]

From the rhapsodes who presented public recitations of heroic poetry to the performances of lyric and dramatic poetry by poets and actors, the ancient world was full of recitations of memorized texts for audiences in public gatherings.

But even private readings were normally done aloud. Thus, St. Augustine describes his surprise at Ambrose's habit of silent reading: "while reading, his eyes glanced over the pages, and his heart searched out the sense, but his voice and tongue were silent."[16] It was so unusual that visitors actually came to watch. Augustine goes on to explain this strange behavior of his revered mentor and suggests that concentration or preservation of his voice might have been motives, and concludes: "But whatever was his motive in so doing, doubtless in such a man was a good one." Further evidence of the association of silent reading with disrepute is evident in Lucian's satire of an ancient dabbler in books:

> What do all your books profit you, who are too ignorant to appreciate their value and beauty? To be sure you look upon them with open eyes and even greedily, and some of them you read at a great pace, your eye outstripping your voice; but I do not consider that sufficient, unless you know the merits and defects of all that is written there, and understand what every sentence means.[17]

Thus, Lucian assumed that understanding the full meaning required reading aloud. This reflects the assumption of the ancient world that any learned man would read aloud even when reading privately.

The evidence in regard to reading aloud in the ancient world is readily available and has been for some time. In 1926, Josef Balogh published two long articles entitled "Voces Paginarum" in which he collected references in classical literature to the oral reading of manuscripts. And in his book, *Ancilla to Classical Reading*, Moses Hadas both cites most of this evidence and discusses it in a highly accessible and entertaining manner. Another major source of evidence regarding the prevalence of the oral reading of manuscripts is the history of annotation.[18] From the trope marks of the

15. Hadas, *Ancilla*, 50.

16. Augustine, *Confessions* 5.3.

17. Lucian, *Adversus Indoctum* 2.

18. For a comprehensive survey of the history of annotation, see Rutherford,

Masoretic text to the marginal notes in Greek texts, ancient authors and editors developed systems of annotation in order to provide guidance for readers about how to read the text aloud rightly.[19]

The oral reading of manuscripts is reflected in many places in the biblical tradition. A short list of major public and private readings is indicative of the tradition:

1) The discovery and reading of the Deuteronomy scroll (II Kings 23:2): "The King went up to the house of the Lord and with him all the people of Judah and all the inhabitants of Jerusalem, the priests and the prophets, all the people, both small and great; he read in their hearing all the words of the book of the covenant which had been found in the house of the Lord."

2) The reading of the scroll of the prophecies of Jeremiah (Jeremiah 36): Baruch read the scroll of Jeremiah's prophecies aloud at the Temple gate and it was reported to the king. The King then ordered the scroll read aloud to him as he sat on the winter porch. As it was read, he cut up the scroll and fed it into a brazier.

3) The covenant renewal festival after the exile (Nehemiah 8): Ezra read the Torah all day long before the people of Israel at the Water Gate while the Levites provided oral interpretation of the reading as Ezra read.

4) The conversion of the Ethiopian eunuch (Acts 8:26–40): Phillip heard the Ethiopian eunuch reading the prophet Isaiah aloud in his chariot and interpreted the text orally in relation to Jesus.

5) The instructions for the reading of the Revelation of John (Revelation 1:2): "Blessed is he who reads aloud the words of the prophecy, and blessed are those who hear, and who keep what is written therein; for the time is near."

There is, as far as I can discover, no evidence of silent reading in the biblical tradition. Studies of the words relating to reading in both Hebrew and Greek yield no signs of anything that might be construed as silent reading.

Annotation.

19. Rutherford's study (1905) of annotation as a textual means for the guidance of oral readings in the ancient world is still an excellent introductory survey. The literature of music history (e. g., Werner, *Sacred Bridge*) tracing the development of notations for cantillation of Hebrew, Greek and Latin biblical texts is a primary source for detailed reconstruction of how the texts actually sounded.

Therefore, the answer to the question of Mark's intended medium is that Mark would have assumed that his Gospel would be performed aloud, either from a manuscript or from memory. The only other option in the media world of Mark's day was a private oral reading. And that would have required the unlikely assumption of extensive copying and distribution of Mark's manuscript. Silent reading, in as far as it existed in the first century, was an extraordinary and disrespected idiosyncrasy. Private reading aloud was more frequent but, because of the scarceness of texts, remained a luxury available to relatively few individuals.

The irony of the current state of biblical studies is that the recognition of public reading as the intended medium of ancient literature has been known for decades. It has become virtually a commonplace in the study of medieval literature. In the study of much earlier biblical literature, however, this recognition has received little or no attention.

In the light of the recognition of the medium as a primary cause of the meaning of texts, the implications of the prevalence of reading aloud in the ancient world for historical biblical criticism are significant. To the degree that our goal is to understand the meaning of the biblical texts in their original historical context, we need to study and experience the texts in their original medium, namely, as sounds recited and heard at least in private but preferably in public.

An analogy from music may be helpful. The symphonies and operas of Mozart, for example, were originally composed for performance. The original medium was sound. But Mozart's compositions were printed and can now be studied as documents. Our present pattern of experiencing biblical traditions is as if we were to study Mozart's scores without ever performing or listening to his music. Just as experiencing the impact of Mozart's *Requiem* or *The Magic Flute* by only reading the score would be very difficult for most of us, so also to primarily study the texts of the biblical traditions without reciting and hearing them is to limit our experience of the traditions to a secondary and derivative medium.

If the understanding and reestablishment of the original medium is a desirable component in the methodology of contemporary biblical study, how would we do it? A step in that direction is to test interpretations by oral performance. This is one way in which we can begin to experience the biblical material in its intended medium. Therefore, I propose that we use the test of oral performance in evaluating the alternative interpretations of Peter's denial.

It is difficult to demonstrate different oral interpretations in writing. I would ask that you, as the reader, do the testing yourself. I will suggest ways of reading the text aloud, a kind of modern annotation. You can then test the interpretations orally by reading them aloud to yourself. Admittedly this is only a private rather than a public reading. And later an even more valid test would be to read or tell the story aloud to a group. But we have to start somewhere. And, in this way, we can at least take a small step toward testing interpretations in the Gospel's intended medium.

Mark's Characterization of Peter

The general structure of the evidence for the interpretation of Mark's emphasis on the failure of the disciples and Peter as a critique of the theological position they represent is well known.[20] In this reading of Mark, the negative elements in the characterization of the disciples are understood as connected with an effort to discredit the disciples and all that they represent.

For the purposes of this methodological test, the story of Peter's denial is an excellent focus. In Kelber's reading of the Markan tradition, the story of Peter's denial is the culmination of Mark's effort throughout the Gospel to discredit Peter and the disciples. He summarizes as follows:

> If the hopes of the gospel's recipients (that the disciples will faithfully follow) have been kept alive into the passion story, it is there that they are decisively crushed. Far from experiencing a change of heart, the disciples, under the leadership of Peter, play out their roles of outsiders to the bitter end. Peter contradicts Jesus' prediction of the discipleship failure (Mark 14:26–29), all the disciples promise to suffer with Jesus (Mark 14:30–31), the triumvirate falters at Gethsemane (Mark 14:32–42), one disciple betrays Jesus (Mark 14:10–11, 43–46), all desert him at the moment of arrest (Mark 14:50), and Peter, the last hope, denies Jesus while he makes his fateful confession before the high priest (Mark 14:53–72).[21]

Stated in terms of narrative analysis, Mark's characterization of Peter is a polemical characterization in which the positive hopes and expectations of the gospel's audience for Peter and the disciples are all broken. The purpose of this characterization is to alienate the audience from Peter and the theology he represents.

The structure of a polemical characterization is relatively easy to identify. First, the norms of judgment that operate in the characterization are negative. The narrator appeals for the audience to recognize that the

20. For a survey of the literature exploring Mark's portrayal of the disciples as a motif of theological polemic, see Kelber, *Oral and Written Gospel*, 96–104.

21. Kelber, *Oral and Written Gospel*, 128.

character's actions are wrong. Second, the dynamics of distance create an intensification of alienation and there is an appeal to the audience for emotional separation from and opposition to the character.

According to Kelber, this is what happens in the characterization of Peter, the disciples, and the women at the end of the Gospel. Clearly, Mark's depiction of Peter and the disciples—their sleeping, flight, and denial—is that their behaviors are wrong. The norms of judgment are absolutely clear. And in the characterization of Peter, Mark seeks to create maximum alienation from the disciples and Peter as a way of discrediting them and the oral Gospel that they represent.

If this was Mark's intention, the implications for the appropriate oral reading of Mark's text are clear. If Mark had annotated his manuscript with instructions for oral recitation, he would have instructed the reader to condemn Peter for his failure. The story would be read in a spirit of judgment and make a strong appeal for alienation from Peter. In effect, the reciter would point his finger at Peter and condemn him for his failure and thereby appeal to the listeners to join him in opposition to Peter. A tone of mockery or ridicule might be an additional element in an appropriate oral rendering.

I would suggest that you try this interpretation by reading the story of Peter's denial aloud. The goal of this reading is to evaluate the interpretation in its intended medium. Throughout the reading, point your finger at Peter and, at the end of the story, condemn or mock him as he realizes his guilt. Thus, the end of the story was a highly cynical satire and a bitter polemic. The so-called father of the church was really a coward and a misguided leader who never understood who Jesus was.

As I have sought to recite the story, this oral interpretation has seemed unsatisfactory. It inevitably comes off as somewhat moralistic and has the feel of a taunt. The oral reading reveals an anomaly. Clearly, Peter's denial is wrong as is the sleeping of the three and the flight of the disciples. But the impact of the story is not polemical. It is a historical fact that people have not been alienated from Peter when they have heard the story of his denial over the centuries. The story has not had that effect. If anything, people have loved and revered Peter, particularly in relation to this story. Why?

I would propose that the reason is a consistent pattern in the characterization of Peter.[22] There are three places in Mark's characterization of Peter in which Peter's actions are associated with negative norms of judgment:

22. Tannehill emphasizes that the polemical interpretation of the characterization of the disciples cannot explain its positive aspects. The pattern is an appeal for identification with the disciples by their positive evaluation in the early parts of the Gospel followed by the questioning that arises out of the disciples' inadequacy (Tannehill, "Disciples in Mark," 395).

1) Peter's rebuke in response to Jesus' first passion prophecy to which Jesus responds, "Get behind me, Satan" (Mark 8.31–33);

2) Gethsemane where Peter falls asleep and is rebuked by Jesus (14. 36–41);

3) The denial.

There is no ambiguity about the norms involved in these actions. Mark clearly appeals for his listeners to recognize that each of these actions of Peter is wrong.

But Mark does not appeal for alienation from Peter. Stated in terms of the dynamics of distance, the characterization of an enemy is structurally consistent. The classic pattern of the Western is as indicative as the characterization of Pharaoh, Goliath, or the chief priests. There is a steady intensification of appeals for alienation from the character so that the distance relationship to the character steadily grows. In the classic western just as in the story of David and Goliath, the bad guy is an alien threat at the beginning who gradually does things that are worse and worse until the audience cheers when he is killed by the good guy.

The characterization of Peter does not fit this pattern. He does some things that are, according to the narrative's norms of judgment, clearly wrong. But, after each instance of wrongdoing, Mark takes explicit steps to reestablish a sympathetic relationship with Peter. The clearest element in this narrative structure is a sympathetic inside view in which Peter's feelings are described. Recognition of this pattern in the characterization will help to identify another possible intention in Mark's telling of Peter's denial.

The conflict between Jesus and Peter over Jesus' passion prophecy is preceded by Peter's confession of Jesus as Messiah. In terms of the norms of the narrative, Peter is the first character in the story to recognize what the narrator announced in the first sentence, namely, Jesus is the Christ. It is a very positive norm and creates a high degree of positive emotion in relation to Peter. After the fight, Mark reestablishes this sympathetic relationship with Peter in the transfiguration narrative. Jesus is transfigured, Moses and Elijah appear, and the three of them are talking. Peter's offer to build three booths for them is followed by a narrative comment: "For he did not know what to say. For they were afraid."

These narrative comments beginning with γαρ are typical of Mark's use of this form. They are consistently used to explain a puzzle or surprise that has been created for his audience by the previous statement (e.g., 1:16, 22; 2:15; 3:21; 5:8, 28, 42; 6:17, 18, 20, 31, 48; 9:34; 10:22; 11:13; 14:2, 40, 56; 15:10; 16:4, 8). In this instance, these comments apparently explains why Peter was so nervous and why he said such an inept and inappropriate thing. The explanation is thoroughly sympathetic and is clearly an appeal for identification with Peter whose feelings are presented as the way any person would feel in such company. In the technical terms of narrative analysis, this is a narrative comment to the audience which gives an inside view into Peter's internal thoughts and feelings. And the norms of judgment are wholly sympathetic and humanly understandable.[23]

One way to understand the dynamics of a story like this is to hear another story that has similar characteristics. What follows is my effort to identify such a story. But, in order for it to be appropriate in the context of this scholarly discussion, you need to imagine this story being told in a somewhat folksy style among a group of friends.

Peter's response to being in the presence of Jesus, Moses, and Elijah is like a mythical Midwestern B.D. student of Paul Tillich's at Union Theological Seminary in the late '50s finding himself unexpectedly thrust into the midst of a private conversation at a seminary tea between Bultmann, Barth, and Tillich. And Mark describes his bumbling effort to figure out something to say. To pursue my analogy, with which every present or former graduate student should be able to identify: "It's a good thing I'm here, Paul. Could I get some coffee for you and Karl and Rudolf?" Why would he say such a stupid thing? He didn't know what to say because he was afraid. It is biblical humor at its best and Peter is the one with whom we can all identify in that spot.

The Gethsemane story has a similar structure. Peter's falling asleep is preceded by Jesus' appeal to his three closest friends to be with him in his hour of need. When Peter falls asleep, Jesus rebukes him. But, in the next episode, when Jesus again finds them sleeping, Mark once again inserts a narrative comment in which he interrupts the action to give an inside view into the disciples' situation: "For their eyes were weighed down. And they didn't know what to say to him."

The first narrative comment explains the surprise of their going to sleep a second time by describing the external power that they could not control. Once again, it is thoroughly sympathetic. The requirements for wine consumption at Passover meals were probably known to most of Mark's audience. The expectations only began with the required five cups of wine during a three to four hour feast. I observe that many people are like myself for whom two cups of wine will generally put them to sleep within thirty minutes after a big meal. Mark's appeal to his audience is to understand

---

23. For further discussion of the role of inside views and narrative comments in the Gospel of Mark, see Boomershine and Bartholomew, "Narrative Technique" (chap. 3 above).

why the disciples' eyes were weighed down as they sat under a tree after the Passover meal while their teacher prayed long into the night.

The second comment is equally sympathetic in its appeal. The internal description of their inability to find something to say concretizes their shame. What does one say when a beloved friend has been disappointed in his greatest hour of need, even if it couldn't be helped? These narrative comments are inside views explaining their situation and their feelings. The comments do not in any way indicate that the disciples' going to sleep was anything other than wrong. But the narrative function of these comments is to enable the listeners to understand and sympathize with their inability to stay awake. Thus, the episode is an appeal for sympathetic identification and prevents alienation or negative distance.

Finally, and most graphically, this narrative structure is evident in the story of Peter's denial. Peter's three denials are reported one after another so that the audience can count them. His last denial is a climactic, highly emotional, and explicit denial of any relationship with Jesus. But, after the description of the cockcrow, Mark concludes the story with the most extensive and poignant inside view in his entire narrative. He invites the audience literally to enter Peter's mind as he remembers, somewhat inaccurately, Jesus' prophecy. The climax of the story is an invitation to witness and share Peter's grief.

This interpretation can be tested by oral performance. The episodes describing the first two denials are to be read dispassionately except for the words of both the maid and Peter. The climax of Peter's third denial should be read with extremely high emotional intensity and volume. The ending of the story, beginning with "And Peter remembered," is an intimate description of what was going on in Peter's mind. The usual translation of the ambiguous word, ἐπιβαλὼν, is "breaking down." Another possible translation is "beating on himself" and describes the gesture of striking the chest, a gesture which the storyteller may have used in this climactic moment. The goal of the reading of these words is to express Peter's realization of his failure and his grief as deeply and graphically as possible.

What is the difference in these two interpretations? It is the difference between a pointed finger and a clutched fist beating oneself in grief, between an ideological judgment and the expression of a deeply internalized recognition of a monumental wrong. The options for the interpretation are that Mark's intention was either to invite his audience to share in criticizing Peter for his failure or to share in the grief of Peter's own realization of his failure. It is either an anti-Petrine polemic or a Petrine confession.

What difference does oral performance make in deciding between these two options? Could not the same conclusions be drawn from an analysis of the narrative characteristics of the Markan text without any oral experience? As Robert Tannehill's article on the disciples in Mark demonstrates, it is certainly possible for an analysis of Mark's narrative as a silent text to lead to the same conclusion that Mark's intention in the characterization of Peter and the disciples was not theological polemic.[24]

The question is whether the polemical reading is more historically probable as a description of the intended meaning of Mark's narrative in its original context. It is in relation to this question that the medium makes a difference. When the narrative is read aloud in a manner as close as possible to the patterns of oral recitation implicit in the narrative, the anti-Petrine interpretation is much less probable. The reason is the difference in psychological distance to the text and, in this story, to Peter, that is required for oral recitation in contrast to silent reading.

When the text is studied in silence, the degree of potential distance in relation to the text and to Peter as a character is greater. Silent reading encourages psychological distance and a high degree of dispassionate objectivity. Silent readers can imaginatively enter into the dynamics of the story as an oral narrative, in part by recreating the sounds of the story in their minds. There is nothing in silent reading that makes impossible a higher degree of sympathetic distance in relation to Mark's story of Peter's denial. But it is only a possibility. In the modern age, when psychological distance from texts has increased, reading aloud rather than in silence makes certain interpretations of Peter's denial improbable because it requires a higher degree of sympathetic participation in the story.

I have found Prof. Kelber's delineation of the theological issues implicit in these disagreements illuminating and exegetically accurate. I agree that Mark is opposed to a *theios anēr* Christology. That issue is implicit in the conflicts with Peter and the disciples. But how is that issue worked out in the story? Prof. Kelber has rightly identified the theological ideas that influenced Mark's work as a shaper of the gospel tradition. But he misunderstands the nature of Mark's craft and the medium for which he composed his stories. Indeed, given the centrality of Kelber's interpretation of disciple failure to his thesis, this misunderstanding raises serious questions about the over-all picture of the oral and written Gospel that he has drawn.

The Oral and the Written Gospel

In my judgment, Kelber has established a new set of questions for historical criticism and has proposed a series of hypotheses that require careful

24. Tannehill, "Disciples in Mark," 386–405.

evaluation and further research. Kelber's hypothesis that Mark was involved in an anti-Petrine polemic is historically improbable. While Kelber has demonstrated that the documents can be understood in this way, the question is whether the reading is historically probable. The narrative structure of Peter's characterization and the study of the narrative in its intended medium show that it is unlikely that the story had this meaning in its original historical context.

My evaluation is that Kelber has collapsed 1900 years of media development into a forty-year period in the first century. The degree of psychological distance from the Markan text that is required in order to even conceive the hypothesis that Mark was engaged in a polemic against Peter has only happened since the eighteenth century. The process of increasing distance and alienation from the word as sound has taken nineteen centuries, not forty years.

Furthermore, is it likely that a movement as weak and vulnerable as the Christian sect in the post-70 CE period would produce and later canonize a first gospel that was a polemic against its primary and most highly respected leaders? Movements that are divided to this degree rarely survive and grow because the competing leaders cancel each other out.

I doubt that this story would have become a cornerstone of the tradition unless Peter told it and permitted it to be told about him. The same was true of Paul. He told the story of his persecution of the church. In the context of the importance that people in the ancient world attached to how they were remembered, these stories are striking. What is the spirit of men who would tell such stories about themselves? They are the stories of men who have experienced the forgiveness and power of God to overcome their weaknesses and failures. How does one tell such a story? One tells such a story as a confession and as an invitation to others who have the same feelings to identify with the story and make it their own.

Such a conclusion raises serious questions about other aspects of Prof. Kelber's synthesis. If a Markan polemic against Peter and the disciples is historically improbable, so also is a polemic against the oral gospel. Does this imply that Kelber's emphasis on the chasm between the oral and the written gospel is also inaccurate? Kelber has established that the transition from orality to writing was a major development in the gospel tradition. The question is whether Kelber has accurately described the character of that transition. The character of reading in the ancient world and the analysis of the narrative structure of Peter's denial leads to the conclusion that the degree of separation and psychological distance from the living oral word that Kelber finds in Mark only happened later. We need, therefore, to identify the bridges across the chasm between the oral and the written gospel.

The phenomenology of sound in the first century is one of those bridges. The gospel continued to be told and read aloud. The transition from the oral to the written gospel in Mark's context was not a transition from sound to silence but from sounds recomposed by a storyteller to sounds read from a manuscript. We need to know more about the character of the sounds of the gospel narratives in the oral and the written gospel.

A second bridge is memory. The gospel narratives also continued to be told from memory. The transition to the written gospel did not mean the end of memorization and internalization of the tradition. A primary educational practice of the ancient world was the memorization of traditions written down in manuscripts. Thus, while the character of memorization changed as the gospel was written down, it was not eliminated.

Indeed, the phenomenon of the memorization of manuscripts in the ancient world as a transitional stage between orality and literacy may have major implications for the Synoptic problem. The basic change between the memorization of oral traditions and the memorization of manuscripts is the much higher degree of word for word memory in manuscript memorization.[25] However, the memorization and recomposition of manuscripts is an entirely different process from the editing of documents. Thus, the possibility exists that Matthew and Luke may have memorized Mark and then recomposed his gospel preserving both Mark's order and many of the stories virtually word for word. This combination—the discipline to duplicate the tradition word for word and the freedom to reshape the tradition—may be a more accurate understanding of the process of the Synoptic tradition than the traditional model of the editing of documents.

The improbability of an anti-Petrine polemic in Mark raises further questions about the appropriateness of the analogy of Plato's polemic against the poets. The analogy breaks down in significant ways. Mark was not a Plato who developed philosophical and conceptual thought and who wrote dialogues and allegories. Mark continued to tell stories. Furthermore, the Church did not disassociate itself from the storytellers and poets of the traditions of Israel in the way that Plato disassociated the Academy from the rhapsodes and the Homeric traditions. Indeed, the Church canonized their writings and revered Peter as the first Pope. The formation of theology as

---

25. Albert Lord observes that once the Yugoslavian songs he studied were memorized from a written manuscript the process of the oral tradition irrevocably changed: "The set, 'correct' text had arrived and the death knell of the oral process had been sounded" (Lord, *Singer of Tales*, 137). The memorizers were reproducers rather than recreators of the songs. While Lord bemoans this process in the Yugoslavian oral tradition, it may be that the Synoptic tradition represents an intermediate stage in which the traditional oral freedom to recompose and reorder the tradition was combined with the more detailed word for word reproduction of memorized manuscripts.

the dominant mode of thought in early Christianity is analogous to Plato's development of philosophy and Mark stands at the beginning of that process. But Mark's role in the process of media transition of a first-century Jewish sect is radically different from that of Plato in Athens.

While accepting the Platonic analogy, Kelber has rejected the oral tradition analogy with equal force. One of the ironies of Kelber's study is the degree to which he has ignored the results of oral tradition research since the development of form criticism. While it is true that there are distinctive ways in which oral traditions are ordered in the transition to writing, the implication of Kelber's study is that the entire process of ordering is foreign to oral tradition. His picture of the oral gospel is similar to the picture of classical form criticism of a series of individual short stories that were told independently and, apparently, one at a time.

The evidence from oral tradition research does not support this conclusion. The major field studies of oral traditions in recent years share a common conclusion that storytelling occasions are frequently long. They are certainly not two or three minute occasions of storytelling.[26] The stories may be ordered in different ways on different occasions. But the stories are lined up and told in a sequence that often goes on for hours. Thus, the historical probabilities are high that the pre-Markan storytellers told a long series of stories about Jesus and ordered them in different ways for different occasions.

However, while I suspect that there were long stories of Jesus' life, passion, death and resurrection told prior to Mark, I also find it historically probable that Mark brought a new degree of order and completeness to the tale when he wrote it down. And there may well have been in Mark's written gospel a new level of concentration on the ideas implicit in the story. Nevertheless, the evaluation of the exegetical foundation for Kelber's synthesis through media testing raises serious questions and reservations about the over-all picture of Mark that Kelber has drawn. These are then some of the questions upon which further research is needed in the aftermath of Kelber's study.

The Methodology of Historical Criticism

The most far-reaching problem that awareness of the role of the medium in biblical interpretation poses for contemporary criticism is the awareness of

---

26. The widely divergent studies of oral prose traditions in Crowley's work on storytelling in the Bahamas, Degh in Hungary. and Finnegan and Seheub in Africa all include descriptions of typical storytelling occasions in which stories are told for hours.

the chasm that separates the media world of historical criticism from the media world of the Bible. What are the methodological implications of the ancient assumption of oral performance?

What is at stake here is the impact of media research on the way in which we study and interpret the Bible. In my view, we need to recognize the vast distance that separates our media world from the media world of the communities that developed the Bible. The greatest difference is that they were far closer to an oral world and its ways of thought than are we. Prof. Kelber's study tends to minimize that distance by reading back into the ancient world and specifically into the interpretation of Mark the characteristic relationships to texts of modern historical criticism.

The recognition of the role of the medium in contemporary biblical scholarship may shed light on the long stream of reaction against the documentary hypothesis on the part of Jewish scholars.[27] One of the differences between Jewish and Christian scholarship on the Pentateuch is the medium in which Jewish scholars have experienced the biblical literature. Jewish scholars have continued to hear the Pentateuch read aloud during each liturgical year. Christian scholars, on the other hand, have primarily studied the texts as silent documents. Many of the differences in the assessment of phenomena such as frequent parallelism in the Pentateuchal tradition may be related to this significant difference in the medium in which it is experienced.

A fascinating instance reflecting this difference in the study of the Gospel tradition can be seen in Lou Silberman's lecture for the Trinity University Colloquy on the Relationships of the Gospels in 1977. Silberman's lecture explores "wandering motifs" in the various literatures of Judaism of the Hellenistic era and the ways in which those motifs are interpreted. His final section is titled, "Conclusion: How to Hear a Text." He argues that the assumption of literary sources in contemporary biblical study reflects the degree to which we "still march along the straight black line of the Gutenberg galaxy." He finds that the treatment of these themes by the various storytellers is different from the literary models of redaction. By the simple juxtaposition of traditional materials, the storytellers have brought to light latent possibilities of meaning in the stories. This latent meaning is directly related to hearing:

---

27. For example, the commentaries of U. Cassuto have steadily called attention to the unifying oral elements in the Pentateuchal narratives over against the tendencies of critics in pursuit of disparate documents. Jewish exegesis in general has maintained a much closer relationship to the original medium of the tradition.

'Redactor' thus understood is one who senses the latent possibilities within a tradition and, by his placing of the tradition
in a particular context, manifests a possibility that may obscure
but not efface others. To hearers at home in a tradition, it is the
tensions between manifestation and latency that enriches and
enlarges the meaning of the story.[28]

As an illustration, he describes the chanting of the Book of Esther
which I will quote at length:

In the synagogue, the Book of Esther is read traditionally at a
rather rapid rate with its own distinctive cantillation. Five verses,
however, are chanted more slowly and with the chant reserved
for the Book of Lamentations. The verses are: 1:7: "And they
gave them to drink in vessels of gold . . ."; 2:6: "who had been
carried away from Jerusalem with the captives that had been
carried away with Jeconiah king of Judah, whom Nebuchadnez-
zar the king of Babylon had carried away"; 3:15: "but the city
of Shushan was thrown into confusion"; 4:16, which concludes
with the words "and if I perish, I perish"; and finally 8:6, whose
opening words by *ky 'ykkh* "how can I" echo the opening word
of Lamentations, chapters 1,2, and 4, *'ykh*. The reason for this
anomaly is evident for several of the verses, but to understand
its presence, in the first, one must know that, according to a *hag-
gadah*, the vessels used by the king and his courtiers were none
other than the sacred vessels of the Temple of Jerusalem.[29]

In these instances, therefore, it is only in the hearing of the tradition that the
meaning can be perceived in its fullness. And it is only in the appreciation
and experience of the art of the storyteller that the Gospels and the history
of the gospel tradition can be appropriately understood. Silberman thus
appeals for approaching the Synoptic problem as hearers and storytellers
rather than as silent readers and critics.

However, in the responses to Silberman's lecture at the aforementioned
Colloquy, no one dealt with the methodological issue implicit in Silberman's argument. Both Sanders' response, and the seminar which followed,
discussed the issues only in terms of the first-century context. There was
no recognition of the way in which this methodological decision about the
medium of scholarly investigation predetermines our perception of the first
century compositions.

28. Silberman, "*Habent Sua*," 217.
29. Tannehill, "Disciples in Mark," 217.

I perceive here two competing paradigms for which the line of division has not been clearly defined. The paradigms are defined by the medium of experiencing the texts: oral reading, in public gatherings as well as privately, or the silent reading of documents. Those who read the texts aloud as their methodology appeal to silent readers on the basis of historical evidence of orality and its characteristics. But that is only a secondary and derivative outcome of an earlier decision. Each group appeals to the other about different sets of empirical evidence. Implicit in Lou Silberman's lecture is an appeal to approach the Synoptic problem through listening rather than looking for a solution, through an assessment of auditory rather than visual sense data. The same discrepancy is also present between Werner Kelber and myself. But those who read the texts aloud and those who read in silence will inevitably pass like ships in the night because they are discussing two different epistemological worlds.

Reflection on the role of the medium in biblical interpretation suggests that there is a reciprocal relationship between our conception of the way in which the texts were originally experienced and the way in which we study them now. Stated in methodological terms, the decision before contemporary biblical criticism is whether oral interpretation is an essential step, and perhaps even a goal, of the interpretive process. In both the study of the Pentateuch and the Gospels, the options are to continue to study the documents in silence or to read or tell them aloud. In fact, awareness of the determinative role of the medium in the experienced meaning of texts implies that, as long as the decision continues to be made that silent reading is the normative medium for interpretation, the decisions about the outcome of the most foundational issues of interpretation have already been made. Non-literary options for understanding the history of the tradition have already been excluded from the possibility of meaningfulness.

Beneath the discussions about oral and documentary tradition histories lies an unidentified methodological issue: to read aloud or to read in silence. To the degree that our intention is to understand the meaning of the texts in their original context, those who have argued that listening to the texts is essential have virtually all of the historical evidence on their side. The assumption of ancient silent reading of biblical texts is an anachronism, a reading back of contemporary reading conventions into the ancient world. It is media eisegesis.

It would be possible to divide modern scholarship into those who read aloud and those who read in silence. The question posed by Werner Kelber's study and by the history of Synoptic criticism is whether it is possible to reconstruct the history of the gospel tradition accurately if we experience that history in an alien and unintended medium. Can we rightly perceive that tradition and assess the role of telling, reading aloud, remembering, and hearing stories if we continue to study that tradition in our studies alone and in silence?

Kelber and I agree that media research is of great importance for biblical exegesis and hermeneutics. The differences in our interpretation of Mark suggest that we need to continue the work on media criticism that Herder, Gunkel, Bultmann, Dibelius, Marxsen, Ong, and Kelber have begun. Kelber's proposed reinterpretation of the Synoptic tradition demonstrates that a critical assessment of the medium of the Gospel is as important to its understanding as criticism of its form and content. Whereas form criticism subsumed the medium of biblical tradition under the category of form, careful attention is needed to clarify the role of the medium both in the original formation of the Gospel and in the ongoing process of its interpretation.

6

The New Testament Soundscape
and the Puzzle of Mark 16:8

Introduction

The development of sound mapping is a foundational step in the reevaluation of the sensorium or sensory matrix of biblical scholarship and our perception of the sensorium of the biblical tradition as sound.[1] Sound mapping seeks to develop a system of graphic representation of the sounds of biblical compositions. It is analogous to the highly developed system of writing and publishing musical compositions in printed scores that can then serve as the source for performances of those compositions.

A purpose of this essay is to set sound mapping in the context of the larger question of the sensory perception of biblical compositions then and now. The proposal is that there is a fundamental discontinuity between the predominantly visual sensory system of contemporary biblical study and the predominantly auditory sensory system of the biblical world. A dimension of that discontinuity is the difference between the auditory and visual sensory systems of the human brain. When biblical scholarship is evaluated in this context, the implication is that biblical scholarship has been based on a systemic misperception of the Bible as texts read by silent readers rather than as compositions performed for audiences.

The puzzle of the ending of Mark's gospel presents a telling case study. The mapping and analysis of the story's sound reveals a concentration of

1. Lee and Scott, *Sound Mapping*.

119

highly sophisticated compositional techniques. When Mark 16:8 is experienced and analyzed as a composition of sound rather than as a text of visual signs, it makes sense as the intended ending of the gospel. While Mark 16:8 is a very small sample, the possibility emerges that the entire corpus of New Testament literature needs to be reassessed as compositions of sound for which sound mapping is a foundational step.

The Discontinuity between Ancient and Modern Biblical Sensoria

The sensorium of contemporary biblical scholarship and the sensorium of the Bible and ancient media are inextricably linked.[2] The presuppositions about the media world of the Bible shape the ways in which the "texts" are perceived and interpreted now and in their original context. The sensorium of current biblical scholarship is predominantly a sensorium of sight. The biblical texts are examined by looking at them. It is normal to walk the office corridors of biblical scholars and hear nothing behind those doors. And the classrooms of biblical scholars rarely echo with the sounds of biblical compositions while reference to and discussion of the texts is omnipresent. To the degree that biblical scholarship has as its goal the interpretation of the Bible in its original historical context, the implicit justification for this sensory system of sight is that it corresponds to the sensorium of the biblical world. The presupposition is that biblical authors were writing texts that were read by individual readers, usually in silence. The terms "texts," "authors," and "readers" are ubiquitous in the commentaries, monographs, and journals of biblical scholarship and they refer to this underlying concept of the Bible and ancient media. Exegesis is based on the reimagined experience of readers of texts. The underlying and largely unexamined assumption is that there is essential continuity between the sensorium of the Bible in its original context and the sensorium of twenty-first-century biblical scholarship.

The problem is that recent research into the media culture of antiquity has revealed that this assumption is false. The sensorium of the literature of the ancient world was predominantly a sensory world of sound.[3] Classic stories such as the Iliad were memorized and performed in all night orgies of sound and wine. Literary works were read aloud for groups of listeners. The receivers of ancient literature were usually audiences rather than

2. For a comprehensive exposition of the concept of "the sensorium," the sensorium of the Word of God, and "Word as Sound," see Ong, *The Presence of the Word*, 1–175.

3. Ong, *The Presence of the Word*, 1–175.

individual readers. Furthermore, in those instances of individuals reading manuscripts, they usually read aloud.

The recognition of the centrality of sound is in part an inference from the preponderance of evidence that most people in the ancient world were illiterate.[4] Current estimates are that the rates of illiteracy in the various regions of the ancient near east in the biblical periods were 85–95 percent. The probability is that there were increasing rates of literacy in the millennium from 1000 BCE to 100 CE during which most of the works of biblical literature were composed. But while literacy rates undoubtedly increased, the overall rate remained very low. By the end of the first century CE, it was still the case that most people couldn't read. The literary compositions of this period were composed and performed for predominantly illiterate audiences.

During this period in which the compositions of the Bible were produced, literate culture gradually expanded from a small, elite culture of scribes to a much wider network of writing and reading that in turn generated the characteristic institutions of literate culture: military and economic empires, libraries, schools, and bookstores. The primary centers of literacy—Egypt, Babylonia, Greece, Rome—were also the centers of political and economic power.[5] All of these institutions appeared during this period of the gradual ascendency of literacy. But that wider communication network of the literate, including literate slaves, was predominantly an elite group of the classes of power and their coteries.[6] The communication of the products of the literate class to the illiterate majority took place by performances.

In the current discussion about "orality" and "literacy" there has been an extensive critique of the so-called "Great Divide" theory and the focus on orality as a distinctive system of cultural communication. This theory has called attention to the major differences between "oral culture" and "literate culture" and has emphasized the radical character of this transition. Rather than conceiving this transition as a "seamless" and natural transition, as was characteristic of form criticism, this body of research has emphasized both the psychological and sociological differences between the two cultures and their communication systems.[7] The critique of this theory has identified the various ways in which individuals and institutions have integrated these two

4. Harris, *Ancient Literacy.* For rates of literacy, see 13.

5. Innis, *Empire and Communication.* This study of the correlation between the development of literacy and the emergence of the empires of western civilization introduced the study of media technology and communication culture.

6. Carr, *Writing on the Tablet of the Heart,* 287–88.

7. Kelber, *The Oral and the Written Gospel;* also see Kelber, *Imprints, Voiceprints, & Footprints of Memory.*

communication systems and have formed multi-faceted syntheses of orality and literacy.

There are, therefore, major areas of ambiguity that remain in the assessment of orality and literacy in the ancient world. How extensive was the spread of literacy in the biblical period and specifically in the first century CE? What was the role of memory in ancient performance of manuscripts? When did the oral proclamation of New Testament manuscripts in worship begin and to what degree did that require memorization? How available were manuscripts of the gospels for public and private reading? How extensive was the practice of silent reading? How much of a gospel was performed at any particular gathering in the various periods of the gospel tradition? These are specific dimensions of the larger cultural and technological ambiguities of the ever-evolving understanding of the relationship between orality and literacy.

There is, however, one area in which there is no ambiguity: sound. Since 85–95 percent of persons were illiterate, the only way in which the vast majority of persons could experience biblical compositions was by hearing them performed as members of an audience. Individual reading was relatively unusual because of the limited availability of manuscripts. And when individuals read manuscripts alone, they usually read aloud. Silent reading was rare and anomalous.[8] Some three hundred years after the composition of the New Testament and the further development of literate culture in the Roman world, Augustine wrote about the strange behavior of his beloved mentor, Ambrose, who read in silence, with "his voice and his tongue . . . at rest":

> But when he was reading, his eye glided over the pages, and his heart searched out the sense, but his voice and tongue were at rest. Ofttimes when we had come (for no man was forbidden to enter, nor was it his wont that any who came should be announced to him), we saw him thus reading to himself, and never otherwise; and having long sat silent (for who durst intrude on one so intent?) we were fain to depart, conjecturing that in the small interval which he obtained, free from the din of others' business, for the recruiting of his mind, he was loath to be taken off; and perchance he dreaded lest if the author he read should

8. See Slusser, "Silent Reading," for evidence of individual instances of silent reading. See also Knox, "Silent Reading." In his article, "Oral Fixation and New Testament Studies?" Larry Hurtado has argued that there was a very extensive literary culture and a greater prevalence of private and even silent reading. For a more extensive exposition of literacy in early Christianity, see Hurtado, "A Bookish Religion," in *Destroyer of the Gods.*

deliver any thing obscurely, some attentive or perplexed hearer should desire him to expound it, or to discuss some of the harder questions; so that his time being thus spent, he could not turn over so many volumes as he desired; although the preserving of his voice (which a very little speaking would weaken) might be the truer reason for his reading to himself. But with what intent soever he did it, certainly in such a man it was good.[9]

The questions raised for Augustine's readers by this practice of Ambrose were not only about his unusual way of reading but also concerned the assessment of his character. Such was the prevalence of reading aloud at the beginning of the fifth century with persons as highly literate as Augustine and his audience.

Therefore, whether biblical compositions such as Mark's gospel were told from memory with no manuscript or read from a manuscript, the compositions of the New Testament were experienced as sound. As Gamble has observed about ancient texts:

The text was an inscription of the spoken word. Because authors wrote or dictated with an ear to the words and assumed that what they wrote would be audibly read, they wrote for the ear more than the eye. As a result, no ancient text is now read as it was intended to be unless it [is] also heard, that is, read aloud.[10]

That is, the sensory registers that were activated by the performance of biblical compositions were predominantly auditory throughout the period from 1000 BCE to 500 CE.[11] Auditory address was the intention of ancient authors.

Furthermore, a predominantly oral sensorium continued to be the dominant character of the Bible until the advent of the printing of vernacular translations, the extension of silent reading in the eighteenth to nineteenth centuries, and the advent of historical criticism. Thus, for example, the King James translation in the early seventeenth century was structured

---

9. Augustine, *Confessions* 6.3.

10. Gamble, *Books and Readers,* 204.

11. There were also visual dimensions to the experience of ancient audiences. The visual field of the early audiences focused on the face and the gestures of the performer, but also included the setting of the performance. In those early stages of the tradition, the settings were predominantly small groups in homes. As the tradition developed, the settings became larger and more elaborate culminating in the performances in great cathedrals. The visual elements of the sensory data of the New Testament, however, were by no means as well defined for the original audiences as the auditory.

for public readings in churches, as was implemented by the initial publication of a series of large pulpit Bibles.[12]

The implication of this realization about the media world of antiquity is that there is a foundational discontinuity between the sensorium of the Bible and the sensorium of contemporary biblical scholarship. The problem with the assumption of continuity between these two media worlds is that we as biblical scholars are deceived into thinking that we have experienced the Bible in its original medium when we read the "text" with our eyes only. If the biblical documents were compositions and recordings of sound, the sensory vibrations of the compositions are only experienced when they are heard.

Sensory Systems of the Human Brain

We now know that the auditory and visual perceptual systems of the human brain are located in separate and distinct places in the brain.[13] A brief summary of the scientific exploration of human sensory systems will help to specify the differences between the sensory processing of sight and sound.

The perception and processing of sound begins as a disturbance in the air. The path of a particle can be described as a wave. The waves of a particle can range from high to low frequencies. The speed of sound in air is about 1,100 feet per second. The sound waves enter the outer ear. The sound strikes the eardrum and the eardrum moves in and out, starting movements in a set of tiny bones, the ossicles, in the middle ear. The three bones of the middle ear are the malleus (hammer), the incus (anvil) and the stapes (the stirrup). They are the smallest bones in the human body; the stapes, for example, weighs four ten-thousandths of an ounce. Their function is to transmit the sound waves from air to liquid. They work like a chain of levers that transmit the air vibrations in the outer ear to the fluids in the inner ear.

The equipment of the tiny inner ear is packed into a fluid-filled snail-shaped shell, the cochlea. It is half an inch across at its base and rises only a quarter of an inch into the temporal bones of the skull. The cochlear duct is coiled in a full two and three-fourths turn in the shell that holds the organ of

12. For a discussion of the predominance of oral reading in the late medieval period and "the reader" in the seventeenth-century fiction of Henry Fielding, see above, "Audience Asides".

13. For diagrams of the visual and auditory centers of the human brain, see Wilentz, *The Senses of Man*, 23, 182, 273. Also see Brynie, *Brain Sense*, 225–30. For an evocative exploration of personal and literary communal experience of the senses, see Ackerman, *A Natural History of the Senses*.

Corti. Inside the cochlea are two ramps, an upper scala vestibuli and a lower scala tympani, both of which contain perilymph, a water-and-salt solution very much like cerebrospinal fluid. The fluid in the cochlear duct contains endolymph, more viscous than the perilymph in the scala and differing in salt content. Three membranes lie between the three chambers within the cochlea. The fluid in the organ of Corti vibrates the basilar membrane that is lined with 16,000 to 24,000 tiny hair cells, each of which registers specific vibrations in the spectrum of sound frequencies.

Nerve fibers from both the inner and outer ear hair cells assemble to form the spiral ganglion of the organ of Corti, the beginning of the auditory branch of the eighth cranial nerve. The auditory nerve enters the medulla and spreads via the geniculate body of the thalamus to the auditory cortex of the temporal lobe of the cerebrum. This chain of nerve cells follows a devious path from the cochlea to the auditory cortex. At the end, the vibrations of sound are processed in the temporal lobe of the cerebrum. These complex pathways are duplicated in each ear.

The perception of sound is made possible by this highly complex system of transmission of the vibrations of air to the vibrations of the fluids in the inner ear. Significant dimensions of this sensory system are still essentially a mystery and are the object of ongoing research. The distinctive character of this sensory system is the detection of vibrations and resonance.

Vision is the best understood of the senses. The sensory perception of light begins in the retina. It is composed of three parallel layers of nerve cells that are arranged in alternating rows of axons and dendrites. The first layer in the front of the eye is primarily ganglion cells, the second layer is horizontal, bipolar and amacrine cells, and the third layer at the back of the retina is 120 million light-sensitive neurons—photoreceptors, cones and rods. Cones detect color and work best in bright light. Rods work best in dim light. Cones and rods operate at different speeds, rods being slower than cones. Individual cones and rods have highly specific receptive fields and detect single, minute points of light. The signals from the rods and cones travel to the front of the eye to the ganglion cells that are responsible for the transmission of most of the signals to the brain via more than a million optic nerve fibers.

Most of the impulses from the retina travel through the optic nerve to the lateral geniculate nucleus (LGN) that lies in the thalamus. The LGN is organized in six layers of cells, each with specific functions and inputs from only one eye. The signals from the LGN end up on the two sides of the occipital lobe in the primary visual cortex, called the striate cortex or $V1$. Thirty different visual processing regions have been identified in the brain, most of which draw on data from the $V1$.

Recent research shows that visual processing also happens in areas outside the neurons of the brain's outer layer of the cortex. Visual sensory impulses are processed in the brain in multiple places that can operate independently. For example, there is a specific center in the frontal cortex that lights up at the sight of a baby's face.[14] Most of the brain's cells are glial cells, between one and five trillion cells, that support the neurons of the two hemispheres of the brain. The processing of visual stimuli is highly diversified and even creates new tracks and connections when there has been damage to particular cells.[15]

This brief summary of the sensory systems of the human brain makes it clear that the sensory systems of the eye and the ear, of visual and auditory stimuli, are different and distinct. While the two systems also interact with each other at various intersections in the brain, the auditory and visual systems of the human brain are highly differentiated: different sensory registers, different optic and auditory nerve tracks, and different auditory and visual cortex centers in the brain. Each system perceives distinct sensory impulses, transmits that data in distinctive ways through millions of cells, and processes those sensory impulses in distinct centers of the amazingly complex human brain.

Implications for Biblical Scholarship

Hearing and seeing are different systems of perception and knowledge. One way of conceiving the biblical tradition is as a set of sensory stimuli. When the gospel of Mark, for example, is heard, we literally perceive a different set of sensory stimuli than if we read it in silence. The analogy of music is helpful in describing this difference. Reading Exodus or Mark in silence is like reading the manuscript of Beethoven's Ninth Symphony and never hearing the music. We are like the deaf Beethoven who was present at the first performance of his greatest work but heard nothing.

The difference is that Beethoven wanted to hear the music whereas we have made a communal decision to read the texts in silence. If biblical compositions are read in silence, they are a different set of sensory stimuli than what the original composers/authors assembled and intended for their audiences. The assumption of the "composers" of the biblical books was that

14. Brynie, *Brain Sense,* 114. The baby face center in the front of the brain just above the eyes responds instantly (100 milliseconds) and instinctively to an infant's face but not to more mature faces.

15. Brynie, *Brain Sense,* 110–15. For a more extensive treatment, see Geldard, *The Human Senses,* 18–153.

every receiver would perceive the compositions with their ears in interaction with a performer. Their compositions were always for "those who have ears to hear."

It is important to acknowledge that I do not know the actual practice of biblical scholars in the privacy of their own studies. It may be that many read the texts aloud as common practice. There are a growing number of instances of the phrase, "readers and hearers" in New Testament monographs and commentaries. For example, Robert Stein in his article on Mark's ending has the following footnote to his earlier article cited in the note below: "When we speak of Mark's 'readers,' we should not envision a group of 'readers' silently reading Mark's original scroll or codex but a group of hearers listening to Mark's text being read to them."[16] However, the ubiquitous reference in New Testament scholarship to "the reader" implies the imagined picture of an individual looking at a text and remains the dominant framework for the reconstruction of the meaning of the Bible in its original historical context. Furthermore, my hunch is that most New Testament scholars study the texts in silence and that few have performed them for an audience.

I will state this issue as provocatively as I can. If the Bible was originally composed in a sensorium of sound, the Bible is not perceived when the Bible is read now as a "text" (in silence with our eyes). If we as biblical interpreters only read the Bible as a "text" and claim to interpret the Bible in its original historical context, we are engaged in misrepresentation and a kind of fraud. Our studies claim to be an investigation of the original documents. But our studies are actually an analysis of a different set of sensory data than was originally structured and intended by the composers of the biblical compositions. As a result of this discontinuity, many of our conclusions about the meanings of biblical "texts" in their original contexts are, so to speak, wrong-headed. We have used the wrong parts of our heads to perceive the "texts."

If we want to perceive and interpret the compositions of the Bible in their original historical context, it is necessary for our sensory system to correspond with the sensorium in and for which they were composed. This would be in contrast to our present situation in which we have read back our sensory system of silent reading into the ancient world. How can we perceive and study the Bible in its original sensory medium, sound?

16 Stein, "Ending," 86n31. For the article, see Stein, "Is Our Reading the Bible the Same as the Original Audience's Hearing It?" Stein's answer is "no" to the question identified in the title. The article is an excellent delineation and documentation of the predominant practice of reading aloud both to audiences and to oneself in antiquity.

The Colon Hypothesis and Sound Mapping

Rather than continuing to make assertions, however, it might be more inviting to approach this reorientation as a hypothesis, just as Frank Scheppers
has done in his monumental treatise, *The Colon Hypothesis*. On the basis of
a systematic study of the extant works of Lysias and four of Plato's dialogues,
Scheppers tests the hypothesis that the colon was the basic unit of composition. That hypothesis is confirmed by three patterns of usage: word order,
discourse segmentation, and discourse coherence.[17] If we approach the hypothesis that the Bible was originally composed as sounds to be performed
for audiences, what difference would it make if we began to listen to the
compositions with our auditory sensors rather than reading the texts with
our visual sensors? What difference would listening make in the testing of
that hypothesis?

The foundation on which the development of performance criticism
is being constructed is the ubiquity of sound as the dominant sensorium of
ancient literature. Sound mapping is an integral dimension of that foundation. In 2021, Wipf & Stock's "Biblical Performance Criticism" series has
now reached sixteen volumes. The publication in 2017 of *The Dictionary of
the Bible and Ancient Media* is another milestone in the gathering of knowledge about the communication culture of the ancient world.[18] The dictionary provides a detailed summary of the multi-faceted media research into
the Bible and ancient media during the past 200 years and, in particular,
since the establishment of the Bible in Ancient and Modern Media group
in 1983. And, while not always explicitly identified as such, the description
of the Bible and ancient media in these works is an explication of a communication culture of sound.

The problem that has not been adequately addressed, however, is the
discontinuity between the current visual sensorium of biblical scholarship
and the predominantly sound sensorium of the media world of antiquity.
If the Bible has been misperceived as a "text," what have appeared to be
puzzles in a predominantly visual sensorium might be perceived differently
if those puzzles were approached in an auditory sensorium. That is, the
Bible has been misperceived. Dimensions of the testing of the hypothesis of
an auditory sensorium would include:

1. Empirical analysis of New Testament compositions as units of sound
   rather than as units of text;

---

17. Scheppers, *The Colon Hypothesis*.
18. Thatcher, et al, eds., *The Dictionary of the Bible and Ancient Media*.

2. Comparison of the units of sound in particular New Testament compositions with the sound characteristics of the other compositions recorded in the New Testament and the broader compendium of compositions in classical Greek;

3. Identification of the dynamics of interaction with listening audiences rather than the perceptions and responses of readers;

4. Specific decisions about representation of the compositions in a sound map.

Such a reexamination of the biblical tradition would constitute a test case of the difference listening might make.

The Puzzle:
Mark 16:8 and the Intended Ending of the Gospel

The ending of the gospel of Mark is one of the most vexing puzzles of the New Testament. D. E. Nineham has called it, "the greatest of all literary mysteries";[19] and James R. Edwards has named it, "the gravest textual problem in the NT."[20] The great majority of extant Markan manuscripts end with the story of Jesus' appearances to the disciples and his ascension (Mark 16:9–20). That ending has been included in the most authoritative editions of the Greek and English texts, designated as "The Longer Ending of Mark." Some scholars, most notably William Farmer, have argued that 16:9–20 is the original ending.[21] A cornerstone of the empirical evidence against 16:9–20 is that the best manuscripts (Codex Vaticanus and Codex Sinaiticus) end at 16:8. The majority of Markan scholars now consider 16:8 as the original ending of the best Markan manuscripts.

There remains, however, significant division on whether 16:8 is the intended ending of the gospel. Adela Yarbro Collins concludes that 16:8 continues the emphasis throughout the gospel on "wonder" in response to "the manifestation of heavenly power" and was the intended ending.[22] Joel Marcus in his Anchor Bible commentary tries to make sense of the ending at 16:8, but concludes: "there is not enough evidence to say definitely whether Mark intended his work to end at 16:8."[23] In a thorough and carefully nuanced article, Robert Stein finds that 16:8 is the "best preserved" ending but

19. Nineham, *The Gospel of St. Mark*, 439.
20. Edwards, *The Gospel according to Mark*, 439.
21. Farmer, *The Last Twelve Verses of Mark*.
22. Collins, *Mark*, 801.
23. Marcus, *Mark 9–16*, 1096.

argues that it is not the intended ending. The two strongest arguments that he finds for this conclusion are, first, that the prophecies in 14:28 and 16:7 about Jesus' meeting the disciples in Galilee create an expectation for "the intended readers" that is unfulfilled. Second, modern attempts to find 16:8 as a meaningful ending[24] "lose sight of the Christological purpose of Mark in his gospel and in this passage."[25]

The conclusion of Clayton Croy's book, *The Mutilation of Mark's Gospel*, is that the original ending was lost, probably as the result of the original codex losing the sheet that included both the original beginning and ending.[26] In Croy's appendix listing the conclusions of generations of Markan scholars, beginning with J. J. Griesbach (1789–90), eighty-six scholars agree that 16:8 was not the intended ending and seventy-seven agree that the original ending was somehow lost.[27] Croy has called the ending at 16:8 "a gaping wound" and judiciously explicates eight major arguments against 16:8 as the original intended ending.[28]

To state the problem of Mark's ending in terms of sensory perception, when 16:8 is evaluated as a text ending the gospel, it looks strange. Here is the UBS Greek text of Mark's resurrection narrative:

> Καὶ διαγενομένου τοῦ σαββάτου Μαρία ἡ Μαγδαληνὴ καὶ
> Μαρία ἡ [τοῦ Ἰακώβου καὶ Σαλώμη ἠγόρασαν ἀρώματα ἵνα
> ἐλθοῦσαι ἀλείψωσιν αὐτόν. καὶ λίαν πρωῒ τῇ μιᾷ τῶν σαββάτων
> ἔρχονται ἐπὶ τὸ μνημεῖον ἀνατείλαντος τοῦ ἡλίου. καὶ ἔλεγον
> πρὸς ἑαυτάς, Τίς ἀποκυλίσει ἡμῖν τὸν λίθον ἐκ τῆς θύρας τοῦ
> μνημείου; καὶ ἀναβλέψασαι θεωροῦσιν ὅτι ἀποκεκύλισται ὁ
> λίθος. ἦν γὰρ μέγας σφόδρα. καὶ εἰσελθοῦσαι εἰς τὸ μνημεῖον
> εἶδον νεανίσκον καθήμενον ἐν τοῖς δεξιοῖς περιβεβλημένον
> στολὴν λευκήν, καὶ ἐξεθαμβήθησαν. ὁ δὲ λέγει αὐταῖς, Μὴ
> ἐκθαμβεῖσθε. Ἰησοῦν ζητεῖτε τὸν Ναζαρηνὸν τὸν ἐσταυρωμένον.
> ἠγέρθη, οὐκ ἔστιν ὧδε. ἴδε ὁ τόπος ὅπου ἔθηκαν αὐτόν. ἀλλὰ
> ὑπάγετε εἴπατε τοῖς μαθηταῖς αὐτοῦ καὶ τῷ Πέτρῳ ὅτι Προάγει
> ὑμᾶς εἰς τὴν Γαλιλαίαν. ἐκεῖ αὐτὸν ὄψεσθε, καθὼς εἶπεν ὑμῖν.
> καὶ ἐξελθοῦσαι ἔφυγον ἀπὸ τοῦ μνημείου, εἶχεν γὰρ αὐτὰς
> τρόμος καὶ ἔκστασις, καὶ οὐδενὶ οὐδὲν εἶπαν, ἐφοβοῦντο γάρ.

---

24. Some of the scholars who argue that Mark 16:8 is the intended ending include Petersen, "When Is the End not the End?," 153; Best, *Mark: The Gospel as Story*, 132; Lincoln, "The Promise and the Failure"; Tolbert, *Sowing the Gospel*, 297–99; Danove, *The End of Mark's Story*, 221–22.

25. Stein, "The Ending of Mark," 97–98.

26. Croy, *The Mutilation of Mark's Gospel*.

27. Croy, *The Mutilation of Mark's Gospel*, 174–77.

28. Croy, *The Mutilation of Mark's Gospel*, 47–64.

The most natural response to the reading of this ending is a series of questions. So what happened? Did the women tell the disciples? If not, how did the resurrection story get told? Did Jesus meet the disciples in Galilee? These questions then lead to others. Why did the author end the story like this? Is this really appropriate for a story that claims to be good news for the entire world? That is, when read as a text, the ending naturally leads to the questions of a critical reader. It is a puzzle and, to many readers, an unacceptable ending. What difference would it make if the ending was originally heard by audiences in interaction with a storyteller or reader? How did Mark 16:8 sound?[29]

The Characteristics of the Sound of Mark 16:8

This essay was inspired by the publication of *Sound Mapping the New Testament*. Margaret Lee and co-author, Bernard Brandon Scott, have based their proposal of sound mapping on the works of the grammarians of the classical and Hellenistic periods, especially Dionysius of Halicarnassus, Demetrius, and Aristotle. Their survey concludes: "Greek authors crafted their works with their auditory impact in mind at every level of construction."[30] The basic units of sound composition that can be identified in Hellenistic Greek literature are the syllable, the colon, and the period. The identification of these basic units of composition in Mark 16:8 will be the focus of this analysis of the sound of Mark 16:8.

A principal dialogue partner in this research is Frank Scheppers, the author of *The Colon Hypothesis: Word Order, Discourse Segmentation, and Discourse Coherence in Ancient Greek*. Scheppers has sought to identify the patterns of sound composition in classical Greek literature and argues that the colon rather than the period is the most consistent and verifiable unit of composition in this literary corpus.[31] He has found the period to be a more ambiguous guide to discourse segmentation than the colon. His subtitle names the patterns of sound that are characteristic signs of the colon.

29. For a performance of Mark's passion and resurrection narrative in Greek and in English, listen to (and see) my recording at http://messiahofpeace.com. Scheppers refers to this recording several times; see Scheppers, "Discourse Segmentation," 154, 160, 167. It is significant that he finds a strong correlation between his analysis of the cola of Mark 15 and the colometric segmentation implied in the performance.

30. Lee and Scott, *Sound Mmapping*, 121.

31. Scheppers, "Discourse Segmentation," 140. The period was Aristotle's literary unit of choice and is adopted by Lee and Scott as the next higher unit of composition above the colon. Scheppers found the period to be an ambiguous unit of composition and focused on the colon as the basic intonation unit.

Scheppers's identification of the colon is related to the "discourse analytical approach" of Wallace Chafe and a group of related linguists who have concluded that the basic unit of discourse analysis is best conceived as the "intonation unit."[32] In Scheppers's work, the colon and the intonation unit are virtual synonyms. Chafe and Scheppers also have adopted a similar practice as Lee and Scott of transcribing texts, often in Chafe's case of spontaneous conversations, with every discourse unit on a separate line.

Word Order and Colon Segmentation

An important starting point for Scheppers's work is the recognition of the correlation between word order and colon segmentation. As he states in his contribution to this volume, "Word order played a relatively important part in my own work on classical Greek, in that it offered me clear, formal and objective evidence that 'grounded' the research empirically."[33] This empirical basis was connected with Wackernagel's Law, as originally conceived, "enclitics tend toward the second position of the clause/sentence."[34] This "law" meant that the presence of particles in a postpositive position (P2) was an objective indication of a new colon. Particles that tend to occur in the postpositive position (P2) include particles such as γάρ, δὲ, οὖν, indefinite pronouns, adjectives and adverbs, and personal pronouns. A further related rule is that a number of 'introductive" particles (such as καί) take first position (P1) within the colon. Prepositives are words that, in Scheppers's terms, "cling to" the words that follow them while postpositives cling to the words that precede them.

As Scheppers notes in his essay in this book, these rules, which are highly reliable criteria for colon segmentation in classical Greek, are less so in New Testament Greek.[35] Particles are less frequent and non-emphatic pronouns do not occur as consistently in the P2 position. But, as is evident in the sound map of Mark 15, with these relatively minor qualifications, the basic rules are operative in New Testament Greek. The recognition of this pattern in Scheppers's analysis of classical Greek is important for the study of New Testament Greek because it establishes the presence of this pattern in the much larger corpus of classical Greek literature.

When Mark 16:8 is analyzed in this comprehensive context, the pattern of word order can be readily identified. There is an ABAB alternation

32. Scheppers, *The Colon Hypothesis*, 18–19.

33. Scheppers, "Discourse Segmentation," 10.

34. Scheppers, *The Colon Hypothesis*, 4.

35. Scheppers, "Discourse Segmentation," 10.

between prepositive καί and postpositive γάρ particles: καὶ ἐξελθοῦσαι/εἶχεν γὰρ/καὶ οὐδενὶ/ἐφοβοῦντο γάρ. A literal translation is: And going out/had seized them for/and nothing/they were afraid for. The identification of this pattern makes it possible to reconstruct the colon boundaries in this composition. There are four cola with clearly marked boundaries. When each of these intonation units is placed on a separate line, the sound map of Mark 16:8 is as follows:

καὶ ἐξελθοῦσαι ἔφυγον ἀπὸ τοῦ μνημείου
εἶχεν γὰρ αὐτὰς τρόμος καὶ ἔκστασι
καὶ οὐδενὶ οὐδὲν εἶπαν
ἐφοβοῦντο γάρ

And they went out and fled from the tomb
For terror and amazement had seized them
And they said nothing to anyone
For they were afraid (NRSV)

A striking feature of this sound map is the cluster of four short cola that are progressively shorter. As can be seen, it looks very different than the following UBS/Nestle–Aland Greek text and its translation:

καὶ ἐξελθοῦσαι ἔφυγον ἀπὸ τοῦ μνημείου, εἶχεν γὰρ αὐτὰς τρόμος καὶ ἔκστασις· καὶ οὐδενὶ οὐδὲν εἶπαν· ἐφοβοῦντο γάρ. (UBS5)

And they went out and fled from the tomb, for terror and amazement had seized them; and they said nothing to anyone, for they were afraid. (NRSV)

The UBS punctuation and textual arrangement is based on a grammatical analysis. The editors of the various Nestle/Aland and UBS Greek texts punctuate and arrange this text as a sentence with clauses, rather than as cola. They punctuate 16:8 as one sentence with a comma, two half stops and a concluding full stop.

However, a function of punctuation related to sound can be to indicate the length and quality of the pauses between grammatical units: a comma indicates a short pause/catch breath; a half stop in a Greek text (usually transcribed as a semicolon in English texts) indicates a longer pause/half breath; a full stop/period indicates a major pause/full breath. As presently punctuated, the UBS Greek text above would be recited with a catch breath and two short pauses prior to the concluding full breath and full stop. In the context of the conclusion that 16:8 is four short cola, what is the quality and length of the pauses between the four cola? How should 16:8 be punctuated?

Short cola in Mark

The composer of Mark used short cola as a basic technique of composition, particularly in the creation of climactic endings. The climactic effect is often the result of a short colon following a longer colon. The climactic ending can also be heightened in its intensity by a cluster of short cola and, in the case of 16:8, a crescendo of increasingly shorter cola.

The composer consistently uses short cola in emotionally charged endings. Most of these moments are either climaxes in the stories of Jesus' conflicts with various opponents or the stories of wrong responses by Jesus' disciples.

The following are climactic short endings prior to the passion narrative:

Rejection at Nazareth	καὶ ἐθαύμαζεν διὰ τὴν ἀπιστίαν αὐτῶν And he was amazed at their unbelief	6:6
Cursing of the fig tree	καὶ ἤκουον οἱ μαθηταὶ αὐτου And his disciples heard it	11:14
Parable of the wicked tenants	καὶ ἀφέντες αὐτον ἀπῆλθον And they left him and went away	12:12
Paying taxes to Caesar	καὶ ἐξεθαύμαζον ἐπ'αὐτῷ And they were utterly amazed at him.	12:17

With the exception of the cursing of the fig tree, each of these short cola is the climax of a conflict story and the cursing of the fig tree is the surprising and emotionally charged prelude to the prophetic demonstration in the temple that leads to Jesus' death.

The frequency of highly charged and climactic short endings increases in the passion narrative:

Judas' betrayal	καὶ ἐζήτει πῶς αὐτὸν εὐκαίρως παραδοῖ And he looked for the best way to betray him	14:11
Prophecy of flight and denial	ὡσαύτως δὲ καὶ πάντες ἔλεγον And they all said the same thing	14:31
Arrest and flight	καὶ ἀφέντες αὐτὸν ἔφυγον πάντες And forsaking him, they all fled	14:50
Sanhedrin trial	καὶ οἱ ὑπφρέται ραπίσμασιν αὐτὸν ἔλαβον And the guards took him away beating him	14:65
Peter's denial	καὶ ἐπιβαλὼν ἔκλαιεν And beating himself he wept	14:72
Mocking by Romans	καὶ ἐξάγουσιν αὐτὸν ἵνα σταυρώσωσιν αὐτόν And they led him out to crucify him	15:20

Mocking by Judeans	καὶ οἱ συνεσταυρωμένοι σὺν αὐτῷ ὠνείδιζον αὐτόν	15:32
	And those crucified with him taunted him	
Death of Jesus	ὁ δὲ Ἰησοῦς ἀφεὶς φωνὴν μεγάλην ἐξέπνευσεν	15:37
	But Jesus giving a loud cry he breathed his last	

All of these endings are emotionally intense moments in the story. Two of these endings, the beating by the Sanhedrin's guards and the mocking by the Roman soldiers, are the climax of stories of the humiliation of Jesus. Judas' betrayal, the prophecy of flight and denial, the flight of the disciples as the climax of the arrest, and Peter's denial are climactic endings of the stories of the responses of Jesus' disciples. The climactic ending of the story of Jesus' death is a response to the mockery by the Judean passersby, the chief priests and scribes, and the "insurrectionists" crucified with him. The shortest of these climactic cola is the three word/eight syllable ending of the story of Peter's denial.

Thus, the final colon in the best manuscripts of Mark, ἐφοβοῦντο γάρ (for they were afraid), is the shortest of the climactic cola in the gospel. As can be seen in the sound map above, the segmentation of the cola in 16:8 shows that there is a four step shortening in successive cola: 6, 6, 4, 2 words and 14, 11, 8 and 5 syllables. The proposition that this pattern in the usage of short cola is accidental or unintentional is highly unlikely. This technique of composition and performance occurs throughout the gospel and is used only in highly climactic and emotionally charged moments in the larger story. The ending at 16:8 uses this technique of sound composition in a climactic manner.

This pattern is also a guide in estimating the length of the pauses and the punctuation between these four climactic cola. The lengths of the cola are an indication of their tempo: longer cola are faster and shorter cola are slower. This slowing of the tempo at the end is then a clue to the length of the pauses between cola. The pauses become longer and participate in the gradual retard with each successive colon, the longest being the pause between the report that the women said nothing to anyone and the performer's explanation that they were afraid. This in turn leads to the conclusion that the best punctuation would be four full stops.

Audience Address

As noted above, the alternation between the prepositive καί cola and the postpositive γάρ cola marks the four cola in 16:8:

καὶ ἐξελθοῦσαι ἔφυγον ἀπὸ τοῦ μνημείου (prepositive)
εἶχεν γὰρ αὐτὰς τρόμος καὶ ἔκστασις (postpositive)
καὶ οὐδενὶ οὐδὲν εἶπαν (prepositive)
ἐφοβοῦντο γάρ (postpositive)

This alternation is also an objective sign of the change of tone in the address to the audience that concludes the gospel. The alternation between the description of the surprising actions of the women in fleeing and saying nothing and the audience asides explaining their actions by the performer of the story creates this dynamic.

The storyteller reports something that is surprising or puzzling in a straightforward indicative to the audience. The more shocking or surprising this initial report is the more the audience is hooked into wondering. In effect, the audience is invited to ask: "Why?" or "What?" The γάρ colon that follows this provocation is an aside in which the performer changes tone and explains the apparent anomaly to the audience. In performance, this is often accompanied by a gesture of leaning into the audience that establishes a higher level of connection or intimacy between the storyteller and the audience. The gesture may be a direct looking at the audience, a knowing smile or a hand to one side of the mouth. And the change of tone can be a lower volume or a lower vocal pitch. It creates a moment of inside information that indirectly says, "Now let me tell you the inside story."

In 16:8, the initial indicative is the surprising report that the women fled. The question that this report raises is, "Why did they flee?" The aside to the audience explains that they had been seized by "trauma" and "ecstasy." The second report that they said nothing to anyone is even more surprising in light of the angel's command to "go, tell. . ." The audience aside explains that they were "afraid."

This pattern of audience address is present throughout the gospel.[36] For example, the explanation of why the woman snuck up behind Jesus and touched his garment is, "For she said, 'If I can touch his garment, I will be made well'" (5:27–28). Earlier in the resurrection story, the aside to the audience explains the reason that the women were so surprised at finding the stone rolled back: "For it was a big stone!" (16:4).[37] When heard in the

36 Audience asides introduced by γάρ that explain confusing or surprising events reported in the previous colon are: 1:16, 22; 2:15; 3:21; 5:8, 28, 42; 6:17, 18, 20, 31, 48; 9:6, 34; 10:22; 11:13; 14:2, 40, 56; 15:10; 16:4. For an analysis of the two asides (7:3–4; 15:21) that have been misperceived as "narrative comments," see above, "Audience Asides."

37. The major recent translations of Mark have eliminated this climactic audience aside and made it a subordinate clause earlier in an indicative sentence, e.g., "When they looked up, they saw that the stone, which was very large, had already been rolled

context of the earlier instances of this pattern, 16:8 is the only instance in the gospel in which this pattern of provocation/explanation occurs twice in succession. That is, there is a climactic concentration of this technique of sound composition in 16:8. In the ending of the gospel, the performer of the gospel, whether a storyteller or a lector, turns to the audience twice and addresses them.

Furthermore, this ending is another instance of a distinctive Markan way of audience provocation. The typical function of audience asides is to explain a puzzle or surprise in the previous cola. The explanation brings closure to the audience's questions. For example, in the story of Jairus' daughter (5:22–24, 35–43), the storyteller reports that the "little girl" (ταλιθά) got up and started walking around the room. In order to resolve the audience's ambiguity about whether the little girl was an infant, the storyteller explains that she was twelve years old. Most of the audience asides introduced by γάρ listed above have this function.

However, in two earlier instances, the explanations are themselves enigmatic and raise more questions than they answer. The most graphic of these provocative explanations is the ending of the story of Jesus walking on the sea (6:45–52). The surprise needing explanation is the disciples' utter amazement at seeing Jesus walking on the sea. The aside is: "For they didn't understand about the loaves, but their hearts were hardened." This explanation provokes further questions. What didn't the disciples understand about the loaves? How are the disciples like hard-hearted Pharoah?

The second instance is the plot of the chief priests and scribes that begins the passion narrative:

> Now the feast of Passover and unleavened bread was the next day. And the chief priests and the scribes were seeking how to arrest him by treachery and kill him. For they had been saying, "Not during the feast, lest there be a riot of the people. (14:1–2)

The surprise that demands explanation is that the authorities were taking criminal steps to kill Jesus on that day: "Why the sudden urgency?" The explanation is that they had to arrest him "today" because they had ruled out an arrest during the feast that begins "the next day."[38] But this

---

back" (NRSV). For a more extensive discussion of these translation issues, see Boomershine, *The Messiah of Peace,* 333–37.

38. The NRSV mistakenly translates this phrase, as "It was two days before . . ." (NIV: "two days away.") Just as μετὰ τρεῖς ἡμέρας (8:31; 9:31; 10:34) means "on the third day" and counts "today" as the first day, so also here the meaning in 14:2 is "on the second day." Counting "today" as the first day, "the second day" is "tomorrow/the next day." For a further discussion of the evidence supporting "the next day" as the meaning of the phrase in the context of the plot of the chief priests, see *The Messiah of Peace,* 37–44.

raises more questions: "Will they abandon their plot if they cannot arrest him today? What is Jesus doing today?" The second question is answered by the story of the anointing at Bethany, with its implication that Jesus didn't go into the city on that Wednesday: "On that day Jesus was in Bethany . . ." (14:3).

Thus, the supremely provocative ending at 16:8 is a climactic instance of a pattern in Markan storytelling that also occurs frequently in the parables of Jesus and in Israelite storytelling.[39] The widespread conviction among Markan scholars that 16:8 is an unintended ending is itself a sign that Mark's provocation continues to work.

Sonic Echoes

A basic technique in the composition of sound is repetition. In contrast to text that does not disappear when perceived, sound immediately begins to deteriorate or disappear. For example, a note struck on the piano, even if the key is held down or maintained by the damper pedal, will instantly begin to decline in volume and will disappear in a few seconds. With the voice, the disappearance of the sound is almost instantaneous unless the sound is produced in a highly resonant room, in which case it may resonate for a second or two.

But regardless of the resonance of the space, the only way to return to a sound is to repeat it. Repetition is a basic technique of musical composition. A typical structure is the sonata. It has an ABA structure in which there is the statement of a theme (A), a variation or complementary theme (B), and a restatement of the original theme (A). Another type of composition is a theme with variations. In this form, the basic theme is repeated with variations either in the theme itself or more frequently in various harmonies and tempos that surround the theme. In popular music, including contemporary Christian music and music from the Taize faith community in France, a musical motif or theme may be sung or played over and over again, sometimes ten to twenty times.

The primary function of repetition in sound compositions is the reinforcement of the audience's memory. In biblical stories, repetition of key words and phrases from earlier episodes shapes the memory context in which the current story is heard. In addition to the associations of content, repetitions will sometimes have a similar tone that evokes the emotional

---

39. For a more extensive exploration of this characteristic pattern in Mark, in the storytelling traditions of Israel and in Jesus' parables, see Boomershine, *The Messiah of Peace*, 342–44.

atmosphere of the earlier story. A graphic example of this is Peter's remembering Jesus' prophecy of his denial "before the cock crows twice." The repetition sets Peter's denial in the context of the audience's memory of Peter's vehement vow to die with Jesus rather than to deny him.

The impact of these repetitions is often subtle and may only be perceived in hearing the story. One of the classic instances of misperception of biblical compositions is the so-called doublet. A doublet is a repetition of words that are perceived as redundant. The doublet is often seen as a sign of the merging of two disparate sources. The identification of doublets has been one of the primary clues to the analysis of tradition history in biblical scholarship. But it is often also a misperception that is the result of examining the text with the eyes rather than listening to the story with the ears.

When biblical compositions are heard, repetitions are experienced as sonic echoes that make connections between elements of the composition. A frequent pattern of New Testament composition is the repetition of individual words, metaphors, and portions from the traditions of the Old Testament, either as quotations or as allusions. The most frequent pattern, however, is the repetition and development of sound motifs from earlier episodes in the individual composition.

In Mark 16:8 there are four prominent sonic echoes: the tomb, flight, said nothing to anyone, and fear. Discussing them in their order of occurrence, the first is the tomb. The tomb is a structural element in the resurrection story. The women "went out to the tomb" (ἔρχονται ἐπὶ τὸ μνημεῖον), "enter into the tomb" (εἰσελθοῦσαι εἰς τὸ μνημεῖον), and "going out they fled from the tomb" (ἐξελθοῦσαι ἔφυγον ἀπὸ τοῦ μνημείου). This sonic echo continues the theme established in the burial story: "and he laid him in a tomb that had been carved out of the rock and rolled a stone over the door of the tomb" (καὶ ἔθηκεν αὐτὸν ἐν μνημείῳ ὃ ἦν λελατομημένον ἐκ πέτρας, καὶ προσεκύλισεν λίθον ἐπὶ τὴν θύραν τοῦ μνημείου). The echo is a kind of tolling bell in the story that evokes the grief associated with Jesus' death and burial. It also establishes the place of the story and the repetition invites the listeners to see the tomb in their imagination.

The women's flight from the tomb is a sonic echo of the flight of the disciples and the naked young man that concludes the arrest story (arranged in cola):

> καὶ ἀφέντες αὐτὸν ἔφυγον πάντες.
> καὶ νεανίσκος τις συνηκολούθει αὐτῷ
> περιβεβλημένος σινδόνα ἐπὶ γυμνοῦ,
> καὶ κρατοῦσιν αὐτόν.
> ὁ δὲ καταλιπὼν τὴν σινδόνα γυμνὸς ἔφυγεν

> And forsaking him, they all fled.
> And there was a young man following him
> wearing a linen cloth over his nakedness,
> and they seize him.
> But leaving the linen cloth, he fled naked. (14:50–52)

The sound of the word ἔφυγον ("they fled") resonates with the memories of the disciples' fear of being arrested, tried, and executed with Jesus. It also resonates with their failure to keep their promise that they would die with him. The flight of the naked young man carries the vibes of shame associated with forsaking Jesus. The women have been commissioned to announce the resurrection and this word is the first clue in the story that they will fail to fulfill the commission they have been given.

The next surprise in the story is the report that they told no one anything: καὶ οὐδενὶ οὐδὲν εἶπαν. The sonic echoes connected with these words are the earlier soundings of various forms of the verb λέγω, "to say, tell." The most immediate is the command of the young man: ἀλλὰ ὑπάγετε εἴπατε τοῖς μαθηταῖς αὐτοῦ καὶ τῷ Πέτρῳ ("But go, tell his disciples and Peter" 16:7). Saying nothing is an explicit and immediate contradiction of the young man's command.[40]

The earlier instances of this sonic theme are Jesus' admonitions to the leper and the disciples to say nothing. The most fully resonant with 16:8 of these earlier commands is Jesus' stern command to the leper: Ὅρα μηδενὶ μηδὲν εἴπῃς ("See that you tell no one anything" 1:44). The only differences between Jesus' charge to the leper and the report of the women's silence are the forms of the negative particles and the endings of the verb: μηδενὶ μηδὲν εἴπῃς /οὐδενὶ οὐδὲν εἶπαν ("tell no one anything"/"they told no one anything"). The irony, perhaps with a touch of ironic humor, is that both of these responses indicate explicit disobedience of earlier commands and a reversal of audience expectations. Jesus commands the leper to tell no one anything and he proclaims it everywhere; the women are commanded to "tell" the news to the disciples and they tell no one anything.

Jesus' admonition to the disciples to say nothing about him immediately follows Peter's declaration, "You are the Messiah": καὶ ἐπετίμησεν

---

40. The NRSV translation of the command, "tell," which has been continued from the King James translation, is not the same sound as the women's response ("they said nothing"). This is an example of the translators' failure to listen to the sounds of the Greek composition and to maintain as many of the sonic echoes as possible in translation. It would be equally congruent with the meaning of the original Greek to translate the young man's command as: "Go, say to his disciples and Peter . . . The other sonically connected possibility would be to translate the command and the women's response as, "Go, tell his disciples . . . And they told no one anything." I like the last best.

αὐτοῖς ἵνα μηδενὶ λέγωσιν περὶ αὐτοῦ ("and he strongly commanded them to say nothing about him"). The actual words in the command following the messianic confession are more explicitly a sonic echo of the command to the leper (repetition of μηδενί) than the report of the women's silence. But the report of the women's silence is definitely sonically linked with the messianic confession.

The primary impact of these sonic echoes with earlier moments in the story is the irony of the women's silence. The leper is commanded to say nothing but instead proclaims the news and the disciples are commanded to say nothing about him being the Messiah. The reason for Jesus' effort to maintain secrecy in relation to his messianic identity has been fully clarified by the high priest's immediate charge of blasphemy in response to Jesus' messianic confession. But now in the wake of the resurrection, the women are commanded to tell the story and they tell no one anything.

The sonic echoes of the women's fear in the earlier stories of the gospel is the most highly developed sonic theme that resonates with the words of 16:8, specifically the ending: ἐφοβοῦντο γάρ ("For they were afraid"). Various forms of the verb occur eleven times prior to the ending. In the early parts of the gospel prior to the messianic confession and the passion-resurrection prophecies, the verb is primarily used to describe the responses of persons to Jesus' powerful deeds:

The disciples' fear at the calming of the sea	ἐφοβήθησαν φόβον μέγαν feared a great fear	4:41
The Gerasenes' response to the demoniac clothed and in his right mind	καὶ ἐφοβήθησαν and they were afraid	5:15
The bleeding woman's response to her healing	ἡ δὲ γυνὴ φοβηθεῖσα καὶ τρέμουσα and the woman afraid and trembling	5:33
Jesus' response to the disciples' terror	θαρσεῖτε, ἐγώ εἰμι· μὴ φοβεῖσθε Take heart. I am. Don't be afraid.	6:50

The same word, ἐφοβοῦντο, occurs twice in the stories of Jesus' passion/resurrection prophecies. In response to the second passion-resurrection prophecy, the disciples "were afraid to ask him" (καὶ ἐφοβοῦντο αὐτὸν ἐπερωτῆσαι–9:32). And just prior to the third prophecy, Jesus walks ahead of them and they are amazed, and "those who followed were afraid" (οἱ δὲ ἀκολουθοῦντες ἐφοβοῦντο–10:32). The last three instances of this verb name the responses of the chief priests and the scribes to Jesus' actions and teaching in the temple. After Jesus' prophetic demonstration in the temple, they wanted to arrest him but they "feared" him because of the crowd's enthusiastic response to his demonstration and teaching (11:18). In the stories of their questioning Jesus' authority and in response to his parable of the wicked tenants, the chief priests and the scribes "feared" the crowd (11:32; 12:12).

When analyzed as sonic echoes, therefore, the associations of this theme are first with Jesus' power and authority and second with the prophecies and conflicts that led to his death. That is, the sonic echoes of this climactic word prior to the ending are associated with the words and events connected with his authority and his death. For Mark's listeners, therefore, death is the answer to the implicit question of why the women were afraid.

In the context of these sonic echoes, the women's flight, silence, and fear are fully understandable. Mark 16:8 resonates with the sounds of the earlier stories that lead up to Jesus' death and resurrection. The principal theme around which these earlier themes coalesce in 16:8 is the commissioning of the women by the divine messenger, not Jesus' appearance.

This theme is the focus of the addresses to the audience that conclude the gospel. The last words, the climactic short cola, are neither descriptions of what happened with Jesus' death and resurrection nor statements of the promise of his appearance in Galilee. They are explanations of the women's flight and silence that are addressed to the audience. In Mark's provocative manner, however, those explanations of the women's flight and fearful silence raise as many questions as they answer. At the end of the story, the performer turns to the audience and addresses them directly. In the provocative silences that are the climax of the story, therefore, hang the questions: How will I/we respond to the news of the resurrection? Will I/we flee? Will I/we be silent and say nothing to anyone? Will I/we be afraid?

The other three gospels end with the same theme of the commissioning of Jesus' followers. In Matthew and Luke, Jesus commissions the disciples. In Matthew, the great commission takes place on a Galilean mountain (28:16–20). In Luke, the commission to be Jesus' witnesses to all the nations is located in Jerusalem (24:36–49). In John, Jesus addresses the commission to feed his lambs and sheep to Peter by the Sea of Galilee (21:15–19).

Conclusions about Mark 16:8

The principal conclusion of this case study is that, when Mark 16:8 is perceived and analyzed as sound, it is a climactic and intended ending. The sounds of the ending are a climactic use of techniques of composition that are present throughout the gospel. The analysis of those techniques of composition and the actual sound of the words reveals a high degree of sophistication in the art of oral storytelling. In light of this attention to sonic detail, it is impossible to imagine that such a pervasive use of composition techniques of sound in the formation of the cola, the dynamic address to the audience, and the sonic echoing of major thematic elements was accidental or in some way unintended.

Thus, the following sonic structures can be identified in Mark 16:8.

Word Order and Segmentation of Intonation Units

The word order follows the patterns of colon demarcation in Greek compositions of classical and archaic as well as Koine Greek of the New Testament period. The alternation of postpositive and prepositive word order is a clear indication that 16:8 is structured as four cola. The intonation units of Mark's ending are segmented in a manner that occurs throughout the composition.

Climactic Shortening of Cola

The four cola are progressively shorter (6, 6, 4, 2 words; 14, 11, 8, 5 syllables) and, therefore, slower. In musical terms, it is a long retard. The cola build to a climax of sound and silence. This usage of short cola in climactic positions occurs frequently in earlier moments in the gospel composition, most notably in the ending of Peter's denial. 16:8 is a climactic instance of this pervasive technique of composition in the whole story.

A Crescendo of Lengthening Pauses

The alternation between reports of the women's surprising actions and audience asides that give an inside explanation of the women's emotions creates a crescendo of pauses between successive cola that are progressively longer. Those pauses give the performer time to turn to the audience for the asides and give the audience time to ponder both the women's response and their own response to the commission and the fear of death associated with it. The composer of Mark uses earlier pauses like those in 16:8 prior to enigmatic audience asides that explain puzzling elements in a provocative manner that raises more questions (e.g., the ending of the walking on the sea story in 6:52).

Sonic Echoes

The sonic echoes of the words naming the women's actions and internal responses link the women's flight and silence with central themes of the gospel story as a whole. In musical terminology, the sonic echoes are the climactic endings of leitmotifs, as in Wagnerian operas, that link elements of the longer story. Prominent themes in the sonic echoes are the women's presence at the death and burial, the injunctions to silence and the maintenance of the messianic secret, the flight of the disciples, and being afraid.

The hypothesis that listening to Mark 16:8 might make a difference in the perception and evaluation of its credibility as an ending is confirmed. Listening to Mark's ending creates a perception of the story that makes sense as an ending. When Mark's composition has not been processed through auditory perceptual systems, it has been for many readers a puzzle that does not make sense as an ending. The implication is that Mark's ending has been misperceived as a result of the discontinuity between the auditory sensory data of the original composition and the visual sensory data of the silent reading of Mark's text.

Implications

The identification of the discontinuity between the silent reading of New Testament texts and the original character of the New Testament as compositions of sound has broader implications.

The Importance of Sound Mapping

Sound mapping lays a foundation for the study of New Testament compositions as sound. The implication of the difference between the auditory and visual sensory systems is that auditory perception is a necessary first step in scholarly methodology. Furthermore, the creation of a sound map requires a disciplined attention to the sounds of New Testament compositions that brings a degree of objectivity to the otherwise highly subjective voicing of the compositions.

Sound mapping also has major implications for the editing of New Testament compositions. The presentation of the Greek text and of the various vernacular translations as sound maps would more adequately represent the sound of the stories in a printed manuscript. Such reediting would include a re-examination of the punctuation of the texts as intonation units. The need for sound mapping of the New Testament carries with it the implication that the entire corpus of biblical literature needs to be reassessed and reedited as compositions of sound rather than as texts.

The Practice of New Testament Scholarship

The customary scholarly practice of silent reading needs to be modified as the dominant sensory perception of the Greek compositions that comprise the New Testament. A higher degree of congruence between the original sensory character of the Greek compositions and contemporary perception and analysis of the compositions as sound would lead to a more accurate and compelling interpretation of the New Testament in its original context. Performance criticism emerges from the current methodological multiplex as a central methodology for the study of the New Testament. The need for this reorientation of scholarly practice applies equally to the study of the Old Testament. The discontinuity between the sensorium of the ancient world and the sensorium of contemporary scholarship and the radical difference between auditory and visual perception justifies the description of this reorientation of biblical scholarship as a paradigm shift.

The Pedagogy of the New Testament

Teaching the New Testament as performance literature is a natural extension of this reorientation from sight to sound as the sensory matrix of learning and teaching.[41] This new pedagogy is based on the performance of the compositions by both faculty and students. Among other benefits, it is more interesting and engaging for students.

The Liturgical Performance of Biblical Literature

The Bible is probably the most widely performed literature in the world, as happens every Sunday in millions of churches around the world.[42] However, in contrast to the performance of the Hebrew/Aramaic scriptures in synagogues and of the Quran in mosques, biblical performance in the churches

41. For a further development of this implication, see the chapter on pedagogy in this volume (chap. 7): "Teaching Mark as Performance Literature."

42. A current estimate is that there are approximately thirty-seven million churches in the world. This number does not include, for example, all of the house churches in China, many of which are underground. The performance of the Bible happens in virtually all of those churches every Sunday; see https://www.quora.com/How-many-Christian-churches-are-there-in-the-world.

has largely lost contact with its ancient performance traditions. The present practice of liturgical proclamation has mirrored the assumption that the Bible is a disembodied text intended to be read in silence. The emotionally detached and monotone performance of the Bible in Christian liturgy has become a rote recital of texts characterized by poor preparation and audience boredom. Attention to the Bible as sound would contribute to the revitalization of the performance of the Scriptures in Christian worship.

7

Teaching Mark as Performance Literature
Early Literate and Post-Literate Pedagogies

Presuppositions about ancient communication culture are correlated with contemporary pedagogical approaches to the teaching of biblical literature in general and Mark in particular. Historical-critical study of the Bible has presupposed that ancient communication culture was analogous to the text-based communication culture of the eighteenth–twentieth centuries. The biblical tradition has been conceived and studied as texts that were read by readers, usually alone and in silence. This presupposition is reflected in the basic methods of source and redaction criticism of the documents and in the frequent references to "the reader" in biblical commentaries.

The teaching of Mark in contemporary education utilizes a text-based pedagogy that is congruent with the presupposed character of the communication culture of Mark's original historical context. This tradition for the teaching of Mark fits well with the text- based pedagogy of the university and the seminary with their libraries, papers, and degrees in the mastery of literary research and communication. Lectures focus on the textual history of Mark and on various documentary processes for the exegesis of the meaning of the text. Students are taught how to analyze the text by critical reading of the text with their eyes. Student projects are papers researched and written in silence and read in silence by the professors. The goal of the pedagogical process is for students to learn the theological and/or historical meaning of the texts in their original historical context on the basis of critically evaluated textual evidence. This data can then be interpreted for contemporary audiences in sermons, lectures and small group study. The presupposition is that this pedagogical approach is congruent with the experience of the original readers and communities. It is also presumed that this pedagogy will produce a vital engagement with Mark in the context of contemporary culture.

Recent historical investigation of ancient communication culture and of Mark within that culture has led to different conclusions about that culture and Mark within it. Ancient communication culture at the time of the composition of the Gospel of Mark was an early literate culture in which literacy had great cultural power but in which the great majority of people were unable to read. Current estimates are that literacy in the first century ranged from a maximum of 15 percent in urban communities to as little as 2–3 percent in rural areas. Documents were copied by hand, were relatively expensive, and were owned primarily by communities and wealthy individuals. There was no mass distribution of documents, minimal evidence of private reading and even less of silent reading. Publication of documents was primarily by performance for audiences. The grammatical literature of Greek rhetoricians and grammarians shows that ancient literature was composed as sounds with careful attention to cola and periods as breath units of sound.[1] When Mark is heard in the context of this communication culture, it is a skillful composition of sound structured for performance to audiences.

An additional characteristic of ancient communication culture was the centrality of memory. A trained memory was the goal of ancient education. A daily activity for children in Jewish and Greco-Roman schools was the memorization of a text, often a part of the Scriptures in Jewish schools and of rhetorical speeches in Greco-Roman schools. Written compositions were structured to facilitate memory and performances of written compositions were often done from memory. Indeed, since ancient manuscripts were a string of undifferentiated letters, it was necessary to virtually memorize a composition in order to perform it, even with a manuscript in hand.

This reassessment of the character of Mark raises the question of appropriate contemporary pedagogy. In as far as historical-critical methods of scholarly study and pedagogy are based on the assumption of continuity between the communication culture of the eighteenth–twentieth centuries and the biblical world, those methods and pedagogies are a historical anachronism, a reading back into the ancient world of a much later communication culture and its pedagogies. If our goal is to learn and teach about the meaning of Mark in its original historical context, we need to develop pedagogical methods that are congruent with the original character of Mark

---

1. Lee and Scott, *Sound Mapping*, 108–11.

as performance literature. The pedagogical theory is that there will be more understanding and energy for students in learning about Mark in a manner that is congruent with the original character of Mark. The first dimension of pedagogical reassessment is, therefore, the development of teaching methods that will give students an experience of Mark in its original context as an epic story that was performed for audiences.[2]

Furthermore, twenty-first-century students of the performance literature of the Bible live in a post-literate world in which digital communication technology rather than mass printing is the dominant means of mass communication. In this culture, the pedagogical methods of the eighteenth–twentieth centuries are increasingly archaic. The underlying cultural hermeneutic in digital culture is the priority of experience rather than concepts. To enable students to have a vital experience of Mark as a performance event is more likely to be meaningful for them than an exposition of the theological doctrine implicit in the document. Therefore, a combination of the pedagogical approaches of early literate culture and the pedagogies of post-literate, digital culture will open new possibilities for the teaching of Mark in the future.

The goal of this chapter is to outline the pedagogical methods that I have found to be effective in teaching Mark as performance literature. Future discussion about educational theory and the relationship between these methods and traditional pedagogy will be additional steps in this exploration. But a first step is to outline the new possibilities that have emerged from teaching Mark as a story told by storytellers.

Teaching Mark as Performance Literature

The major shift involved in the teaching of Mark as performance literature is to reorient the experience of Mark from text to performance. When seen from a pedagogical perspective, our present practices would be analogous to a professor of piano who taught students to study the manuscripts of piano compositions and never listened to or played the music. At every stage of the course work, experience of Mark as sound and as stories told to audiences is foundational. The possibilities range from weekly assignments and classroom experience to individual and communal research projects.

The more the pedagogical approaches of the course pursue a multifaceted exploration of Mark as stories told by heart to audiences, the better will be the overall course experience. The presupposition of teaching

2. For an excellent description of a highly successful university course with this structure, see Ruge-Jones, "The Word Heard."

Mark in this manner is that students will learn more about the character and meaning of Mark by being actively engaged in learning and telling the composition.

An Introductory Performance
of Mark by the Professor

Following the introduction to the course of study, a performance of Mark, either of the whole or of major parts, by the professor is the best introduction to Mark. Doing it live in front of the students is better than any recording. Until the students have experienced the Gospel as a story, the talk about it as a performed story remains abstract. Once they have experienced it, they have a much clearer idea about the subject of the course. A further positive dimension of the experience is that the students have a model for their own work on the story and the development of their skills as tellers of Mark's story.

The limitation of the professor telling the Gospel early on is that it eliminates the possibility of the students inductively arriving at their own interpretations on the basis of their study of the manuscript and independent exploration of how they might tell the stories. On the other hand, without an initial experience of hearing the story told, many students will be at a loss because they lack previous experience with the performance of literature. Only those who had been involved in drama earlier in their educational careers have the confidence and ability to develop as storytellers on their own. However, storytelling is significantly different than acting. In the teaching of performance for musical instruments such as the piano, it is important for students to have heard high quality performances early in their training. This also applies to learning the performance of Mark.

Of course, the challenge for the teachers of Mark is that most have had no training or experience in performing Mark themselves. There are now resources of videotapes and organizations such as the Network of Biblical Storytellers, International in which there is the possibility of experiencing high quality performances of Mark. There is a sense in which the best way to learn is to tell the stories of Mark in small settings. It is also possible to do shorter segments of the Gospel rather than the whole composition as an introduction to the performance dimensions of the course. But the most energizing step is for the students to experience the whole Gospel early in the course as told by their professor.

A Storytelling Workshop

The foundational introduction to performing Mark for the students is a storytelling workshop in which each student is enabled to learn and tell a story from Mark. I will briefly outline the basic stages of a storytelling workshop.[3]

Learning the Story

The first step in learning the performance of a Markan story is to learn the story. Good stories for an initial workshop are: the healing of the paralytic, the stilling of the storm, and Bartimaeus. My experience is that the best pedagogical approach is to dive in with no theory or introduction utilizing the methodology of the teachers of antiquity: repeat after me. The process is simply to tell the story phrase by phrase with gestures and have the students say it back with energy and gestures. I have sometimes found it helpful for a class to have an outline of the episodes of the story available preferably on a screen. The identification of the structure of the story can also be done on a flip chart, blackboard, or screen as the second step in learning the story.

An initial process is first for the students to say the story back to the teacher, then the teacher tell it after a brief analysis of the story's structure, the students say it back again, and finally they tell it to each other dividing into groups of two. Sometimes it is helpful to give the students a copy of the story arranged as a sound map in case neither one of them is able to remember what comes next. But it is also possible for them to rely on their memory with only the outline as a guide. After sufficient time for the students to tell the story to their partners, a brief discussion about the process of learning a story is helpful. Many of them have never learned and told any story before and certainly not a biblical story. To debrief the experience of learning and telling the story at this initial stage encourages their exploration of a native ability they did not know they had.

A next step in learning the story is to outline the structure of human memory. Memory training has been almost wholly eliminated from modern education. An outline of the structures of the brain that enable us to remember and the mnemonic structures built into the story is helpful to students.[4] The first of those structures are the sensory registers that register and sort the five sense data—sound, sight, smell, taste, touch—that are

3. For a more extensive description of a storytelling workshop, see Boomershine, *Story Journey*, 23–59.

4. For a comprehensive outline of the memory systems of the human brain, see Klatzky, *Human Memory*.

constantly being recorded in our brains. They are sorted by the dynamic of attention. The second stage of human memory is short-term memory that is best conceived as a workbench of up to ten items that are being processed every moment. The chunking of items of various sizes such as a set of notes in music, phrases in language, and moves in a dance is helpful in facilitating easier and quicker learning of stories.

The third stage is storing the items from short-term memory in the ordered shelves of long-term memory so that they can be retrieved. The two primary storage and retrieval systems are "episodic" storage and "syntactical or conceptual" storage. The issue for storytelling is not storage. Vast amounts of material are present in our long-term memories. The problem is that we cannot find the retrieval link to those memories stored in our memories. When students understand the way their memory works, they are able to learn stories more easily and become more consciously aware of a process that they use constantly. The absence of memory training is a major gap in contemporary education.

After outlining the structure of memory, it is often helpful to identify the mnemonic structures of cola/periods, episodes, verbal threads, gestures, and reversals of expectation built into the story they have just learned. The students can then tell the story to each other again using the analysis as a resource for remembering and telling the story.

The goal of this first stage of the workshop is that each student will be able to get through the story from beginning to end without leaving out anything of major importance and without adding anything of major importance. That is, the goal is that there is significant interpretive resemblance between the story as it has been "traditioned" to us in a competent translation, and the story we are telling. At this stage in the work on a story, a workable guideline for the question about "word for word accuracy" that will usually arise is 95% content accuracy and 75% verbal accuracy.

Listening to the Story

A second stage in a storytelling workshop is listening to the story in its original historical context. This segment of a storytelling workshop can vary in length depending on the goals of the session. This is the context in which all of the data from a "performance criticism" exegesis of a biblical composition can be summarized. All of the resources of historical-critical study of Mark can be utilized in this stage of a workshop: word study, Jewish and Greco-Roman background, the history and politics of the first century, archeological discoveries, tradition history, etc. This can also include an introduction to the performance traditions of the ancient world as outlined in several recent books such as Whitney Shiner's *Proclaiming the Gospel*, Moses Hadas' *Ancilla to Classical Reading* and David Rhoads' articles on performance criticism.[5]

The most important finding of this literature is that contemporary performance traditions are far less emotionally expressive, dramatic, and physically active than ancient performances. The styles of the reading of scripture in contemporary worship are a pervasive performance tradition that has determined what many now experience as appropriate performance. In fact, the literary compositions of the Bible are more widely performed than any other literature. But there is a great distance between ancient and modern performances of Mark.

A further dimension of this listening is to identify the variations in tempo, volume and pauses that are implicit in the story. For example, long periods are fast, short periods slow; loud places are really loud, soft places really soft; pauses are intentionally marked, but generally the story flows with a fast pace.

The conclusion of this stage of the workshop is for the students to tell the story again. This time, however, the goal is that they will seek to tell the story in a manner that is more like the way it would have been told in its original historical context. Here the students can be encouraged to be as big as possible in their way of telling the story. This segment of the workshop can also be an introduction to the exegetical work of the course including the "performance criticism" papers the students will write.

Connecting to the Story

A third stage of a storytelling workshop is to explore the connections between the experiences of each person and the story from Mark. The identification and telling of these stories will help each storyteller discover the distinctive ways in which they would tell the story. The telling of personal stories also enables each student to tell the stories they know best.

5. Shiner, *Proclaiming the Gospel*; Rhoads, "Performance Criticism Parts I and II"; Hadas, *Ancilla*, 50–77, for a series of citations from ancient literature showing that performance of written works was the primary mode of publication. Even historical works were published by oral recitation, as is evident in Lucian's opening of his book, *Herodotus*, in which he tells the story of Herodotus taking the opportunity of the Olympic Games to read his work: "He seized the moment when the gathering was at its fullest, and every city had sent the flower of its citizens; then he appeared in the temple hall, bent not on sightseeing but on bidding for an Olympic victory of his own; he recited his Histories and bewitched his hearers."

The primary role of the professor in this stage of a workshop is to model and then encourage the students to tell their own stories. The hermeneutical theory underlying this process of connecting the stories from Mark and personal stories is that Mark's stories address the deep structures of human experience. The identification of that deep structure is relatively easy. In the three stories I have suggested for an initial workshop, the deep structure of the paralytic story is the experience of being paralyzed and reduced to a position of shame and dependence. The calming of the storm is about the experience of being seized with terror and fear at the prospect of being overwhelmed by the powers of chaos. The story of Bartimaeus addresses the experience of blindness and literally sitting in the dust begging for help and then answering the question "What do you want me to do for you?"

In the workshop process, students often find it initially difficult or threatening to identify these dimensions of their own experience. I have found that sharing my own experience of these dynamics helps them to know what is being addressed by the story. My story of being hit by a car, overcome with fear of paralysis and death, and crying out for help has enabled students to identify their own stories and given them permission to be vulnerable in this way.

There are two possible dimensions of connecting with the story. The first is simply identifying and telling a partner the story of your experience. For example, "When have you felt paralyzed and dependent on others?" "When have you experienced being afraid?" "When have you been unable to see any way forward?" or "What would be your answer now if Jesus asked you, 'What do you want me to do for you?'"

The other possible dimension is to tell and hear the biblical story as an immediate response to a story of a felt need. Thus, a partner might initially say, "Right now I feel paralyzed in relation to the paper I need to write" or "I feel ashamed about . . ." Or, "If Jesus asked me, 'What do you want me to do for you?' I would say, 'I want . . .'" The other partner can then tell Mark's story, no counsel or advice, just the story. And the first can also share what, if anything, the story meant as it was told. It is often the case that the story has more impact than was expected. When the group as a whole comes back together, it is appropriate to ask them, "Is there anything that someone would like to share with the group that happened as you listened or told the story?" Students are generally glad to share their experience of the stories.

The purpose of this storytelling process is to make it possible for persons to explore the personal connections that these ancient stories invite. It has usually been surprisingly meaningful to people who have done this. This is not always the case and there have been instances in which persons have not discovered any significant connection. But that rarely happens. And in a group as a whole, there have usually been persons who have found that the stories connected with their experience and enabled them to see their present life situation from a new perspective. The minimal result of this process is that students can better understand the transformative impact of these stories in their original historical context. They may also help students appropriate the stories as elements of their own existential belief system.

Telling the Story

The conclusion of the workshop is for the professor to gather the experience of the group in a concluding retelling of the story. In this concluding recital, the accents, emphases, and experience of the group inform the retelling of the story. Rather than talking about the story and its meaning as a source of referential information about history or theology, the telling of the story itself focuses the attention of the group on the meaning of the story as a story. It is also possible for a student to do this final retelling of the story. But my experience has been that on occasion a volunteer does not tell it well because of their limited experience. For this purpose and at this moment in a workshop, the professor is best.

The storytelling workshop experience is highly generative and its value is not limited to the initial stages of introduction to storytelling processes. It can also be adapted to the needs of the curriculum at later stages in the course experience.

Regular Performance of Markan Stories in English and Greek

During every class, both the students and the professor have the opportunity to tell the stories from Mark that are either the subject or the background of the class session. It is possible to make this a required element of every class session. The students can tell the story of the day to each other in pairs and then a student can be called on at random to tell the story to the whole group. This possibility is sufficient motivation for the students to learn the stories before class. It is also an opportunity for each student to have the experience of performing a story for the whole class in preparation for the concluding communal performance of Mark.

There is surprising value in learning and telling the stories in Greek as well as in translation. The Greek tells well and is in fact better than any translation if you understand some Greek. Telling the story in Greek is an excellent opportunity for students who are studying Greek to utilize their new knowledge of the language in this way. This is also an opportunity for the professor to give the students a first-hand experience of the story in its original language. If the students know the story in translation, they will be surprised at how much they can understand from an expressive and well-gestured telling of the story in Greek. It is also an advertisement for studying Greek that recruits more students for the Greek classes in the curriculum.

My suggestion is that some part of the story regularly be told in Greek as an element of the class session. This is a significant additional preparation for the professor and may not always be possible. But it has great pedagogical value as the students become more familiar with the sounds of Mark in its original language and more impressed by their professor.

Performance Criticism Exegesis Papers

A foundational pedagogy for teaching Mark as performance literature is lectures and required papers on performance criticism exegesis. I have found this to be the most difficult change in reorienting the teaching of Mark to the original character of Mark as stories composed for performance to audiences. The exegetical methods that have been the basis of academic biblical pedagogy need major reformation because of the degree to which traditional exegesis is tied to the study of Mark as a text. For the purpose of this paper, I will only outline the distinctive elements of a performance criticism exegesis. And I would also acknowledge that this is a work in progress rather than a finished product.

Many elements of textual exegesis remain central to a performance criticism exegesis such as word studies, Jewish and Greco-Roman background, comparison with other forms of the story in the other Gospels, and the context of the story in Mark. These elements are, however, refocused on the experience of the stories for ancient audiences. Word studies are refocused on the sounds of the words and their connotative as well as denotative associations from previous usage in the storytelling tradition. The Jewish and Greco-Roman background of the stories needs to identify the stories that would have been known by the audiences. When heard against this background, Mark's stories have both allusions and contrasts to the stories floating around in the ancient communal memory. The comparison with other forms of the stories in the Gospel tradition in the context of performance also calls attention to the development of the sounds, structure and overall impact of the stories in the Jesus storytelling tradition. And the analysis of the context in Mark is based on the assumption that the audiences have just heard the preceding stories in the Gospel and will have the sounds of those stories freshly in mind.

There are also new elements of performance criticism exegesis. The most immediate and the most difficult to teach is the sound mapping of Mark's stories. The analysis of the sounds of Mark's story is based on the descriptions of cola and periods in the Greek grammatical and rhetorical literature. The mapping of the sounds is not unlike writing out the sounds of a musical composition. But there are no conventions of manuscript arrangement of these stories as there are with music: i.e., rests, volume markings, accents, indications of tempo, mood identifications. The major problem is that the current arrangement of Mark's composition in English prose sentences and paragraphs virtually blinds us to recognizing the rhythms and structures of the sound of Mark.

There is great value, therefore, in reformulating the writing of the Markan manuscripts in the structures of sound. While necessarily ambiguous at this stage of our communal research, the sound mapping of Mark restructures the basic conception and experience of Mark's story regardless of the accuracy of the analysis. Processing examples of sound maps is a helpful introduction. Thinking of the sound map as a script for the story is sometimes helpful to students doing a sound map for the first time.

Another element of performance criticism exegesis that is initially difficult for students is the analysis of the dynamics of the story as a story. Because virtually all of the exegetical works on Mark and, therefore, the models of exegesis focus on the identification of the theological and historical meaning of the story, students need help in identifying the meaning of Mark as a story. All of the elements of narrative criticism—point of view, characterization, plot, norms of judgment—are important dimensions of performance criticism.

However, there are also distinctive elements to the study of Mark as an oral narrative rather than as an ancient novel read by readers.[6] The most important of these distinctive elements is the relationship between the storyteller and the audience. The basic facts of audience address are relatively easy to identify.[7] The storytellers addressed the audiences, usually as Jesus addressing various groups in his teaching (e.g., Mark 3:23–29; 4:3–9, 11–32; 8:34–9:1; 10:42–45; 13:4–36) but sometimes as himself addressing the audience as themselves (e.g. 1:1; 6:52; 7:3–4). But the extension of those basic facts to the identification of the impact of the story is outside the experience and training of most students.

---

6. For a study of Mark as an ancient novel, see Tolbert, *Sowing the Gospel.*

7. See above, "Medium and Message" and "Audience Address."

It is, therefore, important for the professor to provide a steady stream of performance criticism demonstrations in the classes so that students have something to work with. But students await the production of full performance criticism commentaries in order to have a wider range of models to work with in their exegetical study of Mark as performance literature.[8]

Student Production of Digital Storytelling of Mark

The re-conception of Mark as performance literature also opens the possibility of Mark being told with the full range of digital production resources. This is an area of potential creativity for which we have few models but that has great potential for creativity and a truly new hermeneutic. Potential elements of these productions are:

1. Videos of a person telling the stories of Mark

2. Archeological pictures, maps, and other images from the first century

3. Film clips that have related themes to Mark's story

4. Videos of personal stories of the meaning of Mark's stories for individual persons

5. Music videos of the dynamic equivalent contemporary images and music that are invited by Mark's story

6. Musical background for the digital performance of Mark's story. Because of the ready availability of high-quality digital production technology, a new world of hermeneutical possibilities is now available for creative engagement with Mark's story.

Performance of Mark in Worship

Student performance of Mark in worship services as the Scripture recital for the day brings the study of Mark as performance literature to another level of knowledge and experience. This can be at student led worship services in a university or seminary or for local churches. The current performance of Mark in virtually all churches is done in an emotionally distant style with which we are all familiar. Telling the story by heart brings a new level of vitality and interest to the performance of the Scriptures in a worship service. The frequent response of congregation members is something like: "I feel

---

8. For a full-length performance criticism commentary on Mark's passion and resurrection narrative, see Boomershine, *Messiah of Peace*.

like I never heard the story before." The performance needs to be steadily rehearsed with supervision and direction by the professor. But, if done well, the telling of Mark in worship is a significant experience for students and for congregations.

A Communal Performance of Mark

A concluding communal performance of Mark is an excellent ending for a course on Mark. The students and professor divide up the story and tell it in sequence. It is possible to invite the academic community as well as interested persons from the wider community to such a performance. If an audience is invited, the students need to practice the stories intensively as they would in preparation for the performance of a play. The professor functions as the director of the performance. It is important for the director to provide clear feedback and direction for the individual students. This work can be done best in individual coaching sessions but that is very time intensive work. Managing the mix between positive encouragement and reinforcement and suggestions/directions for ways of improving the telling of the story requires sensitivity and courage for the professor.[9] These communal performances for invited audiences have been highly energizing experiences for students and audiences that are never forgotten. They do, however, require a lot of preparation.

It is also possible for this concluding performance to be an "in house" event in which the members of the class tell the stories they have learned to each other. We have told Mark in a classroom, the community chapel and a private home or apartment. I have invited classes to my home and we have sat on the floor around the living room and told Mark in the circle. We have passed around food and/or put various dips, fruit, crackers, bread, etc. in the middle of the group where everyone can reach it in the ancient style. These celebrations of the learning of the Mark by the class have been universally positive experiences. Students learn a lot about themselves and about Mark in this process. And the ante is much lower than for an external audience. But the benefits from a public performance are also greater because of the higher investment of time and energy.

9. For the best available resource on working with new storytellers, see Lipman, *Storytelling Coach;* also Lipman, *Improving Your Storytelling,* 101–9.

Conclusions

This is then a sketch of some pedagogical approaches to teaching Mark and other biblical books as performance literature. I have been doing various aspects of these approaches for more than forty years. They have been consistently positive. In fact, my only regret in retrospect is that I sometimes hesitated to use these processes in my courses. This pedagogical approach is so different than normal academic teaching that I was sometimes anxious about the responses of students and colleagues. That anxiety has not been inappropriate. Some colleagues have been critical and have even opposed teaching in this manner. It does not always fit well with the role of biblical courses in a traditional seminary or university curriculum. And when the word has gotten around, some students have been reluctant to take the courses because of the performance expectations. Others, however, have heard about the overall quality of the educational experience and have wanted to take the course. The net was an overall increase in the number of students.

All of that is of minor significance in comparison to the value of a vital experience of Mark. These conflicts are an inevitable dimension of a major paradigm shift in biblical interpretation. In the end these pedagogies bring new vitality and interest to the teaching of Mark. Most important, this approach gives students a deeper understanding and experience of Mark in its ancient historical context and opens a new range of possibilities for the interpretation of Mark now.

PART III

Audience Address and Audience Identity
in Mark and John

8

Audience Address and Purpose in the Performance of Mark

Prelude

This chapter was initially composed and published as a contribution to the collection of essays, *Mark as Story: Retrospect and Prospect*. The occasion for this collection was the thirtieth anniversary of the publication of *Mark as Story*. That publication by David Rhoads and Donald Michie was the first major book that utilized narrative criticism as its primary methodology. The purpose of the collection was to assess the contributions of what has become a significant body of critical analysis and interpretation and to explore the potential futures of this overall approach.

The Origins and Evolution of Narrative Criticism

The publication of *Mark as Story* in 1982 was a major step in the development of a new paradigm for the study and interpretation of the Gospels in ancient and modern media. The systematic application of what the authors call "narrative criticism" began the process of the reconception of Mark in the context of the media culture of antiquity through the adaptation of the methods of literary criticism that were developed for the study of a major development in modern media culture, the novel.[1] By close attention to the intrinsic features of Mark as a narrative, a new body of scholarship has

1. For the classic example of an "intrinsic" methodology for the study of the novel, see Booth, *Rhetoric of Fiction*; also Chatman, *Story and Discourse*.

drawn a rich picture of Mark that has begun the process of removing the shadow from biblical narrative that Hans Frei aptly named "the eclipse of biblical narrative."[2]

This intersection of ancient and modern media culture is only the latest stage of this development in biblical study. "Historical criticism" in its classical form was the product of an earlier intersection between what Wellek and Warren termed extrinsic methods of literary criticism that created a picture of the meaning of a literary work by identifying the complex of extrinsic forces—e.g., cultural and political movements, biography of the author, and most important, the history of the sources and traditions—that led to the final work.[3] The study of Mark as a texts produced by an editor of earlier oral and written traditions and designed to be read in silence by readers draws a picture of Mark that makes sense to readers of history and theology who have lived in the media culture of the eighteenth–twentieth centuries.

The foundational contribution of *Mark as Story* is that it approaches Mark in a manner that is appropriate to the form of the Gospel, namely, narrative. Rather than interpreting Mark as a source of referential information in the categories of the literatures of "history" and "theology," this work initiated the study of Mark as a narrative. By paying attention to the dynamics of the interaction of the narrator, the characters and the plot of Mark's narrative in its final form, the book succeeded in drawing a complex and nuanced description of the story world of Mark as experienced by readers. In the first edition, the authors acknowledge that their approach may be more appropriate to the way modern readers experience the Gospel than to the way Mark was experienced in the ancient context:

> Mark's gospel was probably written to be heard rather than read. It would, therefore, be appropriate to refer to the hearers of the drama. We have chosen, however, to deal with the gospel as literature and to discuss its readers.[4]

The second edition is more attentive to the original medium of the Gospel:

> We have chosen here to focus on the literary reading of Mark rather than on an oral hearing, because most modern people will read the Gospel rather than hear it, and because our purpose is to suggest ways of reading. Nevertheless, our interpretations,

2. Frei, *Eclipse*.
3. Wellek and Warren, *Theory of Literature*.
4. Rhoads and Michie, *Mark as Story*, 143n1.

particularly in regard to the role of the narrator, the character of the disciples, and the understanding of plot, have been influenced by our work on oral narrative.[5]

Both editions, however, were deliberately directed at modern readers who would "read" rather than hear Mark, namely, college and seminary students. The book has been highly successful in enabling generations of students to experience Mark in a mode that is more accessible than traditional historical criticism has provided.

Furthermore, interpreting Mark as addressed to readers is in continuity with the assumptions of most scholarly investigations of Mark. The present conclusions about the historical audiences of Mark have been developed within what can be called the textual paradigm. This paradigm is a hermeneutical circle of assumptions about the medium of Mark. In this paradigm it has been assumed that Mark was a text read by an audience of readers.[6] This assumption is often explicitly named as in Joel Marcus' superb commentary on Mark where he frequently refers to Mark's reader.[7]

This assumption has been most graphically developed in reader response criticism. The most critically informed development of this approach for the study of Mark is Robert Fowler's comprehensive survey of reader response criticism and detailed application to the exegesis of Mark's text, appropriately titled *Let the Reader Understand*.[8] As he summarizes at one point, "Mark's Gospel is designed to guide, direct, and illuminate the reader vigorously and authoritatively, but at the same time challenge, puzzle, and humble its reader."[9] The focus of Fowler's analysis is making explicit in great detail the facets of "the reading experience." For example, in his exegesis of the crucifixion scene, he identifies the narrator's use of opacity, irony, paradox, metaphor, and ambiguity as dimensions of Mark's indirect moves in engaging his readers in the experience of the crucifixion.

The "reading experience" implies a picture of the reception of Mark as that of a single person sitting alone and in silence reading the manuscript, generally in silence as in modern reading but perhaps aloud. This picture

5. Rhoads, Dewey, and Michie, *Mark as Story*, xii.

6. See, for example, Best, "Mark's Readers."

7. Marcus, *Mark 1–8*, 468: "The woman's hope that her daughter will be healed, and the reader's, seem to be dashed by Jesus' response." However, Marcus also locates the genre of Mark as part of a liturgical drama in which the Gospel was read as part of the liturgy in Mark's Christian community (see 67–69).

8. Fowler, *Let the Reader Understand*.

9. Fowler, *Let the Reader Understand*, 220.

sometimes includes the possibility that the reader may read the manuscript aloud to a small group of listeners.

The dominant concept of Mark's audience and the manuscript's purpose for the audience is a natural inference within this framework. The most frequent conclusion of Mark scholars is that the audience of Mark was readers who were members of first-century Christian communities who already believe that Jesus is the Messiah. This makes sense when the controlling presupposition is that Mark is a text read by readers. It is highly unlikely that persons outside the believing communities of Christians in the first century would go to the trouble and expense of purchasing a manuscript of Mark and reading it. The readers of a Markan manuscript would most naturally be persons who are committed members of a community of believers. Joel Marcus argues that the Gospel was written for an individual community of which Mark was a member.[10] Richard Bauckham and Mary Ann Tolbert have imagined Mark as being written for broad distribution to Christian communities throughout the Greco-Roman world.[11] They share the assumption that Mark was written for an audience of readers.

The purpose of the Gospel when interpreted in this context is primarily to reinforce in various ways the beliefs and identity of the reader as a follower of Jesus. Thus, Adela Yarbro Collins summarizes Mark's purposes: "One was to reassert the messiahship of Jesus and to redefine it over against the messianic pretenders during the Jewish war that began in 66 CE. Another was to interpret actual or expected persecution (or both) as discipleship in imitation of Christ."[12] Both of these purposes are congruent with the function of Mark's manuscript when read by a believing reader.

Another dimension of this paradigm is the congruence between the medium of contemporary Markan scholarship and its audiences and the original medium and purpose of Mark. Just as contemporary scholars and the audiences they address in commentaries and monographs read the text in silence, so also it is assumed that Mark addressed an audience of persons who read the text in silence. The function of Markan scholarship is to call detailed attention to what a reader sees in the text. The historical validity of this methodology is based on the assumption that this was how Mark's text was originally experienced. That is, scholarship is paying close attention to the reading experience of the original readers of Mark and within those parameters to alert modern readers to dimensions of the meanings of the text.

---

10. Marcus, *Mark 1–8*, 25–28.

11. Bauckham, "For Whom Were Gospels Written?"; see also Tolbert, *Sowing the Gospel*, 304.

12. Collins, *Mark*, 102.

An integral part of this medium of Markan scholarship is "criticism." Scholars are trained as critics who read Mark from a psychological distance. That distance is an integral dimension of reading a text with one's eyes in silence. Indeed the name of the dominant methodology for the study of Mark is "historical criticism." Among the range of meanings of this methodology, it means the critical reading of biblical texts in their original historical context. The media dimension of this methodology is silent reading with an attitude of critical detachment.[13] Silent reading is what a scholar does in the study. Silent "critical" reading is the dominant experience of Mark in the media world of contemporary biblical scholarship.

It is not coincidental that various dimensions of "critical" reading of Mark have been found to be central dimensions of the meaning and purpose of Mark in its original historical context. Wrede's exploration of the Messianic secret is based on an exposition of the theological questions that were raised for Mark's readers by Jesus' persistent injunctions to silence about his identity.[14] An entire school of Markan interpretation has been based on the conclusion that Mark was inviting his readers to be critical of the disciples and their various failures in understanding and action.[15] In his major work on the relationship of Mark to the oral and literate cultures of antiquity, Werner Kelber extended Mark's critical purpose to the criticism of the entire oral gospel tradition represented in Mark by Peter and the apostles.[16] That is, modern "critical" readers of Mark have found that there were "critical" readers of Mark in the ancient world as well. Criticism may be an inevitable dimension of silent reading.

13. Fowler writes well about the centrality of his commitment to criticism in the ending of his book. He is reflecting on the ways in which Matthew, Luke, John, and Tatian have each in different ways retold Mark's story and made Mark forever a precursor. Even though he would like to experience Mark without these revisions, he recognizes that if he were to retell Mark's story, he would probably also revise it and turn Mark into a precursor. "Yet my own vocation is not storyteller but critic. If I were a storyteller, I would like to write a Gospel that places Mark's successors in such a light that the shadows they have cast upon Mark for centuries would be dispelled and the highlights they have shone upon Mark would be muted. I would like to construct a grid for reading Matthew that blocks out Matthew and allows only Mark's Gospel to be seen as it was before Matthew came along. Nevertheless, such a reading experience is a pipe dream—no such magical reading grid will ever be produced—so I shall continue to trust the powers of criticism to serve reading" (Fowler, *Let the Reader Understand,* 206).

14. Wrede, *Messianic Secret.*

15. This identification of Mark as a critic of the disciples had its initial book-length exposition in Weeden, *Mark: Traditions in Conflict.*

16. Kelber, *Oral and Written Gospel.*

Performance Criticism and
the Original Audiences of Mark

A new framework of Markan scholarship in particular and biblical scholarship in general is emerging as a new intersection between ancient and modern media cultures. The results of recent research by both classical and biblical scholars paint a different picture of the media cultures of the ancient world than has been assumed by this textual paradigm of Mark and his readers. A summary of the results of this research includes the following factors:

1. Literacy was minimal. Current estimates are that the rates of literacy in urban areas in the first century were somewhere between 10–15 percent of the population with significantly lower rates in rural areas. Thus, the great majority of people could not read.[17]

2. Manuscripts had to be copied by hand, were relatively rare by modern standards and relatively expensive. Only communities and rich individuals were able to acquire manuscripts of ancient writings in the first century.[18]

3. Manuscripts were normally published by public performance for audiences. Audiences could range from a few people to a large group.[19]

4. A biblical manuscript was a recording of sound that the author assumed would be reproduced as sound by those who performed it. The audiences heard the manuscript rather than reading it with their eyes.

5. Manuscripts were often memorized and performed from memory rather than read from a text. This made possible a high degree of interaction between the performer and the audience.[20]

17. See Harris, *Ancient Literacy.*

18. Gamble, *Books and Readers*; and Gamble, "Literacy and Book Culture."

19. Hadas, *Ancilla,* 50–77 for a series of citations from ancient literature showing that performance of written works was the primary mode of publication. Even historical works were published by oral recitation, as is evident in Lucian's opening of his book, *Herodotus,* in which he tells the story of Herodotus taking the opportunity of the Olympic Games to read his work: 'He seized the moment when the gathering was at its fullest, and every city had sent the flower of its citizens; then he appeared in the temple hall, bent not on sightseeing but on bidding for an Olympic victory of his own; he recited his Histories and bewitched his hearers' (Hadas, *Ancilla,* 60).

20. Shiner, *Proclaiming the Gospel,* 103–26.

6. Performances of stories were highly emotional and physically demonstrative. Highly expressive gestures were a crucial dimension of performance.[21]

7. Performances of ancient stories were often long and could last anywhere from an hour to all night as was the case with some performances of Homer.

The mass production of books, mass literacy, and silent reading were much later developments in the history of literacy and book production. The assumption that these practices were widespread in the first century is an anachronism. The media world of the first century was very different than the media world of the eighteenth–twentieth centuries.

When the Gospel of Mark is interpreted in the context of the media world of the first century CE, the medium of Mark has to be reconceived. The most comprehensive study of Mark in the context of the media world of the first century is Whitney Shiner's ground-breaking work, *Proclaiming the Gospel: First-Century Performance of Mark.*[22] Shiner bases his conclusions about Mark's original medium on a comprehensive examination of ancient primarily rhetorical writings that describe, often in great detail, the character of first-century rhetorical culture. In Shiner's reconstruction of the first-century media culture, the Gospel of Mark was usually performed for audiences. The original medium of Mark was the sounds of the story and the gestures of the storytellers who performed it. Storytellers normally learned Mark's story by heart and performed the story. Usually, the whole Gospel was told at one time which took approximately two hours.

This understanding of Mark is congruent with Eusebius' description of Mark's use of the manuscript he had written. Immediately following his citation of the Papias tradition that Mark had written his Gospel by recording Peter's proclamation at the request of the Christian community in Rome, he states the following about what Mark did with his manuscript: "And they say that this Mark was the first that was sent to Egypt, and that he proclaimed the Gospel which he had written, and first established churches in Alexandria."[23]

Regardless of the uncertainty of the historical accuracy of this account, it reflects the assumption of an author some three centuries later that the account he had received—as "they say"—was historically credible, namely that Mark was sent to Egypt where he "performed" the Gospel for audiences

21. Shiner, *Proclaiming the Gospel,* 77–98.

22. Shiner, *Proclaiming the Gospel,* 171–79.

23. Eusebius, *Ecclesiastical History* 3.16.1. The reference to "they" probably refers to Papias and the Elder who are quoted in the preceding paragraph.

in Alexandria and established churches there. That is, Eusebius' description is congruent with the conclusion that Mark's story was proclaimed orally. Seen in this context, the primary purpose of the manuscript was to facilitate and resource the proclamations/performances of the story. It is also implicit in Eusebius' description that some of those who heard Mark's proclamation were converted and became the basis for the establishment of churches. In view of the further probability that Mark was highly popular and was developed by Matthew and Luke, it is also probable that Mark was not performed for only one local community such as Alexandria, as reported by Eusebius, or Antioch or Rome, but was performed in many cities and towns throughout the Greco-Roman world. If we want to reconstruct the meaning of Mark for its original audiences, therefore, we need to evaluate the data of the manuscript as essentially a script for storytelling performances of the story of Jesus.

This in turn raises a methodological issue that has not been resolved since the first introduction to what was then called "rhetorical criticism" of the study of Mark.[24] How can we as modern readers study ancient narratives in a manner that is appropriate to their original media culture? Specifically, how can we hear rather than read Mark's stories?

David Rhoads has taken the next step in the development of an approach to this problem in his essays on "performance criticism."[25] This work has in turn grown out of his own performances of Mark. Performance criticism is based on the conclusion that the accurate perception and interpretation of biblical literature in its original historical context requires that we conceive and experience the books of the bible in performance. When applied to Mark, performance criticism is redrawing the picture of Mark from a narrative read by readers to a story performed for audiences.

In light of the recognition that the medium of biblical scholarship should be appropriate to the original medium of the bible, the ancient character of Mark as performance literature suggests that the methodologies of Markan scholarship shift from silent reading to oral performance for audiences as the primary medium of research, pedagogy, and proclamation. If we as Mark scholars want to understand the meaning of Mark's Gospel in its original context, we may need, in as far as possible, to ground our research in proclaiming and hearing Mark rather than reading it. The internet and

---

24. David Rhoads has graciously acknowledged the contribution of my 1974 dissertation to his work as in footnote #1 in the first edition of *Mark as Story*, 143; see Boomershine, "Mark, the Storyteller." An integral part of that dissertation was an audiotape of the passion narrative in Greek and in English.

25. Rhoads, "Performance Criticism, Parts I & II."

video recordings now make it possible to integrate performances of ancient compositions with contemporary scholarly analyses of those compositions.

There are a variety of issues in relation to this study of Mark in its original context that are significantly impacted by the shift in methodology described above. The issue here is the makeup of the audience for whom Mark originally intended his story. The reigning consensus that has resulted from approaching Mark as a text read by readers is that the audience must have been Christians. This is often qualified to identify the original readers as Gentile Christians. The study of audience address from the perspective of Mark as a story performed for a listening, not a reading, audience points to a different conclusion.

Data of Markan Audience Address

In the original performances of Mark, there were three major components: the performer or storyteller, the story that the storyteller told with its characters particularly Jesus, and the audiences. In the course of the performance of the story, the storytellers were first and foremost themselves speaking as themselves to the audience, that is, speaking as who they were in their daily life and not as this or that character in the secondary world of the story. This contrasts with ancient theater in which each actor "became" a particular character in the drama. The most important task of a storyteller, in contrast to an actor, is to establish a positive relationship with the audience. The central feature of that relationship is credibility and trust, the credibility of the storyteller and the audience's confidence that the storyteller will tell them a good story. Thus, at the beginning of the story, Mark, the storyteller, introduced the subject of his story as a direct address to the audience: "the beginning of the good news of Jesus Christ."

In the performance of stories, storytellers have a complex role. In contrast to drama in which a single actor presents the words and actions of one particular character, storytellers embody all of the characters of the story. In Mark, the major character is Jesus. At many points in the story, the storyteller addresses the audience as Jesus. This involves a move from being oneself to presenting and embodying the character, Jesus. It was probably signaled by a change of voice, accent, attitude, or tone as well as gestures. In Mark's story, John the Baptist introduces Jesus and the story of Jesus' baptism and testing in the wilderness is the first description of Jesus' actions. But the first presentation of Jesus as a character is his address to the audience as the people of Galilee: "The time is fulfilled. The Kingdom of God is at hand. Change your minds and believe in this good news" (1:15). In the telling of the story, the storyteller becomes Jesus and presents him as a different character than the storyteller. This change in character happens throughout the story in the many speeches of Jesus. But while the major character that the storyteller presents is Jesus, the storyteller also presents many other characters. In what we now call chapters one and two, for example, the storyteller embodies the demon-possessed man in the synagogue, Simon, the begging leper, the skeptical scribes in the house, the critical scribes of the Pharisees, the disciples of John and the Pharisees.

The audience also has a complex role. Since the only people present in a storytelling performance are the storyteller and the audience, the impact of the story depends to a significant degree on the engagement and responses of the audience. Every storyteller experiences this. There are good audiences who respond freely, laugh a lot, and interact with the story enthusiastically and sympathetically. There are also difficult, unresponsive audiences who are indifferent, hostile or critical and who don't laugh or even smile. For a bad audience a storyteller will sometimes shorten the story in order to get it over as soon as possible.

A central dimension of the interaction of audiences with storytellers is created by a storyteller's address to the audience.[26] Most of the time, storytellers present the events of the story to the audience as themselves. In the telling of Mark, they may dramatize some of the short interactions between characters such as the conversation between Jesus and the leper. But most of the story is direct address by the storytellers to the audience as themselves. However, when the storyteller "becomes" a character, often Jesus, and addresses another character in the story, such as the scribes sitting in the crowded house into which the paralytic is lowered, the audience is in turn invited to "become" that other character listening to and interacting with Jesus for the duration of that address by Jesus. The storyteller as Jesus addresses the audience as the scribes who were grumbling to themselves: "Why do you question like this in your hearts? What is easier to say to the paralytic, 'Your sins are forgiven' or to say to him, 'Get up, take up your pallet and walk.'" But that you may know that the Son of Man has authority on earth to forgive sins. . ." And then the storyteller steps back out of the character of Jesus into his role as narrator, briefly addressing the audience as his own listeners, "he said to the paralytic" and then again assuming the character of Jesus, the storyteller kneels down and speaks to the paralytic.

---

26. Most of the available performances of Mark including those of David Rhoads are conceived as dramatic productions in which the audience is not addressed directly but is invited to watch the imagined interactions of the characters of the story on the other side of "the fourth wall" of the theater. Storytelling is a different performance art than drama.

This shift for the listeners from being themselves to identification with the characters addressed by Jesus increases the story's experiential impact. The length of the speech is an important factor here. The longer the audience is addressed as a particular character, the more deeply the audience identifies with and "becomes" that character. Furthermore, just as storytellers change their presentational identity to embody the various characters of the story, the audience experiences changes in their identity by being addressed as a range of different characters in the story.

If this happened in the ancient performances of Mark's story, as is highly probable, we can identify the character of the audience for whom Mark may have performed his story. We will approach this question through an analysis of audience address in the Gospel. We begin this analysis by gathering and presenting some data. Where does Mark, usually as Jesus but a few times either as himself as narrator or as other characters in his story, address various characters, and who are the characters he addresses? This study will limit the analysis of Markan audience address to speeches of two or more sentences, or more accurately "periods,"[27] in the Greek text. The following chart identifies the instances in Mark's story where Mark as a storyteller addresses the audience as particular characters (usually Jesus) in the story for two or more periods. The chart lists the story in which the speech occurs and the location and length of the speech, the character who is the speaker, and the character by whom the audience is addressed.

Audience Address in Mark

Story and address to the audience	Speaker embodied by the storyteller	Audience addressed as . . .
John's baptism (1:7–8)	John the Baptist	People of Judea, etc.
Proclamation of the Kingdom (1:15)	Jesus	People of Galilee
Healing of paralytic (2:8–10)	Jesus	Scribes
Eating with tax collectors (2:17)	Jesus	Scribes of the Pharisees
Question about fasting (2:19–22)	Jesus	Disciples of John and the Pharisees
Shucking grain on Sabbath (2:25–28)	Jesus	Pharisees

27. See Lee and Scott, *Sound Mapping*, 108–111.

Man with withered hand (3:4)	Jesus	The people in the synagogue
Jesus and Beelzebul (3:23–29)	Jesus	Scribes from Jerusalem
The true family of Jesus (3:33–35)	Jesus	The group sitting around Jesus
Parable of the sower (4:3–9)	Jesus	The crowd
Purpose of parables, the meaning of the sower parable, and parables of the Kingdom (4:11–32)	Jesus	Those around Jesus with the twelve
Rejection of Jesus at Nazareth (6:4)	Jesus	People in Nazareth synagogue
Mission of the twelve (6:10–11)	Jesus	The twelve
Tradition of the elders: purity laws (7:3–4)	Mark	Audience: Gentiles ignorant of Jewish purity laws
Tradition of the elders (7:6–13)	Jesus	Pharisees and scribes
Tradition of the elders (7:14–15)	Jesus	The crowd
Tradition of the elders (7:18–22)	Jesus	Disciples
Demand for a sign (8:12)	Jesus	Pharisees
The loaves discourse (8:15–21)	Jesus	Disciples
Messianic confession, 1st passion prophecy and discipleship (8:34–9.1)	Jesus	The Crowd with the disciples
Transfiguration (9:12–13)	Jesus	Peter, James and John
2nd Passion Prophecy (9:31)	Jesus	Disciples
Who is the greatest? (9:35–37)	Jesus	Disciples
The other exorcist (9:39–50)	Jesus	Disciples
Teaching about divorce (10:5–9)	Jesus	Pharisees
Teaching about divorce (10:11–12)	Jesus	Disciples

Blessing the children (10:14–15)	Jesus	Disciples
Rich man (10:18–19)	Jesus	The rich man
Rich man (10:23–27)	Jesus	Disciples
Rich man (10:29–31)	Jesus	Peter
3rd Passion Prophecy (10:33–34)	Jesus	The Twelve
James' and John's request for position (10:42–45)	Jesus	Disciples
The cleansing of the Temple (11:17)	Jesus	The chief priests/scribes and crowd in the Temple
The fig tree (11:22–26)	Jesus	Disciples
Parable of the vineyard (12:1–11)	Jesus	The chief priests, scribes and elders
The resurrection controversy (12:24–27)	Jesus	Sadducees
Messiah David's son? (12:35–37)	Jesus	Crowd in the Temple
Denouncing of the scribes (12:38–40)	Jesus	Crowd in the Temple
The widow's gift (12:43–44)	Jesus	Disciples
Apocalyptic discourse (13:5–37)	Jesus	Peter, James, John and Andrew
Anointing by woman (14:6–9)	Jesus	Those who rebuked the woman
Preparations for Passover (14:13–15)	Jesus	Two disciples
Betrayal prophecy (14:18–21)	Jesus	The Twelve
The last supper (14:22–25)	Jesus	The Twelve
Prophecy of desertion and denial (14:27–30)	Jesus	Twelve and Peter
Gethsemane (14:37–38, 41–42)	Jesus	Peter and Peter, James and John
The arrest (14:48–49)	Jesus	The crowd from the priests, scribes, and elders
The trial before the Council (14:63–64)	High priest	The Council

The trial before Pilate (15:9, 12–14)	Pilate	The crowd
The resurrection (16:6–7)	Young man in a white robe	Mary Magdalene, Mary, and Salome

The category of "Speaker" in the chart above reveals the basic structure of audience address. In speeches of two or more periods, the storyteller addresses the audience as Jesus most of the time (forty-five of fifty). The other characters who address the audience are John the Baptist, Mark as narrator, the high priest, Pilate and the young man at the tomb. The category of "Audience addressed as" reveals another surprising fact in the context of the Gentile Christian audiences envisioned by many Markan scholars: the audience is almost always addressed as various groups of Jews. A suggestion is that each reader would look through the chart in detail with attention to the column of "Audience addressed as . . ." in order to get a sense of audience address.

The only exception to the audience being addressed as Jews occurs in the story of Jesus' dispute with the Pharisees over the purity laws. The storyteller's explanation of the cleanliness laws (7:3–5) is addressed to the audience as persons who do not know these Jewish customs, that is, as non-Jews. This is a sign that the composer of the Gospel recognizes and wants to include non-Jews in the audiences of the story. That is, the audiences that are projected as the potential audiences for the performances of the Gospel are primarily, but not exclusively, Jewish.

This is a paradigmatic example of the difference made by the medium in which Mark is experienced. When the Gospel is read in silence, this comment appears to be an inside address to the reader. Scholars have often inferred from this comment that the readers of Mark were Gentiles. When the Gospel is heard as addressed to audiences, however, this comment is not directed to a reader but is directed to any in the audience who may not be familiar with Jewish customs. The comment indicates only that Mark as the composer of this story projects that there may be Gentiles in the potential audiences. This comment is a storytelling gesture of audience inclusion. The storyteller introduces it after a considerable amount of time during which he has been inviting his listeners to experience being addressed as a series of various Jewish characters by Jesus. The purpose is to keep on board any Gentiles who might find it difficult to maintain involvement with the story without this essential information.

Another revealing dimension of audience address in Mark is the way in which the audience is invited to move from being addressed as those who are Jesus' opponents to those who are Jesus' disciples. In this structure of audience address, the storyteller as Jesus moves from addressing the audience as 1) Jesus' opponents who are in conflict with him, to addressing them as 2) those around Jesus, often the disciples or the twelve. This pattern is first established in the opening section of the Gospel. The audience is first addressed as the people of Judea by the storyteller as John the Baptist (1:7–8) and then as the people of Galilee by Jesus (1:15). The audience is then addressed by the storyteller as Jesus for a long time as various groups with whom Jesus is in conflictual dialogue: the scribes (2:8–10), the scribes of the Pharisees (2:17), the disciples of John and the Pharisees (2:19–22), the Pharisees (2:25–28), the people in the synagogue who are, by inference, Pharisees (3:4–5), and climactically the scribes from Jerusalem (3:23–29). That is, the audience is predominantly addressed in the early parts of the story as various groups of Jews who are engaged in various degrees of dialogue and conflict with Jesus.

Furthermore, there is a distinct escalation in the tone and content of the conflict. Jesus' address to the audience as the scribes in the paralytic story is moderate in tone. The address in each of the stories that follows is increasingly intense in tone and content. The longest and most conflictual address in this series is the address to the audience as the scribes who have come down from Jerusalem. They accuse Jesus of being possessed by Beelzebul and of casting out demons by the prince of demons. The climax of Jesus' speech is his description of their accusation as blasphemy against the Holy Spirit that will never be forgiven.

This series of stories ends with the most intimate address to the audience to this point in the Gospel, the story of Jesus' mother and brothers (3:31–35). At the climax of the story, the storyteller as Jesus speaks to the audience as those seated around Jesus: "Who are my mother and my brothers?" And looking around at those who were seated around him, he says, "Here are my mother and my brothers. Whoever does the will of God is my brother and sister and mother." In the performance of the story, the storyteller addresses this saying to all those in the audience with a gesture of wide-open arms of inclusion. This is implicitly an invitation to the audience to move from identifying with those who are in conflict with Jesus to being one of those in Jesus' intimate circle of friends. This address to the audience as followers of Jesus is then continued throughout Jesus' parabolic teaching (4:1–32).

The next instance of this pattern in Mark's story is the dialogue about the purity laws. This story begins with the storyteller's description to the audience of the Pharisees' critique of Jesus for allowing his disciples to eat with unwashed hands and his explanation of Jewish purity customs (7:1–5). This introduction is followed by a highly confrontational address by Jesus

to the audience as the Pharisees and scribes. This speech begins with Jesus'
citation of Isaiah as prophesying their hypocrisy and ends with the accusation that they abrogate the law of God in many ways by the handing on of
their tradition (7:6–13). Then the audience is briefly addressed as the crowd
(7:14–15). The climax of the dialogue is an extensive address to the audience
as the disciples. This speech is introduced by the relocation of the address
from a public to a private place, "When he had left the crowd and entered
the house . . ." (7:17). In the telling of the story this introduction was probably accompanied by some gesture, perhaps a simple movement to the side
and sitting down. It is also an indication of a lowering of the volume of the
speech. The storyteller as Jesus moves from heated public argumentation
through explanation to a sympathetic crowd to private explanation to the
audience as the disciples. These storytelling moves in sound and gesture
create increasing intimacy between the character of Jesus and the audience.

There are two smaller instances of this pattern in audience address
prior to the stories of Jesus in Jerusalem. The first is the story of the Pharisees demanding a sign followed by Jesus' speech to the disciples about the
leaven of the Pharisees and the bread in the boat (8:11–13 and 8:14–21). The
audience is addressed as the Pharisees who were testing him in the expression of their desire for a sign. The tone of the storyteller's voice as Jesus is
best described as exasperation mixed with anger. The discussion is abruptly
ended with the description of Jesus getting back into the boat. The trip back
to the other side of the lake is the context in which the storyteller as Jesus
discusses the significance of the loaves with the audience as the disciples
(8:14–21). While Jesus continues to express exasperation with the disciples,
the tone is the exasperation of a teacher whose students just don't get it.
There is a real possibility that the storyteller smiled and even laughed in the
delivery of this speech of Jesus. The dynamic of these two stories is an invitation to the audience to experience Jesus as moving from public prophet to
private teacher, a move from being addressed as an ongoing adversary to
being addressed as a disciple who is also confused about the meaning of the
seven and twelve baskets as is the audience.

The second instance of this pattern in audience address is the divorce
controversy (10:1–11). Once again, the Pharisees engage Jesus in another
test, this time about divorce law. The public discussion is first addressed to
the audience as the Pharisees (10:5–9). In contrast to the earlier stories of
legal dispute, there is no sign here that the words of Jesus were delivered
with a tone of anger or frustration. This rabbinic ruling about divorce law
appears to have been delivered in a straightforward and authoritative manner in spite of the fact that their question is introduced as still another testing of Jesus. Once again the scene shifts to the more intimate setting of the

house. The storyteller as Jesus addresses the audience as the disciples for a short explanation of his legal opinion. This move from public pronouncement to private discussion about the law has the same rabbinic dynamic as the earlier story about the purity laws.

The most extensive and highly developed instance of this pattern of audience address is the stories of Jesus in Jerusalem. The longest address to the audience as Jesus' opponents in the Gospel is the parable of the vineyard and the wicked tenants (12:1–11). It is addressed to the audience as the chief priests, scribes and elders. This highly confrontational parable is followed by the controversy about the resurrection in which the audience is addressed as Sadducees. Jesus' pronouncement in this story ends with a dismissal of the Sadducees: "You are quite wrong." After the relatively cordial story of Jesus' discussion with the scribe, the audience is addressed as the crowd in the Temple. The storyteller presents Jesus addressing the audience as a large and sympathetic crowd. He first speaks with them about the scribes' teaching that the Messiah must be the son of David and then levels a climactic denunciation against the scribes. The next move toward more intimate and confidential address to the audience is the story of the widow's gift where the audience is addressed as the disciples.

The climax of the stories of Jesus in Jerusalem prior to the passion narrative is the most extensive and intimate conversation in the entire Gospel. The so-called apocalyptic discourse (13:4–37) is addressed to the audience as the four disciples who are sitting with Jesus on the Mount of Olives overlooking the Temple. In this long address, the storyteller invites the audience into a relationship of intimacy with Jesus. This intimacy and reinforcement of belief is directly related to Jesus' prophecies about the Jewish-Roman war that have probably been fulfilled in the audience's recent experience of the war and the destruction of the Temple.[28]

This invitation to an intimate relationship with the character of Jesus is the culmination of the storyteller's appeals to the audience throughout the story. Repeatedly in narrative sequence after narrative sequence, Mark as the teller of the tale invites the audience to move from a relationship of opposition and confrontation with Jesus to a relationship of belief and discipleship. In this structuring of audience address, Mark first engages his audience as adversaries of Jesus. The listeners are invited to enter into a series of testing confrontations with Jesus revolving primarily around the interpretation of the law. The listeners are then invited to engage with Jesus as the members of a sympathetic crowd. This climactic setting in the narrative sequences described above resonated with the real world setting of

28. See Marcus, "The Jewish War."

a storytelling performance in which a crowd of people gathered around a storyteller. The culmination of this implicit appeal to the members of the audience is a storytelling invitation to enter into and identify themselves with Jesus' disciples listening to Jesus in small, private settings usually in a house. This setting of the story is consistent with the most probable setting for the telling of Mark's story in private homes to relatively small groups of people who would gather for an evening of storytelling.

Further evidence that this pattern of audience address was intentional is the progressive structure of engagement with being addressed as a disciple. The first significant address to the audience as persons close to Jesus occurs, as we have seen above, in the story of Jesus and his mother and brothers (3:31–35). There the character with whom the audience is invited to identify is named "the crowd sitting around him" (καὶ ἐκάθητο περὶ αὐτὸν ὄχλος), literally "the sitting around him crowd." In the first teaching discourse that immediately follows this story, there is an elaborate description of the super large crowd (ὄχλος πλεῖστος) that gathered along the shore of the sea. The storyteller Jesus then addresses the audience as that large crowd, with Jesus probably seated and speaking in a loud voice with a slow tempo as one would find it imperative to use in speaking to such a crowd. After the parable, the storyteller shifts the setting to an unnamed place where Jesus is alone and the character addressed in the long discourse that follows (4:11–32) is "those who were around him with the twelve" (οἱ περὶ αὐτὸν σὺν τοῖς δώδεκα). This name is a step closer to being addressed as a disciple but this character is "those who were around him with the twelve" rather than "the twelve" by themselves. The probable purpose of this rather strange name is the construction of a dynamic structure that invites the audience to draw closer to Jesus in small, incremental steps.

Furthermore, the content of Jesus' speech in this discourse (4:10 ff.) is a series of implicit invitations to the audience to experience being "insiders" in the Jesus group and to reflect on the quality of their engagement with the story. The first episode of Jesus' speech about the mystery of the kingdom of God is an explicit address to the audience about the gift offered to them as followers of Jesus. Furthermore, the identification of "the mystery," like the motif of the Messianic secret, is a classic storytelling lure to an audience to stick around and hear the rest of the story. The contrast between those who are "inside" and those who are "outside" identifies a choice that the audience must make about whether to remain "outsiders" or to become "insiders." Both the interpretation of the parable of the sower (4:13–20) as a parable about different ways of "hearing" and the saying about "hearing" (the saying can mean both "Pay attention to what you hear" and "Pay attention to how you hear" (as in Matt. 7:14 and Luke 12:49 BDAG) address the quality of the audience's present engagement with the story. This series of teaching stories (4:1–32) is the longest and most intensive interaction up to this point in the story between the main character, Jesus, and the audience, who are addressed first as "the great crowd" and then as "those around him with the twelve."

The first speech addressed to the audience as "the twelve" does not occur until the story of the mission of the twelve (6:10–11). Jesus' speech has an interesting structure. The storyteller reports the first half of Jesus' instructions to the twelve in indirect discourse (6:7–9). Only after this introduction does the storyteller as Jesus address the audience directly as "the twelve." This is the final incremental step in the storytelling process of inviting the audience to accept being addressed as disciples.

Prior to the Messianic confession and discipleship discourse, the audience is addressed once more as "the disciples" in the concluding speech about the purity laws (7:18–22). However, the major discipleship discourse that follows Peter's realization (8:27 ff.) is addressed to the audience as "the crowd with the disciples" (8:34). Once again, the storyteller steps back from having Jesus address the audience as "the disciples" or "the twelve" and addresses them as "the crowd with the disciples." Like the earlier address to the audience as "those who were around him with the twelve," this name for Jesus' addressee is initially puzzling because it is difficult as a description of the actual scene. How did Jesus gather a crowd in between his confrontation with Peter and his pronouncements about discipleship? The function of this comment, however, is less to describe what happened at Caesarea Philippi than to describe the gathering of the audience by the storyteller as "the crowd with the disciples."

This is the turning point in the addresses to the audience as Jesus' disciples. After the discipleship discourse, the audience is addressed as the disciples most of the time (chapters 9–10) in the story of the journey up to Jerusalem. The only exceptions are the teaching about divorce and the conversation with the rich man. Both of these stories conclude with discussions addressed to the audience as the disciples. These stories firmly establish the relationship between the storyteller as Jesus and the audience as disciples prior to the initial events in Jerusalem that end with the longest and most intimate conversation with the four disciples seated on the Mount of Olives.

Thus, the addresses to the audience as disciples are structured to move the audience from a distanced relationship with the character of Jesus to an identification of themselves as Jesus' disciples. This dynamic in the relationship between the storyteller and the audience is experienced far more clearly in oral performance for a listening audience than when it is read alone in silence. In oral performance the storyteller can generate waves of

emotional interaction upon which she or he seeks to carry the audience towards an intimate relationship with Jesus that readers reading in the context
of a wholly different rhetorical tradition do not experience.

Another sign of the importance of audience address for the composition of the Gospels is the structure of the other three Gospels. While similar
patterns of audience address, namely interspersed addresses to the audience
as opponents and disciples throughout the pre-passion story, are present
in Matthew and Luke, John has a highly distinctive structure of audience
address that engages audiences in a clearly marked, progressive relationship
with Jesus over the entire story prior to the passion narrative.[29] In the first
four chapters of John's Gospel, the storyteller as Jesus addresses the audience as a series of Jewish groups who are both interested in him and even
believe in him. Thus, the audience is addressed by Jesus as themselves in the
prologue, then in subsequent narratives first as the disciples, particularly
Nathaniel (1:50–51), then as the Jews in the Temple (2:16–19), Nicodemus
(3:3–21), by John as the disciples of John (3:27–36), and by Jesus as the
Samaritan woman (4:21–24).

In John 5 there is a major shift in audience address. Beginning with
Jesus' response to the Jews persecuting him after the Sabbath healing of the
man at the pool of Bethzatha, the storyteller as Jesus consistently addresses
the audience as various groups of Jews (e.g., the Pharisees, the Jews who
want to kill or stone him or who believe in him, the crowd, and simply the
Jews) who for eight chapters (5–12) alternate between extreme opposition
and belief in Jesus. This continues through the entry into Jerusalem with the
only exception being the brief address to the audience as his disciples at the
end of the bread discourse (6:60–70). These long addresses to the audience
as Jews torn between opposition and belief have their climax in a series of
four addresses, the first by the storyteller as Jesus to the audience first as
Philip and Andrew (12:23–28) then as the crowd (12:29–36), by "John the
storyteller" to the audience as themselves (12:37–43), and finally as Jesus to
the audience as themselves (12:44–50).

The third section of audience address in John is Jesus' last words to the
eleven disciples in the aftermath of the washing of the disciples' feet and the
departure of Judas (13–17). This is the longest and most intimate discourse
of Jesus in the entire Gospel tradition. Thus, the same pattern of audience
address that is present in smaller sections of Mark is present in the whole of
John's story prior to the passion narrative.

29. For a fuller discussion of the structure of audience address in John, see below
"The Medium and Message of John."

The sign that the composer of John consciously constructs this pattern of audience address is that there are only two relatively short addresses to the audience as the disciples from the story of the man at the pool of Bethzatha to the triumphal entry (6:60–70, 12:23–28). In fact, there are only two additional addresses to the audience as the disciples in the initial section of John's story (chapters 1–4): Jesus' response to Nathanael's "over the top" confession (1:50–53) and his response to the disciples wanting him to eat something after his conversation with the Samaritan woman (4:34–38). This is in marked contrast to the three synoptic gospels in which there are addresses to the audience as the disciples throughout the stories prior to the passion narrative.

This pattern of audience address in John is similar to Mark and may have been a distinctive adaptation of Mark's story. Mark establishes initial engagement with Jesus in the addresses to the audience by John the Baptist and Jesus himself (1:7–8, 15), moves to an extended series of addresses to the audience as various Jewish groups opposed to Jesus (2:8–10, 17, 19–22, 25–28, 3:4–5, 23–29) and ends with an extended address to the audience as those close to Jesus (3:33–35; 4:11–32). But while Mark repeats this pattern several times, it is always within a shorter storytelling compass, the longest being four chapters (1–4, 11–13). In John this pattern is extended with minor variations over the entire story prior to the passion narrative (1–17). These patterns of audience address in the story world of the Gospels of Mark and John are evidence that this was a structural dimension of the Gospel storytelling tradition.

The addresses to the audience in Mark's passion story are further confirmation of this compositional structuring in the Gospel of Mark. As can be seen from the chart, prior to the arrest, the storyteller as Jesus addresses the audience as various groups of the disciples: the angry ones in Bethany, the twelve at the last supper, the three in Gethsemane. With the exception of the Passover preparation instructions to the two disciples and the highly intimate speech interpreting the meaning of the bread and wine at the meal, Jesus' speeches address the responses of the disciples to the events of the passion. Jesus' counter rebuke of those who rebuked the woman who anointed him is implicitly linked with Judas' offer to betray him. Once again, this is more evident when the story is performed than when it is read in silence because of the level of Jesus' conflict and rebuke of those who denounce the woman. The prophecies of betrayal (14:18–21) and desertion/denial (14:27–30) engage the audience in identification with the disciples' disbelief and resistance to the prophecies that are more or less immediately fulfilled.

The climax of Jesus' addresses to the audience prior to the arrest is Gethsemane. This is the quietest, the most intimate and the most emotionally intense interaction of the storyteller as Jesus with the audience as Jesus' disciples in the entire story. The three-fold repetition of Jesus' plea that they stay awake may have had a direct connection with the audience's struggle to stay awake after an evening of some two hours of storytelling. The audience is invited to identify fully with Peter, James, and John as they hear the disappointment in their teacher's voice. In each of these instances the audience is invited to recognize the disciples' responses of betrayal, flight and denial as wrong responses but with which they can fully identify.

The storyteller's addresses to the audience as Jesus, the high priest, and Pilate are the climax of the plot of Jesus' opponents. In each of these addresses, the audience is directly addressed as "you." Thus, after the arrest, the storyteller as Jesus asks the audience as the crowd from the authorities, "Have you come out as against an insurrectionist?" (14:48–49). After Jesus' confession, the storyteller as the high priest asks the audience as the council, "You have heard his blasphemy. How does it appear to you?" (14:63–64). And the storyteller as Pilate addresses the audience as the crowd: "Do you want me to release for you the King of the Jews?" (15:9) and "What then shall I do with the one you call King of the Jews?" (15:12). These speeches all share the same performance dynamic of requiring the audience to answer these questions internally. It is also significant that the questions at the arrest and the Pilate trial address issues directly related to the audience's experience of the Roman-Jewish war. Jesus' question to the crowd arresting him as an insurrectionist (λῃστής) and the crowd's choice at the Pilate trial between Barabbas, an insurrectionist (στασιαστής), and Jesus frame these direct questions to the audience in the same terms that Josephus uses frequently to describe the various groups that led the revolution.[30] These questions—such as "What do you want me to do with the one you call 'King of the Jews'"—are formed to resonate with the experience of Jewish audiences who lived in the aftermath of the destruction of the Temple. The storyteller's implicit appeal to the audience is to identify the arrest, condemnation and crucifixion of Jesus as mistakes that are associated with the disasters of the war.

The final address to the audience in Mark's story by the storyteller as a character in the story is the address of the storyteller as "the young man" dressed in white to the audience as Mary Magdalene, Mary and Salome (16:6–7). This speech is the climax of the entire two-hour story. The speech

---

30. The terms that Mark uses to describe Barabbas would have had the implications of revolutionary activity for Mark's audiences in the aftermath of the Roman-Jewish war. This is evident from Josephus' usage of these same terms to refer to the insurgents. For documentation and an excellent discussion of this dimension of Mark's language in the arrest and trial stories, see Marcus, *Mark 9–16*, 1029.

is quiet, slow and intimate. The audience's identification with the women has been established in the stories of their presence at Jesus' crucifixion and burial (15:40–41, 47). As a result, the audience experiences the young man's words as addressed to them. The climactic imperative addressed to the audience is the command to "go, tell . . ." (16:7). The women's response of flight and saying nothing to anyone completes the cycle of wrong responses by the characters with whom the audience has been invited to identify. In each instance, the impact of this story experience is to be implicated in these wrong responses and implicitly invited to reflect on this response and to do its opposite: staying awake, staying with Jesus in times of persecution, openly confessing being a disciple, choosing Jesus rather than the insurrectionists, and telling the story. This final address to the audience is consistent with the performance function of the addresses to the audience throughout the story. These addresses involve the audience in direct interaction with the characters and events of the story.

The Characteristics of Mark's Audiences

The instances and patterns of the Markan storyteller's addresses to the audiences of the story as various characters in the story are a source of direct information about the characteristics of Mark's audiences:

1. The audiences are almost always addressed as various groups of Jews. The sequence of Jewish groups can be seen on the chart and can be summarized here: the people of Judea and Galilee, the scribes and scribes of the Pharisees, the disciples of John the Baptist and the Pharisees, the Pharisees, the scribes from Jerusalem, the crowd at several points in the story, those around Jesus with the twelve, the people in the Nazareth synagogue, the twelve and the disciples, the crowd with the disciples, Peter/Andrew/James/John, the chief priests/scribes/elders, the Sadducees, the crowd in the Temple, the Sanhedrin, the crowd at the Pilate trial, and Mary Magdalene/Mary/Salome. By far the most frequent character embodied by the storyteller in these addresses to the audience is Jesus. No other character has more than one major address to the audience. Thus, with the one exception in the explanation of Jewish customs, the storyteller addresses the audience as a wide-ranging spectrum of Jewish groups.

2. Non-Jews are addressed as a minor but integral part of Mark's audiences. At one point in the story (7:3–5), Gentiles are addressed directly by the storyteller and are thereby included in the projected audiences of the Gospel.

3. The translations of Hebrew and Aramaic terms by the storyteller are an indication that the audiences are addressed as Greek speaking Jews and Gentiles who do not know Hebrew or Aramaic.

4. Mark's audiences are addressed as Jewish persons who are invited to move from identifying with groups who are opposed to Jesus to identifying with Jesus' disciples. This pattern is present in progressive sections of the Gospel (2:1—4:41; 7:1–22; 8:11–21; 10:1–12; 12:1—13:37). Before the Messianic confession, the audience is addressed most of the time as groups who are in conflict with Jesus. After Peter's moment of recognition, the audience is predominantly addressed as disciples.

5. The audiences are addressed as persons who are implicitly asked to move gradually from being identified as part of crowds interested in listening to Jesus to being identified as Jesus' disciples. This movement in audience address from being addressed as "those outside" to "those inside" is carefully nuanced in incremental steps. These include addresses to the audience in relatively long discourses by Jesus as, for example, "those around Jesus with the twelve" and "the crowd with the disciples." The addresses to the audience as those "inside" are sometimes located in a story space where Jesus is alone or inside a house. This storytelling location is also a sign that these talks are quieter, smaller in gesture, and more intimate than the public discourses.

This data has implications for our reconstructions of the actual historical audiences of Mark's Gospel. The data of audience address in Mark's Gospel indicates that the story was structured for predominantly Jewish audiences who did not believe that Jesus is the Messiah. Mark's purpose is evident in the structure of audience address in the story. The story is structured to move the audiences from identifying themselves as Jesus' opponents to identifying themselves as Jesus' disciples. Furthermore, those who are interested in Jesus, as are most of those who would have begun listening to Mark's story, are invited by the storyteller to move from a relationship of interest on the periphery of the story to a place "inside" the community of those who have an intimate relationship with Jesus.

There is nothing in this data that would indicate that Mark's story was directed to those outside the nascent Christian communities to the exclusion of those who were already members of believing communities. However, believers are initially addressed as Jews who are either opposed to Jesus or are only interested in his teaching from a distance. That is, the structure of audience address does not support the assumption that Mark was composed for performances to audiences that were either an individual believing community as Joel Marcus envisions or the network of Christian communities in the Greco-Roman world as Richard Bauckham has proposed. The story may have been told in believing communities but those believers are addressed as persons who are either outside or on the periphery of discipleship communities. The audiences are addressed as disciples but only after a long period of storytelling invitations to move from a position of identification with opponents or with a supportive crowd on the outer perimeters of the communities of disciples. Thus, there are many allusions in Jesus' apocalyptic discourse to the experience of the communities of Jesus' followers. But that only happens after a long process of audience inclusion in which the audience is invited by the dynamics of audience address to move from a position of opposition, to the interested periphery, to the inner circle of the twelve, and finally, to the four and the three disciples closest to Jesus.

The Gospel of Mark has a radically different structure of audience address than the letters of Paul that are addressed to small communities of believers. Mark is addressed to the great community of Jews throughout the Greco-Roman world all of whom were seeking for a way forward in the aftermath of the war. A major theme implicit in the structure of audience address is an appeal to the audience to reject the way of insurrection and to believe in a Messiah who taught and practiced the healing and feeding of both Jews and Gentiles. A dimension of Jesus' teaching was a critique of the purity laws that were a barrier to Jews having virtually any relationship with Gentiles. However, while Gentiles are the object of Jesus' actions in several stories, the audience is directly addressed as Gentiles only once in the story. The Gospel of Mark is addressed to Jews and Gentiles in a manner that assumes they are fully cognizant of the realities of hostility between Jews and Gentiles. This relationship is, however, addressed from a Jewish perspective. The Gentiles are those on the other side of the sea (5:1 ff.), those who are appropriately called "dogs" (7:27), those who will mock, spit on and kill the Messiah (10:34), and those who practice leadership by domination rather than service (10:42). Gentiles are, therefore, invited to be part of the audiences of the Gospel but only as they are willing to enter into the Jewish world of Mark's story. As one might expect in the aftermath of the war, the Gospel of Mark addresses audiences in which the relationships between Jews and Gentiles are even more highly polarized than in the letters of Paul.

The analysis of the dynamics of audience address requires that Markan scholarship reexamine the conclusion that the Gospel of Mark was anti-Jewish. The central fact that requires this reexamination is that the audiences of the story were, with one exception, addressed as Jews. Furthermore, for the first hour of the story the storyteller presents Jesus addressing the audiences as Jews who are opponents and critics of Jesus. This is a structure of audience interactions that is characteristic of intra-Jewish conflict rather than anti-Jewish conflict. In its original context, the Gospel of Mark is no more anti-Jewish than the book of Jeremiah or the book of Exodus. In both of those books, the audience is addressed as members of Israelite communities by storytellers who embody characters such as Moses and Jeremiah who are in steady conflict with the people of Israel. The literature of Israel is full of violent intra-Jewish conflict in which various authors are appealing to Jews to reject the policies and actions of other Jewish groups.

What is distinctive about Mark's story in the context of the literature of Israel is the inclusion of Gentiles in the projected audiences of the story. Gentile members of Mark's audiences were invited to join audiences of Jews and to experience the story of Jesus as an integral part of the wider Jewish community. The storytellers of Mark's Gospel did not address their audience as Gentiles for whom *Jews* are "the others," as would be required if the story's purpose was anti-Jewish. The audiences of Mark are addressed as Jews for whom *Gentiles* are "the others." The structure of audience address in Mark requires that we imagine a social and political context in which non-Jews were invited to join Jews in listening to a Jewish story of which they were an integral part both in the story itself and in their participation in the audiences for whom the story was performed. This is congruent with the social and political context of the Jewish community in the immediate aftermath of the war outlined by Joel Marcus.[31] But the data of audience address indicates that the audiences of Mark were not addressed as communities in which either Gentiles or members of believing communities were the majority. The audiences of Mark were addressed as Jews and Gentiles who were invited by the story to move from a position of opposition to Jesus to a position of identifying with Jesus' disciples. The audiences of Mark are, therefore, primarily addressed repeatedly as Jews who do not believe that Jesus is the Messiah. The historical probability is that this was the dominant character of the audiences for which the Gospel was performed. The primary purpose of the story was to move its listeners from opposition to Jesus to belief in Jesus as the Messiah, the Son of God.

In conclusion, the process of the investigation of Mark as a narrative initiated in public discussion by the publication of *Mark as Story* has been a complex process that is already evolving in new directions. Performance criticism is a logical and historically appropriate methodological development that is more congruent with the original character of Mark than narrative criticism with its assumption of Markan readers as developed in *Mark as Story*. The recognition that Mark was not a book read by readers but

31. Marcus, *Mark 1–8*, 28–38.

was a composition performed by oral performers, initially storytellers, is of primary importance for the interpretation of Mark in its original historical context. Oral performance encourages identification with characters and the experience of being addressed by a character in the story that is easily jettisoned when other strategies of reception, such as silent reading of a mute text, replace those of the oral storyteller. Silent reading in particular allows the reader to remain an observer on the outside of the events being narrated, especially when the events involve characters with whom the reader does not readily identify. Mark as a storyteller, on the other hand, utilizes a panoply of resources for engaging the audience in a dynamic identification with the characters of the story. Mark's story created a story world that connected with the real world of both Jewish and Gentile first-century audiences. The characters are predominantly Jewish and the listeners' experience in the course of the story moves from negative to more positive engagements with Jesus. Hearing and performing Mark provides new data that will change our perceptions of Mark's audiences and the meaning of Mark's story for those audiences.

9

Audience Asides and the Audiences of Mark

The Difference Performance Makes

The reassessment of Mark as performance literature for audiences rather than as a text read by readers invites a reexamination of some details of the composition that have been foundational for the identification of Mark's audience in recent Markan scholarship. Two statements of Mark have had a central role in the definition of Mark's original historical context: the explanation of Jewish practices of washing food, hands, and cooking vessels (Mark 7:3–4) and the identification of Simon of Cyrene as the father of Alexander and Rufus (Mark 15:21). The thesis here is that these statements were not narrative comments by the author/narrator to readers, but were storytelling asides to the audiences to whom Mark's story was told. When these audience asides are heard in the context of ancient performance, the exegetical focus shifts from private communication to readers to public communication for multifaceted audiences and points to a larger setting and purpose for the whole story. Rather than conceiving Mark as addressed to readers in a Gentile Christian congregation in Rome or Syria, this data points to audiences that included first Jews and also Gentiles throughout the Greco-Roman world. Heard in this context, the horizon of Mark's vision for the public proclamation of his composition is much wider than most current interpretation envisions.

Narrative Comments in the Identification of Mark's Audience and Purpose

A characteristic feature of biblical scholarship is the dialogue between the big picture of the historical context of the documents and the details of the documents themselves. This is particularly true of Markan scholarship. When Mark is seen in a big picture of ancient literature as read by readers, the translations and various explanations that are frequent features of Mark's story are seen as narrative comments addressed to readers. The prevalent image of the reading situation in which Mark's story is to be interpreted is a private context of a person sitting alone with a manuscript of Mark, reading the text. Sometimes the imagined reading situation will include Mark's manuscript being read aloud either by the reader either for the reader or to a group of hearers. But if for a group, it is usually conceived as a small, local group, that is, a local congregation of believers.[1]

This is the picture in the background of the two major recent commentaries in English on Mark. Both Joel Marcus in the Anchor Bible commentary and Adela Yarbro Collins in the Hermeneia commentary, though not regarding it as "a mathematical certainty," have portrayed the Gospel as a document written for readers, and sometimes hearers, in a particular congregation. While Collins concludes that a local congregation in Rome or Antioch is possible, Marcus favors a Syrian provenance.[2] The exegetical context reflected throughout both commentaries is the reading of Mark's Gospel either for a local congregation of believing Christians or for a single reader.

Richard Bauckham and a group of his British colleagues have challenged this picture of Mark and the Gospels in a collection of essays, *The Gospels for All Christians*. Bauckham and colleagues argue that the contemporary consensus about the local audiences and purposes of the Gospels is too small. They propose that the Gospels were encyclical documents that were addressed to the Christian churches throughout the Greco-Roman world. As Bauckham observes, the "local church" interpretation has become the characteristic feature of late twentieth-century scholarship on the four Gospels. The initial studies of Mark and John as documents addressed to

---

1. This picture of Mark is drawn with characteristic clarity by Joel Marcus: "Whoever the author of the Gospel was, he seems to have written his work first and foremost to the Christian community of which he himself was a member." The critique here of Marcus' description of Mark's receivers is set in the context of my deep appreciation for the quality of the commentary and in particular his insight about Mark's connection with the Jewish War. See Marcus, *Mark 1–8*, 25.

2. Collins, *Mark*, 101–2; Marcus, *Mark 1–8*, 36–37.

local congregations by Weeden and Martyn have been extended to Matthew and Luke in subsequent scholarship.[3] In a variety of ways, the Gospels have been read as inner-church documents that were directed to local congregations. In this interpretive horizon, the Gospels are a kind of mirror of the congregations to which they are addressed. A predominant dimension of their original meaning was the interpretation of the struggles and beliefs of those local churches.[4] While these two reconstructions of the audience and purpose of the Gospels are not irreconcilable, all subsequent interpreters will have to decide which of these pictures is most historically probable. Is it more historically probable that the Gospels were composed in and for a local congregation or for a much wider series of audiences?

Mark's Narrative Comments for a Local Church

For Marcus, the pivotal sign that Mark was composed for a local congregation is the narrative comment that names the sons of Simon of Cyrene who carried Jesus' cross:

> Mark's notice in 15:21 that the man who carried Jesus' cross, Simon of Cyrene, was "the father of Alexander and Rufus" is most plausibly explained by the theory that Mark's audience knew Simon's sons. Since, however, Alexander and Rufus are not mentioned elsewhere in early Christian literature, they were probably people who were familiar to the Markan community, perhaps even members of it, but little known elsewhere.[5]

Marcus' conclusion is that this comment implies that Mark's local congregation knew Alexander and Rufus. Mark's reference to Alexander and Rufus is an "in-group" naming of persons who were known to him and to his church. This argument against Bauckham's proposal has been persuasive to Adela Yarbro Collins:

---

3. The initial studies that launched the "local church" horizon of Gospel interpretation were Weeden, *Mark,* and Martyn, *History and Theology.* This "local" context for Gospel interpretation has been developed in a whole series of subsequent studies of all four Gospels.

4. For Bauckham's helpful survey of the origins and tradition history of the "local" theory of the audience and purpose of the Gospels, see Bauckham "For Whom Were Gospels Written," 13–26. Marcus also sees the description of persecution in Mark 13 as being *first* about the persecution of his local church.

5. Marcus, *Mark 1–8,* 25. Brown also notes this as a probable dimension of the Markan audience's foreknowledge: "15:21 suggests that Alexander and Rufus, the sons of Simon of Cyrene, were known to them" (Brown, *Introduction,* 163n91).

> One of his (Marcus) better arguments is that Alexander and Rufus are mentioned in 15:21 because they were known to Mark's audience. Since both Matthew and Luke omit these names, it is likely that they did not expect the two men to be known to any of their audiences.[6]

The presence of this narrative comment in Mark and its absence from the other Gospels is seen as a decisive sign of an "in-church" provenance for the Gospel.

Furthermore, Mark's narrative comment explaining Jewish customs has been seen as a sign of the predominantly Gentile character of Mark's church. The inference from this comment is that the readers did not know Jewish customs and were, therefore, non-Jews. As Brown states, "For the most part the recipients were not Jews since the author had to explain Jewish purification customs to them."[7] This Markan comment has also been seen as decisive evidence of the Gospel's recipients as located in a Gentile Christian church.[8]

Another element of Mark's story lies in the background of this picture of Mark as addressed to readers. In Jesus' final extended speech, often called the little apocalypse, Jesus foretells what is going to happen in the future. In the middle of that speech in the description of the great tribulation, the document reads, "When you see the abomination of desolation set up where it ought not to be, let the reader understand, then those in Judea must flee to the mountains . . ." (13:14). This address to "the reader" has been understood as a parenthetical comment (usually placed in brackets by contemporary editors of the text) by the author to the reader of the manuscript alerting the reader to pay particular attention to what is being said by Jesus here.

The most natural conclusion for contemporary interpreters has been that this is an address to the receiver of the document who is privately reading the document. The assumption of "the reader" as the recipient of the Gospels is ubiquitous in Gospel commentaries and monographs. Following Robert Fowler's recommendation, I have begun to underline the references to "the readers" in works of biblical scholarship and have found it to be virtually universal. Sometimes "hearers" are added but "reader" is the common and most frequent term for the recipients of the Gospels.

---

6. See Collins, *Mark*, 97.

7. Brown, *Introduction*, 163. In the context of this article's topic, it is worth noting that Brown, who is less certain of a Roman locale, also says of the audience: "Most likely they had heard a good deal about Jesus before Mark's Gospel was read to them."

8. Incigneri, *Romans*.

There is a connection between this assumption about "the readers" as the most common description of the receivers of the Gospels and the "local church" hypothesis. The media world of literature has become increasingly private over the centuries. In the modern world, reading is associated with an individual reading in silence. In the relatively infrequent occasions when a document is read to a group, the group is usually small: one or two children, a class, or a local congregation. In the case of the Bible, it has continued to be read aloud in weekly congregational worship in local churches.

The assumption of a small horizon for the reception of Mark's Gospel is natural. Thus, the explanation of Jewish cleanliness and purity traditions in Mark 7 and the identification of Simon of Cyrene as the father of Alexander and Rufus in Mark's story of Jesus' crucifixion have been interpreted as internal communication between the author/narrator and the receivers/readers of the document. Describing these components of Mark's story as narrative comments is an integral dimension of the critical interpretation of Mark as addressed to readers. Those essentially private comments have been seen as central clues to the setting and purpose of the Gospel as inner-church communication.

Mark and "the Reader" in the Communication Cultures of Western Civilization

A first step in the reexamination of these elements of Mark is to identify the relationship between the Gospel of Mark and the communication cultures of western literature. Recent research on the communication culture of the ancient world has made it clear that the first century was an early literate culture in which 85%-90% of people were illiterate.[9] Written documents were scarce and relatively expensive. The primary means of publication of first-century literature was performance for audiences. To be sure, there are exceptions to this dominant pattern, as has been demonstrated since the initial recognition of the predominance of oral performance in early literate culture.[10]

The preeminent historical fact is, however, that "the reader" as the *dominant* receiver and object of literary composition and distribution did

---

9. The foundation of the recent recognition of the limits of ancient literacy has been the explicit study of the communication culture of antiquity. See Achtemeier, "*Omni Verbum Sonat*," 3–27. Balogh, "Voces Paginarum"; Carr, *Writing on the Tablet*; Shiner, *Proclaiming the Gospel*; Hadas, *Ancilla*; Harris, *Ancient Literacy*; Ong, *The Presence of the Word*; and Ong, *Orality and Literacy*.

10. See Slusser, "Reading Silently," 499.

not happen until the seventeenth century. A representative example of this historical recognition is William Nelson's study of the practices of reading in the Renaissance culture of the fifteenth–sixteenth centuries, "From 'Listen, Lordings' to 'Dear Reader.'" Nelson concludes that while people doubtless read to themselves and evidence of reading habits is scattered, the dominant pattern is clear:

> Enough does exist to show that not only the long narratives of the Renaissance but also books of every conceivable kind, whether in prose or in verse, were commonly read aloud, sometimes by the author himself, sometimes by members of a household taking turns, sometimes by a professional reader or 'anagnost' as he was called in ancient times, the audiences ranging from the princely and sophisticated to the rustic illiterate.[11]

In the court of Francois I (1537), there was an official position of "reader-in-ordinary" who was employed to read to the king and the royal court. Even in the aftermath of the printing press and the accompanying increase in literacy, books were normally read aloud in part because of the sheer pleasure of the shared experience of hearing and then discussing great works of literature. Annotations and introductions gave instructions about how works were to be read.[12] Thus, after approximately 1500 years, the dominant practices of the reading of literature in the ancient world were still present. While there were undoubtedly silent readers in this period, it was only in the seventeenth century that addresses to the receiver of literary works as "the reader" became widespread.

The exploration of this private relationship between an author and a reader sitting alone and reading in silence is developed into an integral dimension of the novel in the fiction of Henry Fielding (1707–54). Fielding's comments to the reader are an omnipresent dimension of his narration of his tale. These comments serve up a plate of ever-new possibilities for relationship between an author and a reader. Early in his greatest novel, *Tom Jones*, Fielding establishes a sense of camaraderie between the author and

11. Nelson, "Listen, Lordings," 110–24.

12. Nelson, "Listen, Lordings," 117–18. Nelson quotes Ronsard who in a 1572 Preface gives instructions as to how his *Franciade* should be read: "Je te supliray seulement d'une chose, lecteur, de vouloir bien prononcer mes vers & acommoder ta voix a leur passion, & non comme quelques unes les lisent, plustost a la facon d'une missive, ou de quelques lettres royaus que d'un Poeme bien prononcé." [ET: I would only ask one thing of you, reader: to be good enough to speak my verses out loud and to adapt your voice to their passion, and not as some read them, more in the manner of a private letter or of some royal letters than of a well-spoken poem" (K. C. Hanson trans.)].

the reader sliding down the hill together into their literary adventure and the next episode of the story:

> Reader, take care. I have unadvisedly led thee to the top of as high a hill as Mr Allworthy's, and how to get thee down without breaking thy neck, I do not well know. However, let us e'en venture to slide down together; for Miss Bridget rings her bell, and Mr Allworthy is summoned to breakfast, where I must attend, and, if you please, shall be glad of your company. (Book I, chap. 4)[13]

Another function of these narrative comments to the reader is to provide inside information about what is happening to the characters:

> The reader will perhaps imagine the sensations which now arose in Jones to have been so sweet and delicious, that they would rather tend to produce a cheerful serenity in the mind, than any of those dangerous effects which we have mentioned; but in fact, sensations of this kind, however delicious, are, at their first recognition, of a very tumultuous nature, and have very little of the opiate in them. (Book IV, chap. 3)

Fielding's elaborate comments also guide and, in the quote that follows, provoke the reader to align the reader's norms of judgment with the norms of the author in relation to the characters and elements of the plot:

> Examine your heart, my good reader, and resolve whether you do believe these matters with me. If you do, you may now proceed to their exemplification in the following pages: if you do not, you have, I assure you, already read more than you have understood; and it would be wiser to pursue your business, or your pleasures (such as they are), than to throw away any more of your time in reading what you can neither taste nor comprehend. To treat of the effects of love to you, must be as absurd as to discourse on colours to a man born blind; since possibly your idea of love may be as absurd as that which we are told such blind man once entertained of the colour scarlet; that colour seemed to him to be very much like the sound of a trumpet: and love probably may, in your opinion, very greatly resemble a dish of soup, or a surloin of roast-beef. (Book VI, chap. 1)

As one can see from these brief examples of reader address, the range of narrative possibilities associated with the development of silent reading has been immense. Since the seventeenth century, the silent reading of

13. Fielding, *Tom Jones.*

fiction has provided both authors and readers with ever-new dimensions of the reading experience to explore.[14] This development, however, has been the end result of processes of change in communication technology and culture that have happened over sixteen centuries since the composition of Mark. The technologies and pedagogies associated with writing, reading, and cultural formation evolved gradually during those centuries.

The reading and interpretation of the Bible has been part of this evolution. When silent reading became the normative way of reading the Bible, new dimensions of the possibilities of meaning also emerged. Hans Frei's description of "meaning as reference" as the underlying assumption of biblical interpretation since the eighteenth century is a helpful description of this new discovery. The investigation of the Bible's "meaning as reference" has made possible the endlessly fascinating exploration of the Bible as a source of "ostensive" referential information about, for example, "the historical Jesus" and "ideal" referential information about the theologies of the Bible.[15]

The entire apparatus of historical criticism based on "the reader" is, however, a relatively late development in the history of literate communication. "Reader response" criticism is an appropriate methodology for the study of Mark as read by Enlightenment readers, as Robert Fowler's book on Mark, *Let the Reader Understand,* reflects. Fowler, however, makes a strong and consistent distinction between the first-century reader in Mark 13.14 and the contemporary reader of Mark whose reading experience is the subject of his study. As Fowler writes: "the Gospel of Mark was probably written to be read aloud to an assembled audience, and one possibility for identifying 'the reader' of 13:14 would be to take the parenthesis as a kind of wink or stage direction to an anagnostes, a professional reader reciting the Gospel of Mark before an assembled audience."[16]

Fowler identifies the other possible references to "the reader" in Mark 13:10 as "an isolated, individual reader . . . reading the Gospel aloud to himself in private" or "an individual student of the Jewish Scriptures, who should be able to recognize and comprehend an allusion to Daniel." But the purpose of his book is to explore the rich interpretive tradition that has developed with the silent reading of Mark as a text by readers rather than the interpretation of Mark and its reader in the ancient world.

14. For a comprehensive survey of the development of relationship between the reader and the complexities of narration in modern fiction, see Booth, *Rhetoric of Fiction.*

15. Frei, *Eclipse*; see in particular, "Hermeneutics and Meaning-as-Reference," 86–104.

16. Fowler, *Let the Reader,* 84.

This distinction between "the reader" now and "the reader" then has not, however, been widely adopted in biblical scholarship. A reading of representative works of biblical scholarship leads to the conclusion that "the reader" in the first century is virtually the same figure as "the reader" in the eighteenth to twenty-first centuries. This is, however, a major blind spot in the ongoing work of biblical scholarship. In relation to the goal of identifying the meaning of the Bible in its original historical context, the enterprise of biblical scholarship has been based on a massive media anachronism. It has read back into the ancient world the communication culture of the readers of the Enlightenment sitting in studies examining the documents of the Bible in silence. An underlying assumption has been that the Gospel tradition, for example, moved more or less immediately from a predominantly oral culture to the high literate culture of the eighteenth–nineteenth centuries. The omnipresence of "the reader" in critical biblical commentaries and monographs is a reflection of this anachronistic character of biblical interpretation in the historical-critical era. The historical probability is that most of the persons in Mark's audiences could not read. Robert Fowler's decision to note every instance of "the reader" in his reading of the works of biblical scholarship is a good idea as is his celebration of the conscious pursuit of the reading possibilities that this way of reading has made possible. But he also recognizes that this understanding of "the reader" is different than it was for Mark.[17]

If and in as far as our goal is the identification of the meaning of Mark in its original historical context and if Mark was composed as "performance literature," we need to listen to every detail of Mark's story in the context of the communication culture of the first century as a story that was performed for audiences.

Audience Asides in the Ancient Performance of Mark

If Mark's story was originally performed for audiences rather than read by readers, the "narrative comments" of Mark to his readers need to be heard as asides to the audiences who were present at the performances of Mark in the first century. In a performance of a story, audience asides are one of the most important storytelling techniques. In an audience aside, a storyteller pauses the account of what is happening and leans in and speaks directly to the audience. This may be a step toward them, a hand to the side of the mouth, a wink and a smile, or a change of tone. Whatever the particular move, the storyteller gives some sign that indicates the statement to follow is

17. Fowler, *The Reader*, 82–87.

"inside" information that will help the members of the audience understand what is going on in the story.

These moments enable a storyteller to establish a close relationship with an audience. In a storytelling performance, there are two figures present, the storyteller and the audience. The relationship between a storyteller (or story reader) and any particular audience is extremely fragile. In virtually every moment of the story, it is possible for a storyteller to lose contact with or even alienate the audience. Individual members of the audience can turn off and go to sleep or start looking around for something else to do. Thus, at the end of the "little apocalypse" and in the Gethsemane story, the Markan storyteller as Jesus addresses the audience as the disciples and tells them to "stay awake" (13:33, 35, 37; 14:35, 37, 38, 40). Others may physically get up and leave. John addresses this possibility for the audience at the end of the "bread from heaven" discourse: "Do you also want to leave?" (6:67). Others may start making negative gestures or verbal comments to others in the audience or to the storyteller. The loss of the audience is an ever-present possibility for a storyteller.

This is the reason why audience asides in storytelling are usually short, especially in comparison with narrative comments to a reader. Readers have lots of leisure time. They will happily read for hours. Therefore, Fielding's comments to the reader can be long and complex. Audiences, on the other hand, can easily lose interest and need constant reinforcement. If the audience is comfortable and interested, they will happily sit for hours. But if the story gets boring, an audience can be lost. It is essential in a long story to keep it moving. Therefore, interruptions to the flow of the action need to be brief.

In Mark, the audience asides are all short and have a variety of functions. Each instance of an audience aside, regardless of its function, can be a clue about the character and identity of the audiences that are projected for the story's performance. In the analysis that follows, representative examples of the major types of audience asides in Mark will be listed. Mark's audience asides need to be heard in order to be correctly understood. Therefore, I would recommend that the readers of this essay read aloud or preferably tell the following examples of audience asides to an audience or, if that is not possible, to themselves.

1. The Markan storyteller translates Aramaic words into Greek. The translations are usually introduced by the Greek phrase, ὅ ἐστιν μεθερμηνευόμενον. Examples are:

a. Ελωι ελωι λεμα σαβαχθανι, ὅ ἐστιν μεθερμηνευόμενον Ὁ θεός μου ὁ θεός μου, εἰς τί ἐγκατέλιπές με; "... which means 'My God, my God why have you forsaken me?'" (15:34–35)

b. Γολγοθᾶν τόπον, ὅ ἐστιν μεθερμηνευόμενον Κρανίου Τόπος. "... which means 'the place of the Skull'" (15:22)

c. Ταλιθα κουμ ὅ ἐστιν μεθερμηνευόμενον τὸ κοράσιον, σοὶ λέγω, ἔγειρε "... which means 'Little girl, I say to you, get up.'" (5:21)

These translations are indications that there are Greek speakers in the projected audiences who do not understand Aramaic.

2. The storyteller explains Jewish customs and practices. The most extensive is Mark's explanation of the cleanliness laws:

a. "For the Pharisees, and all the Jews, do not eat unless they thoroughly wash their hands, thus observing the tradition of the elders; and they do not eat anything from the market unless they wash it; and there are also many other traditions that they observe, the washing of cups, pots and bronze kettles" (7:3–4)

b. "since it was the day of Preparation, that is, the day before the Sabbath" (15:42)

These explanations are signs that there are non-Jews in the projected audiences who do not know Jewish cleanliness Sabbath laws.

3. The storyteller introduces characters by naming their children or their parents. These introductions happen throughout the story. Because this is the immediate context of the audience aside regarding Simon of Cyrene, I will list all of the characters who are introduced by the naming of members of their family:

a. James the son of Zebedee and John his brother (1:19)

b. Levi the son of Alphaeus (2:14)

c. James, the son of Zebedee and John, the brother of James and James the son of Alphaeus (3:17, 18)

d. Bartimaeus, the son of Timaeus, a blind beggar (10:47)

e. Simon of Cyrene, the father of Alexander and Rufus (15:21)

f. Mary, the mother of James the younger (brother) and of Joses (15:40)

These introductions of new characters make the characters familiar and sympathetic. It's like getting to know someone's family. It is a response to the audience's desire to "get acquainted" with the characters of a story.

4. The storyteller often explains things that are puzzling in the previous statement. For example, in the introduction to the Beelzebul conflict story, the storyteller reports the surprising and puzzling news that Jesus' family had come to seize him. The storyteller's explanation to the audience is: "Because they were saying, 'He's out of his mind'" (3:21). Other typical explanations are:

   a. The explanation of Jesus telling the disciples to get a boat ready for him: "Because many were healed so that they pressed in on him so that anyone who had diseases might touch him." (3:10)

   b. The reason the woman with a flow of blood touched his garment: "Because she said, "If I can touch his garment, I will be made well." (5:28)

   c. The explanation of the Sanhedrin's inability to find testimony to put Jesus to death: "Because many bore false witness against him and their testimony did not agree." (14:56)

   d. The reason why Pilate surprisingly offered to release Jesus to the crowd: "Because he recognized that it was out of envy that the chief priests had handed him over." (15:10)

   These explanations are a basic technique of audience engagement. Rather than providing explanations before the description of an action or event, the composer describes something that is puzzling or surprising. These little incongruities invite the audience to wonder. The explanation that follows is then a moment of relationship between the storyteller and the audience in which the answer is provided for the question that has just been raised.

5. The storyteller will sometimes provide the audience with an inside view of the feelings or motives of a character, usually as an explanation of something puzzling.

   a. The storyteller gives the audience a double explanation of why Peter was speaking like a bumbling idiot when he asked about building three booths for Jesus, Moses and Elijah: "For he didn't know what to say because he was afraid." (9:6)

   These insights into the feelings of a character answer the audience's question about what is going on with a particular character. In this case, the explanation answers the question: why is he acting like such a fool? The explanation also assumes that the audience will appreciate the fear and intimidation associated with finding oneself in the presence of Jesus, Moses and Elijah.

6. Mark uniquely gives explanations that raise more questions than the puzzle he has just reported:

a. The explanation of the disciples' amazement at Jesus walking on the sea: "For they didn't understand about the loaves because their hearts were hardened" (6:52).

b. The reason the women said nothing to anyone: "Because they were afraid" (16:8).

In the ending of the walking on the sea story, the composer assumes that the audience will know the stories of Pharaoh hardening his heart and, therefore, will wonder what connection the disciples' hardened hearts might have to their inability to understand about the loaves. Furthermore, why would the disciples harden their hearts in response to Jesus walking on the sea? In these moments in the story, the Markan storyteller is more of a provocateur than a helper. Nevertheless, in all of these moments of direct address to the audience by the Markan storyteller, a multifaceted, inclusive relationship between the storyteller and the audience of the story was formed.

The Audience Asides Regarding the Purity Laws and the Sons of Simon of Cyrene

We can now address the specific audience asides that have had a central role in the identification of Mark's audience and purpose. The explanation of Jewish cleanliness laws has a markedly different impact as an aside to the audience than as a narrative comment. As a narrative comment, the explanation defines the readers. A natural inference is that the readers and, therefore, the intended recipients of the Gospel are Gentiles who do not know the "traditions of the elders." And given the adversarial tone of the controversy, a further inference is that the readers are Gentile Christians who are invited to distance themselves from Jews. As an audience aside, however, the explanation has the function of audience *inclusion*. The explanation means that the composer presumes that there will be non-Jews in the projected audiences of the Gospel whom he does not want to exclude. But this aside does not limit or define the audiences as non-Jews. In fact, when heard in the context of all of the asides in the story, this is the only instance of an aside to Gentiles in a story in which there are many allusions that are addressed to Jews.[18]

18. For a systematic analysis of audience address in Mark, see chap. 8 above, Boomershine, "Audience Address and Purpose."

Thus, to name three among many asides to Jews in the audience, the story of the Gerasene demoniac depends on a presumed Jewish norm of judgment that pigs are unclean animals (5:11–14) whose deaths are to be celebrated. The story of the woman who touched Jesus' garment is based on the assumption distinctive to Jewish law that by touching him she made him unclean and was fully justified in being afraid to admit what she had done (5:27–33). And Jesus' third passion prophecy climactically names "the Gentiles" as those who will mock him, spit on him, flog him and kill him (10:34).

The overall conclusion that emerges from a performance criticism analysis of the Markan audience is that the audiences of Mark were predominantly addressed as Jews. When heard in that context, the aside to the audience explaining Jewish cleanliness laws is a gesture of inclusion of Gentile minorities in the projected audiences of the story.

The naming of the sons of Simon of Cyrene also sounds different as an aside to the audience than it looks as a narrative comment to a reader. The names of Alexander and Rufus as a narrative comment imply private communication about two brothers who may have been known by a person or small group. It is fully possible to infer from the character of the comment that both the author and a local congregation knew Alexander and Rufus. This comment would create a personal connection with their father as well as between the author and the readers in his local church.

When assessed as an audience aside in a composition that was performed for wide ranging audiences, the naming of Simon of Cyrene's sons has a different significance. It is one of a series of asides that introduce characters by naming members of their families. For example, Mary, the second witness of Jesus' death (15:40), is described as "the mother of James, the younger, and Joses." For audiences who are listening to the whole story at one time, these names are a verbal echo of the earlier story of Jesus' teaching in his hometown synagogue in which the members of the synagogue ask themselves: "Isn't this the carpenter, the son of Mary and brother of James and Joses and Judas and Simon?" (6:3). There is no possible implication that Jesus' brothers would have been known to the various audiences of the Gospel. Instead the implication of this sonic connection is that this woman is Jesus' mother. In all of the asides that introduce characters by naming members of their families, it is highly unlikely that these were heard as allusions to persons who would have been known to audiences throughout the Greco-Roman world some forty years after the events being described.

When heard as an integral element of a performance, the primary significance of these names is that the Markan storytellers are passing on a story that is linked with real persons who were known by the composer of the story. In the case of Simon of Cyrene, the naming of his sons, Alexander and Rufus, implies that the storyteller heard and learned the story from someone who knew Simon and his sons. The impact of this aside to the audience is to increase the credibility of the storyteller and his story about people whom the original composer knew by name. Furthermore, if we assume that Matthew and Luke knew and rewrote Mark's story, this implicit allusion to personal knowledge is also a possible explanation of why they did not include their names. If they heard Mark's naming of Alexander and Rufus as reflecting personal knowledge, they may have left out the names because they did not want to imply that they knew them. However, regardless of the motives of Matthew and Luke, Mark's aside creates a sense of the authenticity of the storyteller and his story.

The Horizon of Mark's Audiences

The perception and interpretation of what have been called Mark's narrative comments is different when the words are heard as asides addressed to audiences. This is a specific dimension of the reconception of Mark as performance literature in the early literate culture of the first century. There are, however, broader possible implications.

Studying Mark's Gospel as performance literature suggests that we may reconceive what we mean by "Mark." Rather than an author who is singularly present to a reader, Mark was the composer of a story who was made present vicariously by a series of performers who told Mark's story. The function of a composition for performance is to facilitate as many performances as possible by a whole range of performers. In music, for example, a composer may launch a new composition by directing or playing the first performance. But the composer's hope is that many orchestras or soloists will perform the composition over many years, hopefully many centuries. The writing and duplication of a musical composition makes it possible for a much wider range of performers to perform the work than if it were only distributed by oral transmission. Likewise, a primary function of the distribution of copies of Mark's manuscript was to enable storytellers to learn and tell Mark's story, sometimes from memory and sometimes "reading" the manuscript. In each performance, these new storytellers retold Mark's story and in a sense made Mark as the composer present. But each new evangelist also brought new dimensions to the performance of the story. Therefore, we can imagine varied performances of Mark's composition by a series of "Marks" who told the story to various audiences. The original Mark was the composer who set the proclamation of his Gospel in motion.

We also can think of audiences rather than readers as the context in which Mark's story was experienced. When seen in the context of ancient performance literature, the probability is that Mark was composed for widespread performance to a variety of audiences. Mary Ann Tolbert's proposal that Mark is analogous to ancient novels such as Chariton's *Callirhoe* may be ambiguous as a description of Mark's genre.[19] But it is accurate as a description of Mark's communication horizon. The projected audiences of Mark were, if anything, larger and more inclusive than the audiences of the novelists.

Bauckham and his colleagues have proposed that the Gospels were composed for "all Christians." Their proposal is that the audiences of the Gospels were the local churches of the Roman world rather than individual, local congregations. Listening to the Gospel of Mark suggests that even this expanded vision of the horizon of the Gospels is too limited.

Two sayings of Jesus explicitly identify the horizon of the audiences of Mark's Gospel. In the apocalyptic discourse, Jesus says, "It is necessary that the good news/Gospel be proclaimed first to all the nations (ὅπου εἰς πάντα τὰ ἔθνη πρῶτον δεῖ κηρυχθῆ τὸ εὐαγγελίου Ἰησοῦ Χριστοῦ." (13:10) This global horizon is reinforced in Jesus' commendation of the woman who anointed him with precious ointment: "Wherever in the whole world the good news/Gospel is proclaimed (ὅπου ἐάν κηρυχθῆ τὸ εὐαγγέλιον εἰς ὅλον τὸν κόσμον) what she has done will be told in memory of her." (14:9) What then do these two sayings describe? The term, εὐαγγέλιον, is the name that is given to the whole composition: "The beginning of the Gospel/good news of Jesus Christ" (Ἀρχὴ τοῦ εὐαγγελίου Ἰησοῦ Χριστοῦ—1:1). Thus, the "proclamation" of the Gospel is most naturally understood as a description of the performance of the story for audiences.

In these two sayings, Jesus envisions a global horizon for the audiences of the Gospel. His statements suggest that the horizon of the audiences envisioned for the proclamation of Mark's story was not only a local church nor only the Christian churches. The envisioned audiences were Jews and Gentiles throughout the Greco-Roman world. Thus, an initial exploration of Mark as performance literature suggests that the composer of Mark envisioned performances of the Gospel in the whole world and used asides to the audience to include all of those potential audiences in the story.

19. Tolbert, *Sowing the Gospel*, 70–73. The major problem with the genre of the novel as a description of Mark is that the novels were explicitly fiction. However, Tolbert's identification of a broad, popular audience is more congruent with the character of Mark as performance literature than an audience of small local churches in Rome or Syria.

10

The Medium and Message of John

Audience Address and Audience Identity in the Fourth Gospel

The message and meaning of the Gospel of John in its original historical context was shaped by the medium of the Gospel as much as by its form and content. Until very recently, the unquestioned picture of the medium of John in Johannine scholarship has been that it was a written document composed for reading by individual readers. A further dimension of this picture has been that John's readers read in silence as contemporary readers do. This assumption about the original medium of the Gospel has been associated with methodological practices in contemporary scholarly investigations of John's Gospel. In silent reading, the entire text is available for synchronic examination by the eyes in space as well as for diachronic reading in time. Reading in silence reduces or eliminates movement in a straight temporal progression through the text. It also contributes to the possibility that the reader will become an analyst rather than a participant in the author's story. While a reader of the Fourth Gospel *can* get caught up in the story and keep moving in the direction established by the narrator, it is easy to disrupt involvement in the story for reflection and for retracing steps to answer questions.

A primary consequence of individual reading by readers for centuries has been an abandonment of the story as an experience in favor of a search for the ideas implicit in the story. One of the enduring results of reading the Fourth Gospel in this way is that Jews have come to represent disbelief and have been seen as the objects of Johannine polemic.

Recent research about the communication world of antiquity has shown that this picture of the medium of the fourth Gospel is improbable. The evidence from documents in the ancient world indicates that documents were written for performances to audiences and were rarely read in silence by individuals. In modern terms, ancient writers were more like composers than authors or writers. The implications of this realization for our understanding of the Fourth Gospel and for exegetical methodology have only begun to be explored.[1]

The purpose here is to sketch the outlines of an answer to the question implicit in this recognition: what can we discern about the message and meaning of the Gospel of John if it was experienced as a story told or read by a storyteller/performer to audiences rather than read in silence by individual readers? What difference would this reconception and recovery of the original medium of John make in our understanding of its original message and meaning? The focus of this chapter will be the structure of audience address in the speeches of Jesus and the storyteller's direct comments to the audience. When the Gospel was performed, the performers of John's story addressed their audiences in more than half of the story *as Jesus* speaking to specific groups that are identified in the story. The audience as a result was addressed *as those groups* to whom Jesus, embodied by the storyteller/performer, is speaking: e.g., the Jews (John 6:41), Jews who believed in him (John 8:31), Pharisees (John 9:40), the disciples (John 13–16). Thus, throughout the story, the storyteller was continually speaking to the audience as Jesus, and the audience was continually being addressed by the storyteller/Jesus as one or another of various groups of Jews.

This claim may seem initially strange. We are accustomed to reading the Evangelist's story with the assumption that the audience was composed of believers who were *listening in*, as Jesus, with whom they identified, addressed various non-believers, with whom they did not identify. Indeed, John's story can be read, both silently and aloud, to generate this experience. The proposal here is that the Fourth Gospel and its audience is perceived in a radically different way if the document is experienced and analyzed as a story told to audiences rather than as a document read by readers. Even to consider this new thesis, however, the researcher has to both experience

---

1. Richard A. Horsley notes that modern methods of study assume, incorrectly, a reader reading in silence: "we can no longer project the assumptions and typical approaches of literary study that assume a writer at a desk and an individual reader." He further comments: "established Gospel studies in particular and New Testament studies in general are ill-equipped to understand orally performed narratives" (Horsley, "A Prophet Like Moses and Elijah," 166).

and present John's story in its original oral medium.[2] She or he must also be willing to explore the possibilities and capabilities of this medium for producing experiences of the Fourth Gospel excluded by the tradition of silent reading that has been the unexamined tradition of biblical scholarship.

The thesis here is that, when the Fourth Gospel was performed for audiences, the Johannine storyteller always addressed the audiences of the Fourth Gospel as Jews. Furthermore, there was a clear structure to the addresses to the audience that moved from the performer, speaking as both him/herself and as Jesus, first addressing the audience as Jews who are interested in and drawn to Jesus (John 1–4), then as Jews who are torn between wanting to kill him and believing in him (John 5–12), and as Jews who are his beloved disciples (John 13–16). This character of audience address in turn indicates the probability that the actual historical audiences of the Gospel were predominantly Jewish. At least, the audience is always addressed *as if* they are Jews. The impact of the story was to engage the audience in a dynamic and passionate interaction with Jesus as a character who directly addressed them throughout the story. The message implicit in the Gospel was to appeal to Jewish listeners to move through the conflicts of engagement with Jesus to belief in Jesus as the Messiah. When heard as addressed to first-century Jewish audiences, the Fourth Gospel presented Jesus as engaged in passionate interaction with other Jews as the fulfillment of the prophetic traditions of Israel, specifically a prophet like Moses, and as the King of the Jews who gave his life for the nation.

The Fourth Gospel and Its Readers in the Work of J. Louis Martyn

The refinements in our understanding of the Fourth Gospel that may develop from a more precise definition of the Gospel's medium will be sharpened by entering into dialogue with a highly influential picture of John in recent scholarship. In his engaging conversational manner, J. Louis Martyn has invited us all into an exploration of the Gospel of John in its late first-century context. Martyn proposes that the Gospel was conceived and experienced as a "two-level drama." In this drama the characters from the original story, such as the blind man in John 9, represent both the original persons who interacted with Jesus and persons in John's context. As readers of the Gospel read, they perceived in the drama going on in Jesus' life a similar drama taking place in their own lives. As Martyn writes,

2. For a more detailed discussion of the transformative impact of performance on the perception of biblical texts. see Rhoads, "Performance Criticism—Part II," 173–80.

In the two-level drama of John 9 the man born blind plays not only the part of a Jew in Jerusalem healed by Jesus of Nazareth but also the part of Jews known to John who have become members of the separated church because of their messianic faith and because of the awesome Benediction.[3]

The Benediction to which Martyn refers is the Benediction against Heretics, the *Birkath ha-Minim*, that in Martyn's view was published by the Jamnia academy about 85 C.E. This prayer was reformulated as part of the required eighteen benedictions or prayers that were a fixed element in the order of worship in the synagogues. The reformulated twelfth benediction contained this prayer: "Let the Nazarenes [Christians] and the Minim [heretics] be destroyed in a moment and let them be blotted out of the Book of Life and not be inscribed together with the righteous."[4] Since all members of synagogues were required to lead the prayers periodically, if a member of the synagogue either refused or stumbled in the reading of this prayer, he would be detected as a heretic and expelled from the synagogue. The story in John 9 of the blind man who is expelled from the synagogue (John 9:34) thus reflects the experience of John's community.

Martyn identifies major elements of the Johannine Christian community's life and thought in the two-level drama of the Gospel. The community is a predominantly Jewish community of diaspora Jews in a Hellenistic city, perhaps Alexandria, that shares a common belief in Jesus as the Messiah. Many have been or will soon be expelled from the synagogue and, therefore, from Judaism and the Jewish community. The community is in steady dialogue with other Jews who are observing the law as it is being interpreted by the Academy at Jamnia that has replaced the Sanhedrin as the governing body of Judaism in the aftermath of the Jewish war (66–70 CE). This highly polarized dialogue is reflected in the dialogues of Jesus with the Pharisees and other Jews in the Gospel. The Gospel also reflects the ongoing disputes within the community about the various dimensions of the community's theology such as the identity and appropriate names of Jesus.

Martyn's interpretation, which accords with that of Raymond Brown with whom he was in conversation,[5] has generated much lively discussion and critique in subsequent years.[6] The lasting contribution of Martyn's study

3. Martyn, *History and Theology*, 62.

4. Martyn, *History and Theology*, 58.

5. For a critical discussion of Martyn's position, see Visotzky, "Methodological Considerations," 91–94.

6. For a succinct review of this subsequent discussion, see Visotzky, "Methodological Considerations," 95–96. The chief criticisms are a "vast overestimation of the power and importance of the Yavnaen rabbis in the late first century," and "the growing

is the recognition of the interplay in the Gospel's stories between the events and stories of Jesus' life in their original context of the 30s of the first century and the experience of religious communities in the 90s of that same century. He has shown the ways in which John's story weaves together elements from the experience of his time with the stories of Jesus' time.[7]

Martyn also shares the common scholarly understanding of the medium of the Gospel in the mid-twentieth century. He writes regularly about John's "readers" and what they perceived.[8] And his conceiving them as readers is critical to his understanding of the way in which the Gospel impacted them. It is important for the purpose of this article to acknowledge that the issue of John's medium is not directly addressed in Martyn's book nor were questions about John's medium being asked at the time of the study. However, the presupposition that the audience for the Gospel were readers has clearly shaped the picture of the meaning of the Gospel of John that emerges from this study.

In effect, Martyn proposes that the Evangelist's audience read his Gospel as a kind of historical allegory in which all of the major characters in the stories of Jesus stand for persons and groups in their own context. The Pharisees represent the rabbis of Jamnia and the Pharisaic authorities or Gerousia in John's city. Nicodemus represents secrets Christians who may be members of the Gerousia and who are afraid to confess their messianic belief. The blind man in John 9 represents Jewish Christians who have confessed Jesus as Messiah and have been expelled from the synagogue. And the Jews represent those who have rejected messianic belief in John's context.[9] Instead of being swept along by John's story, caught up into the action and the experience of the characters as they engage and listen to Jesus, the readers slow down in the presence of the text and reflect on the way in

---

consensus that the explicitly anti-Christian portion of the *Birkat HaMinim* was most probably added to the prayer only in the fourth century."

7. For a minimalist view of the role of the later community's experience in the shaping of the Fourth Evangelist's narrative, see Reinhartz, "John and Judaism," 111: "There is in fact nothing explicit and, I would argue, nothing at all in the gospel to support the assumption that the gospel encodes the community's experience or the methodological approach of reading the community's history out of the gospel. This is not to discount the possibility that the gospel was written in a way that would resonate with the experience of the first readers."

8. Martyn's most extensive discussion of John's readers occurs in his exploration of the Hebrew term *Messiah* and its translation, *Christos*; see Martyn, *History and Theology*, 92–94. Other references to the reader occur throughout the book; e.g., see 18, 69, 72, 83, 87, 89, 134, 137, 146.

9. See Brown, *Community*, 25–91 for an elaboration of this reading of John as a reflection of specific groups in John's historical context.

which Jesus and the characters he engages represent people in the drama of their own experience. Rather than being drawn by the narrator into sharing the experience of the various characters, the readers connect many of the characters in the story of Jesus with people in their own world who are other than and often in opposition to the readers.

In reading John's story of the blind man, for example, John's late first-century reader read it as an event in the life of Jesus some six or seven decades earlier in which she or he recognized the conflicts between Jewish Christian believers and the supporters of the Jamnia academy in his own local synagogue who were using the newly rephrased Benediction against the Heretics to detect and expel secret believers in Jesus as the Messiah.

There is a further critical dimension to Martyn's understanding of the Fourth Gospel. Martyn sees the primary readers of John's Gospel as having been the members of his church. While it is not out of the question that non-believers could have read the Gospel (opponents of the early Christians, like Celsus, read Christian literature in order to attack it), Martyn agrees with the majority of Johannine scholars who explicitly reject the possibility that the Fourth Gospel was intended for readers other than believing Christians.[10] Martyn, however, in his exposition of the story of the first disciples—Andrew, Simon Peter, Philip and Nathaniel—also proposes that there are non-Christian readers in John's horizon to whom the announcement is that *Jesus* is the Messiah:

> Here we see that John is acquainted with non-Christian readers who already have conceptions of the Messiah. With *these* readers the task is not to awaken expectations of the Messiah, but rather—with certain qualifications—to announce that *Jesus* is the long-awaited Messiah. That is to say, 1:35–51 is not primarily designed to tell the reader that "Jesus is *Messiah*"; in the first instance it is composed for readers who already have (at least latent) expectations of the Messiah. To them John wants to say, "*Jesus* is Messiah."[11]

---

10. See, for example, Wayne Meeks, "Man from Heaven," 70: "It could hardly be regarded as a missionary tract," to which he appends a footnote: "Against a large number of scholars, including K. Bornhaeuser, D. Oehler, J. A. T. Robinson, W. C. van Unnik, and C. H. Dodd, I thus find myself in agreement with R. E. Brown that John's distinctive emphases 'are directed to crises within the believing Church rather than to conversion of non-believers.'" Other scholars who identify John's readers as Christian believers include Barrett, Schnackenburg, Bultmann, Culpepper, and Bauckham. For a recent argument against this broad consensus, see Carson, "The Purpose of the Fourth Gospel."

11. Martyn, *History and Theology*, 92.

Thus, Martyn identifies a range of people and positions in John's community of readers: Christian believers, non-Christians with Messianic expectations, and even Samaritans.[12] Furthermore, in his discussion of the motivation for John's distinctive translation of the Hebrew term "Messiah" into Greek, namely, *Christ*, Martyn identifies the possibility that there were Gentiles among John's readers who did not know the Hebrew term Messiah.[13] But the implication of Martyn's picture is that these "others" were virtually all members of John's community.

This implication makes sense in the context of an assumed audience of readers. The Fourth Gospel was probably composed to address a community sometime around the end of the first century CE. Martyn has made a strong case for seeing the Fourth Gospel as the production of a community deeply involved in theological disputes about Jesus. This picture of the Fourth Gospel is directly related to the presupposition that its medium was a manuscript read by individual readers. Reading depends upon the availability of a manuscript and upon the desire of a person to take it up and read it. This medium would significantly limit the potential audience and lead to the conclusion that an audience for this medium would most likely consist of Christians. Thus, the assumption that the medium of the Gospel was a manuscript read by individual readers limits the potential audience to the relatively few people who had both the ability and interest to read such a manuscript.

Furthermore, the implicit assumption that the medium of John was a written text for readers underlies a set of conclusions about the meaning and message of John. In this medium, the meaning of the Gospel is identified in relation to a range of doctrinal disputes that were going on within the Christian community of the late first century. The specifics of John's message vary in different scholarly accounts. But the shared assumption about the medium of John carries with it a widely shared conclusion about the Gospel's meaning and message, namely, that the primary meaning and message of the Gospel was directed to internal theological debates about

12. Martyn makes a fascinating intimation in exploring whether there may have been Samaritan converts in John's immediate context: "Whether in John's city there were flesh and blood Samaritans we cannot say with certainty, although it is quite possible that John 4 reflects the remarkable success of the Christian mission amongst Samaritans known to John." See Martyn, *History and Theology*, 112.

13. Martyn, *History and Theology*, 92. In this discussion Martyn also states that, since many Jews such as Philo did not know Hebrew, particularly in Alexandria and other Greek cities, this translation of the Hebrew term Messiah into Greek may have been needed for Jewish as well as Gentile readers. This is important because this translation is often seen as evidence that Gentiles were the primary projected audience of the Fourth Gospel.

the identity and significance of Jesus between groups of people who shared the conviction that Jesus was the Messiah. As Martyn's study concludes, the message of the Fourth Gospel was theology of and for John's Church.

What difference would it make if the evidence that has emerged since Martyn's landmark book requires us to reconceive the original medium of the Fourth Gospel? Specifically, how would this reconception effect Martyn's description of the two-level drama?

The Medium of John

Our historical challenge in the identification of John's medium is to specify the place of the Gospel in the evolution of ancient literate culture. We now have a much clearer picture of that history than was available at the time of the development of source, form, and redaction criticism. Literacy in the first century was at a much earlier stage of development than was assumed in the nineteenth century when the media culture of that period was uncritically read back into the ancient world. The assumption that ancient biblical writers were writing for an extensive network of individual readers who would read the manuscripts in silence is anachronistic. At the time of the composition and distribution of John's Gospel, no more than ten to fifteen percent of the people in the Roman empire were able to read and the majority of the readers were concentrated in urban areas.[14] While there was a first-century trade in books, manuscripts could only be copied by hand and were only widely possessed by the upper class. In the first century, books were normally produced and distributed as scrolls. The transition to the codex as the normal mode of book production in the Greco-Roman world took centuries. The first codexes were notebooks and the first evidence of a codex of a literary work is the *Epigrams* of Martial in 84–86 CE.[15] Virtually all early Christian texts are codexes rather than scrolls[16] which may have facilitated distribution. But book production and distribution was limited and nothing like a mass audience of readers was conceivable for ancient authors.

14. William Harris's comprehensive study of ancient literacy surveys the levels of literacy from the early first millennium BCE through the period of the late Roman empire (fifth to sixth century CE). While steadily acknowledging that evidence is fragmentary and varied in different areas and among different groups, Harris draws a picture of literacy levels that never exceeded fifteen to twenty percent and in many places was as low as five percent.

15. Gamble, *Books and Readers*, 52.

16. Gamble, *Books and Readers*, 49.

Written manuscripts such as the Gospel of John were composed for performance.[17] Manuscripts were virtually always recited, often from memory. Indeed, some degree of memorization was required in order to perform written texts because of the character of ancient writing with no division of words, punctuation of sentences, or arrangement in paragraphs. Thus, an ancient writer wrote with the assumption that the book would be performed for audiences. As Moses Hadas has written:

> Among the Greeks the regular method of publication was by public recitation, at first, significantly, by the author himself, and then by professional readers or actors, and public recitation continued to be the regular method of publication even after books and the art of reading had become common.[18]

Books that were read in private were normally read aloud, often as a small scale performance for a group gathered around the reader.[19] Even when reading in private, people read out loud and, in effect, performed the writing for themselves.[20]

The medium of the Gospel of John can be reconstructed in this cultural and technological context. It was composed at a relatively early stage in the development and extension of writing technology. The Gospel of John was written for performance, not for private reading in silence. The performances of the Gospel were often done by heart. A performance of the Gospel of John in its entirety provided an evening of storytelling of around three hours. It was not a particularly long story, especially in comparison to the performances of the great Homeric epics. There were many occasions for performance: small groups in homes, larger audiences in marketplaces and synagogues.

---

17. See Hadas, *Ancilla*, 50–77, for a series of citations from ancient literature that reflect the performance of written works as the primary mode of publication. Even historical works were published by oral recitation as is evident in Lucian's opening of his book *Herodotus* in which he tells the story of Herodotus taking the opportunity of the Olympic Games to read his work: "He seized the moment when the gathering was at its fullest, and every city had sent the flower of its citizens; then he appeared in the temple hall, bent not on sightseeing but on bidding for an Olympic victory of his own; he recited his Histories and bewitched his hearers." Hadas, *Ancilla*, 60. For further instances of ancient performance, see Shiner, *Proclaiming*, 11–35.

18. Hadas, *Ancilla*, 50.

19. Hadas, *Ancilla*, 61.

20. The classic example of the prevalence of ancient oral reading in private is Augustine's apology for his mentor, Ambrose, who had the strange practice of reading in silence. Augustine concludes his apologia: "But whatever was his motive in so doing, doubtless in such a man was a good one." (Augustine, *Confessions*, 5.3).

The Gospel of John was composed as a long story. It is somewhat longer than Mark, but somewhat shorter than Matthew and Luke (Matthew is thirty-four pages in a recent edition; Mark, twenty-one; Luke, thirty-seven; John, twenty-seven). A distinguishing feature of the Gospel of John as a performance is the relative importance of the speeches of Jesus. Jesus' discourses constitute more than half of the fourth Gospel. In Mark, the speeches of Jesus are approximately twenty percent of the story if you count all the discourses; but the two long speeches (chapters 4 and 13) are a little less than ten percent of the story. In Matthew and Luke, Jesus' speeches constitute somewhat more than a third of the compositions. Thus, the speeches of Jesus are a more dominant feature of the Gospel of John than in any of the other canonical Gospels.

The centrality of Jesus' speeches for John's story also has implications for the dynamics of interaction between those who performed the story and their audiences. Comparison with the dynamics of a contrasting genre, drama, may help to clarify the particular character of storytelling. In drama the action is on the stage and the characters talk to each other. The actors are always presenting a character and generally each actor embodies only one character in the drama. Once in a while, often at the beginning and sometimes at the end, a character will directly address the audience. But most of the time the audience is an observer of interactions that happen on the stage.

In storytelling, in contrast to drama, the performer is first and foremost him or herself and is always addressing the audience, sometimes directly and sometimes indirectly. For example, in the prologue and epilogue of the Fourth Gospel, the performer/storyteller speaks directly to the audience *as a person, not as a character in the story*. In the recital of the entire story, however, the performer also speaks *as all the characters*, often in interaction with each other. But when there is a speech, especially a long speech, the storyteller usually addresses the audience directly, not as himself or herself as in the prologue and the epilogue, but *as the character who is speaking*. And the audience, in turn, is addressed not as its own self but as whatever character in the story is the object of the speech. For example, in John's story of the last supper, the storyteller presents Jesus addressing the audience as his disciples. It is a long speech: chapters 14–16 with 13 as the setting and 17 as Jesus' closing prayer. Thus, for at least twenty to twenty-five minutes, Jesus, as embodied by the performer, speaks to the audience as his disciples.

Two imaginative transformations happen in this process. The performer "becomes" Jesus and the audience "becomes" his disciples. That is, in the suspension of disbelief that happens in storytelling, the storyteller presents Jesus in a manner that, when done well, makes the character of

Jesus "really" there. And likewise, the audience experiences Jesus talking to them as his disciples in a manner that, when done well, induces them to "become" Jesus' disciples. The audience is invited to occupy that role in the story, just as the storyteller is occupying the role of Jesus. At other times in the Gospel of John, such as the prologue and the concluding words of both chapters 20 and 21, the storyteller is simply a person speaking to the audience person to person. This highly nuanced dynamic of identity becomes a central factor in shaping the impact of the story. In the Gospel of John, this dynamic is centered in the character of Jesus.

Therefore, a central feature of our picture of the Gospel of John is directly connected with our conclusions about the medium of the Gospel. If we imagine that the original audience of John's Gospel was an individual reader reading in silence, our analysis of the meaning of the Gospel in its original historical context is apt to be determined by our own centuries-old reading habit of objective theological and historical reflection and projecting those same habits onto the first readers. But if we imagine that the original audience of John's Gospel was a group of persons listening to a story told by a performer, a major source of meaning is the interactions between the storyteller and the listeners. There were also a range of meanings that may have happened for different members of the audience. Some may have been alienated or bored by the story. For those listeners, the storyteller's challenge was to get them reengaged with the story as it proceeds. Others may have been drawn to the story and its characters but the consequences of really believing in the story's claims were frightening.

Furthermore, the meaning of the story was shaped by the identity of the various groups in the audiences to which the story was told. To whatever degree we can identify the groups to which the story was addressed, it will assist us in identifying more clearly the range of meanings that may have happened for those groups.

Audience Address in the Gospel of John

The structure of audience address in John will help us to hear more of the specific dynamics of the performance of the Gospel for its ancient audiences. Among the four Gospels, John is distinctive in its manner of audience address. One of those distinctive features of John's Gospel is that there are a lot of long speeches by Jesus, more than in any other Gospel. For example, in Mark there are two long speeches while Matthew and Luke both have five. In John there are eight long speeches and several shorter speeches by Jesus. Jesus' concluding address to the disciples is markedly longer than any of the speeches in the Synoptic Gospel tradition (Sermon on the Mount, 108 verses; speech at Last Meal in John, 142 verses). In the following chart, I have compiled a list of the addresses to the audience in the Gospel of John. In the first column I have listed the stories that contain speeches of two or more verses. When the speeches are embedded in a longer story, I have listed the story in the first column and the actual speech in the third column as an address to the audience. In the second column I have listed the character who is being embodied by the performer, usually Jesus but also the storyteller/performer and John the Baptist. In the third column I have also listed the character who is addressed and, therefore, the person or group with which the audience is invited to identify.

Direct Address to the Audience in John

Story	Speaker	Address to the Audience
Prologue (1:1–18)	Storyteller (John)	Audience
John the Baptist's testimony (1:19–34)	John the Baptist	Pharisees (1:26–27, 29–31, 32b–34)
Calling of Philip and Nathanael (1:43–51)	Jesus	Nathanael (1:50–51)
Cleansing of the Temple (2:13–25)	Storyteller (John)	Audience (2:21–25)
Nicodemus (3:1–21)	Jesus	Nicodemus/Pharisees (3:10–21)
John the Baptist and Jesus (3:22–36)	Storyteller/John the Baptist	Disciples of John (3:27–36)
Samaritan woman (4:1–42)	Jesus	Samaritan woman/ Samaritans (4:21–24)
Samaritan woman (4:1–42)	Jesus	Disciples (4:34–38)
Healing of a crippled man (5:1–47)	Jesus	The Jews who want to kill him (5:19–47)
Feeding of five thousand (6:1–71)	Jesus	The crowd (6:26–40)
Feeding of five thousand (6:1–71)	Jesus	The Jews (6:43–59)
Feeding of five thousand (6:1–71)	Jesus	The disciples (6:61–65)
Feeding of five thousand (6:1–71)	Jesus	The twelve (6:67, 70)

Story	Speaker	Address to the Audience
Jesus' brothers (7:6–8)	Jesus	Jesus' brothers (7:6–8)
Feast of Tabernacles (7:10–52)	Jesus	The Jews (7:16–19)
Feast of Tabernacles (7:10–52)	Jesus	The crowd (7:21–24)
Feast of Tabernacles (7:10–52)	Jesus	Some Jerusalemites (7:28–29)
Feast of Tabernacles (7:10–52)	Jesus	Police officers from chief priests and Pharisees (7:33–34)
Feast of Tabernacles (7:10–52)	Jesus	The crowd (7:37–38)
Feast of Tabernacles (8:12–59)	Jesus	The Pharisees (8:12, 14–18)
Feast of Tabernacles (8:12–59)	Jesus	The Jews (8:23–29)
Feast of Tabernacles (8:12–59)	Jesus	The Jews who believed in him (8:31–47)
Feast of Tabernacles (8:12–59)	Jesus	The Jews (8:48–58)
Healing of the man blind (9:1–10:12)	Jesus	The Pharisees (9:41–10:12)
The Temple Festival (10:22–42)	Jesus	The Jews (10:25–30)
The Temple Festival (10:22–42)	Jesus	The Jews who want to stone him (10:32–38)
Triumphal entry (12:12–50)	Jesus	Philip and Andrew (12:23–28)
Triumphal entry (12:12–50)	Jesus	The crowd in Jerusalem (12:30–36)
Triumphal entry (12:12–50)	Storyteller (John)	Audience (12:37–43)
Triumphal entry (12:12–50)	Jesus	Audience (12:44–50)
The footwashing (13:1–17:26)	Jesus	The disciples (13:12b–20)
The footwashing (13:1–17:26)	Jesus	The disciples (13:31–35)
The footwashing (13:1–17:26)	Jesus	The disciples (14:1—16:33)

Story	Speaker	Address to the Audience
The footwashing/prayer of Jesus (13:1–17:26)	Jesus	The Father/audience as observers of Jesus' prayer (17:1–26)
Purpose of book (20:30–31)	Storyteller (John)	Audience (20:30–31)
The disciple who wrote this book (21:24–25)	Storyteller (John/"we")	Audience (21:24–25)

The following is a list of Jesus' major speeches with the characters who are addressed:

1. Nicodemus (3:10–21)

2. The Jews who want to kill him (5:19–47)

3. The crowd, the Jews, and the disciples after the feeding of the 5000 (6:26–70)

4. The crowd, the Pharisees, the Jews who believed in him and the Jews at the feast of Tabernacles, a long speech of at least ten minutes (7:21–8:58)

5. The Pharisees after the healing of the man born blind (9:41–10:12)

6. The Jews at the Temple Festival (10:25–38)

7. Philip and Andrew, the Jerusalem crowd, and the audience after the triumphal entry (12:23–43)

8. The disciples at the last supper, the longest speech of at least twenty minutes (13:12–16:33; 17:1–26).

Another feature of Jesus' speeches in John is that Jesus addresses the audience as a much wider range of characters than in any of the other Gospels. For example, in Matthew's Gospel, Jesus has five long speeches all of which are addressed to the audience as the crowds and/or the disciples:

1. The crowds with the disciples on the mountain (Matt 5–7)

2. The twelve (Matt 10:5–42)

3. The crowds at the sea (Matt 13:3–52)

4. The disciples (Matt 18:2–35)

5. The crowds and the disciples (Matt 23:1—25:46)

The addresses to the audience in Jesus' five major speeches in Luke are similar to Matthew. But in John the speeches are addressed to a wide range of different characters: Nicodemus, various groups of Jews, the Pharisees, and the disciples. Thus, the storyteller's interactions with the audience in John are more complex than in any of the Synoptics.

Another distinctive feature of John's storytelling is that five of his stories—Nicodemus, the feeding of the 5000, the trip to Jerusalem for the Feast of Tabernacles, the healing of the man born blind, and the triumphal entry—function as introductions to long speeches that are addressed to the audience as characters in the preceding story. In these speeches, the story moves imperceptibly from a third person description of an event to a first person address by Jesus to the audience.

An example is the story of Nicodemus. (3:1–21) The storyteller tells the story of Nicodemus coming to Jesus at night and reports their conversation. Throughout several interchanges, Jesus is talking to Nicodemus in the first person ending with this address: "Truly I say to you, we speak of what we know and we bear witness to what we have seen but you do not receive our testimony. If I have spoken to you about earthly things and you do not believe, how will you believe if I speak to you about heavenly things?" But in the next sentences, Nicodemus fades into the background and Jesus is talking in the third person: "And just as Moses lifted up the serpent, so also must the Son of Man be lifted up so that everyone who believes in him may have eternal life . . . For God so loved the world that he gave his only son . . ." (3:15–16). In the performance of this speech, the probability is that the storyteller shifts from addressing an imagined Nicodemus to directly addressing the audience. But the storyteller is still speaking as Jesus. The change from first to third person is, in effect, a turn to addressing the audience directly as Nicodemus. In the telling of the story, the storyteller as Jesus now talks directly to the audience as if the audience were Nicodemus.[21] The audience has imaginatively become Nicodemus and Jesus' speech is addressed to each member of the audience as a Pharisee who is seeking spiritual rebirth. This speech to the audience then continues through his dialogue about those who come and do not come to the light (John 3:16–21). The effect of this structure of audience address is to create a higher degree of sympathetic identification with the characters prior to the audience being addressed as those characters. This same storytelling dynamic happens in each of these five speeches.

21. The punctuation of different translations reflects different decisions about the narrative character of this speech. In the RSV, NIV and NAB there are no quotation marks enclosing John 3:16–21, thereby indicating the editorial conclusion that this was not part of the speech of Jesus but is a comment by the narrator. The editors of the TEV and *The Complete Gospels* place the close-quote marks after 3:13 and indicate the beginning of the narrator's comment at 3:14. The NRSV (also NEB, CEV, JB) has the more accurate punctuation of quotation marks around the entire speech (John 3:10–21) thereby indicating that all of these words were part of Jesus' speech.

The most distinctive feature of John's Gospel is the clearly marked structure of the addresses to the audience. In chapters 1–4, the audience is addressed as various groups of first-century Jews: the Pharisees (1:26–27), the Jews in the Temple at Passover (2:16–19), Nicodemus/the Pharisees (3:1–21), the followers of John the Baptist (3:27–36), the Samaritans[22] (4:21–24), and the disciples (4:34–38). The longest and most engaging address to the audience in these initial episodes is Jesus' speech to Nicodemus in which the audience is addressed as Pharisees who are interested in Jesus. All of the audiences in these first four chapters of the Gospel are either positively disposed to Jesus or seeking more understanding. No audience expresses hostility or is described as either hostile or as rejecting Jesus.

The one possible exception is Jesus' conversation with the Jews in response to his cleansing of the Temple (2:18–20). The response of the Jews has traditionally been heard as hostile both to his cleansing of the Temple and his invitation: "Destroy this temple, and in three days I will raise it up." (2:19) However, the tone of the storyteller's report of the Jews' response in the performance of this story is indicated by the storyteller's comment to the audience: "When he was in Jerusalem during the Passover festival, many believed in his name because they saw the signs that he was doing" (2:23). That is, the storyteller describes the response of the people to Jesus' actions and words as a positive response of belief. This is in continuity with the positive responses of the people in the story of the Temple protest in both Mark and Luke (Mark 11:18b; Luke 19:48). The tradition of this story is a positive tradition of the people's affirmation of Jesus as a prophet who, like Jeremiah, exercises appropriate authority in protesting the perversion of the Temple. The probability is, therefore, that the storyteller presented the responses of the Jews to Jesus in a positive tone of inquiry and surprise rather than hostility. The fact that the storyteller extensively explains Jesus' comment to his/her audience (2:21–22) is an indication that the listeners were surprised and puzzled by Jesus' words. Thus, throughout this initial section of the Gospel, the Jews are presented as a group that is positively drawn to Jesus and the audience is addressed as Jews who are genuinely interested in Jesus.

After the story of the healing of the lame man at the pool of Bethzatha (5:1–15), there is a sudden and radical change in the identity of the audience that the storyteller as Jesus addresses. Jesus' speech to the audience as the

---

22. While Samaritans were not considered to be Jews in the first century, they were part of the tradition of Israel and, like Christians in a much later period, had been effectively separated from the Judean community. The author of the Fourth Gospel clearly includes Samaritans within the parameters of his projected audience and his understanding of "ecumenical Judaism" (see, e.g., Brown, *Community of the Beloved Disciple*, 34–48).

Jews following this healing story is by far the longest speech to this point in the story. It is introduced by this narrative comment: "For this reason the Jews were seeking all the more to kill him, because he was not only breaking the Sabbath, but was also calling God his own Father, thereby making himself equal to God" (John 5:18). In its context, this is a highly surprising comment. There has been no intimation earlier in the story of this degree of hostility toward Jesus. But it marks a major shift in the dynamics of audience address.

Following this radical and sudden shift, the audience is addressed as various groups of Jews who are variously drawn to Jesus and are repelled by him (John 5–12). Jesus' dialogue partners in this long section of the story are torn between believing in him and not believing in him. The narrator uses the word *schisma* three times (7:43; 9:16; 10:19) to describe this division in the response of Jesus' audiences. There is constant change in the specific identity of the character to whom Jesus is speaking in these stories: for example, as Jews who want to kill him (5), as the crowd and the disciples (6), as Jews who believe in him (8:31ff.), as Pharisees and then as Jews who took up stones to stone him (10:31ff), as Andrew and Philip (12:23–32), and frequently throughout this section as simply Jews. In this section of the Gospel (John 5–12), the audience is addressed as Jews who are constantly changing in their attitude and response to Jesus from total alienation to belief and everything in between.

Finally, there is another sudden change in the address to the audience with the story of Jesus' last supper. The climax of the speeches of Jesus to the audience is Jesus' long talk with the disciples after washing the disciples' feet (John 13–17). In this long speech, the audience is addressed as Jesus' disciples.

Thus, the structure of audience address in the Gospel as a whole is clearly marked and moves from Jesus addressing the audience as various groups of Jews who are drawn to him (John 1–4) to Jesus addressing the listeners as Jews who believe and don't believe in him (John 5–12) to Jesus addressing them as his disciples (John 13–17). In the course of hearing the whole story, therefore, the audience is invited to move in its relationship with Jesus from being Jews who are positively drawn to him (John the Baptist, Andrew/Simon Peter/Philip/Nathanael, the wedding guests in Cana, the crowd in the Temple, Nicodemus, the Samaritan woman and the Samaritans), to Jews who are violently torn between belief and unbelief, to disciples who have entered into a highly intimate relationship of mutuality and love with Jesus.

This structure of audience address is a distinctive feature of John's story. In the Synoptics, most of Jesus' long speeches are addressed to the audience as the crowds or the disciples. The interactions with his opponents are usually short and do not create the same depth of audience identification with the characters who are being addressed by Jesus. This is both because the audience does not have time to identify with the characters being addressed in short speeches and because the operative norms of judgment in relation to these characters are less sympathetic.

For example, in Mark's conflict stories of Jesus in the Temple (Mark 11–12), the storyteller as Jesus addresses the parable of the wicked tenants to the audience as the chief priests, scribes and elders. It is the longest address to the audience as Jesus' opponents in the Gospel of Mark (the other long speech in Mark 7:6–13 addressed the Pharisees' concerns about the cleanliness laws). But the dynamics of the speech do not create a high degree of identification with the Jewish authorities, who remain more emotionally distant. Both of the long speeches of Jesus in Mark are addressed to the audience as his disciples (those around him with the twelve in Mark 4:10–32; the four in Mark 13:5–37). *But there is nothing in the Synoptics like the progressive and clearly demarcated structure of audience address in John.*

Another way of describing the patterns of audience address is the frequency of each of the characters that the audience is invited to become in interaction with the storyteller and his principle character. For the purposes of this analysis, a "long" speech is a speech that is more than one verse. In the seventeen long speeches of Jesus, the audience is addressed as . . .

- "The crowd" three times: the feeding of the five thousand (John 6:26–27, 32–33) the Feast of Tabernacles (John 7:21–24), and the triumphal entry (John 12:30–36);

- "The Jews" three times: the feeding of the five thousand (John 6:43–59), the Feast of Tabernacles (John 7:16–19), and the Temple Festival (John 10:25–30);

- Pharisees three times: explicitly at the feast of Tabernacles (John 8:12, 14–18) and the healing of the man born blind (John 9:41—10:12), and implicitly in the dialogue with Nicodemus (John 3:1–21);

- Jews who want to kill or stone him three times: the healing of the crippled man on the Sabbath (John 5:19–40), the Feast of Tabernacles (John 8:48–58), and the festival of Dedication (John 10:31–38);

- Jews who believe in him, one time: at the Feast of Tabernacles (John 8:23–47);

- Disciples four times: the Samaritan woman (John 4:32–38), the feeding of the five thousand (John 6:61–65), Philip and Andrew (John 12:23–28), and the last supper/footwashing (John 13–17).

Thus, there are seventeen extended speeches of Jesus addressed to the audience as characters in the story: thirteen to a range of Jewish groups and four to the disciples. The speech to the disciples at the last supper is the longest and most emotionally intense speech in the Gospel (John 13–17). In the whole Gospel leading up to the passion narrative, therefore, thirteen of the seventeen extended speeches of Jesus are addressed to the audience as various groups of Jews who are torn between believing and not believing. By far the most frequent interaction between the storyteller and the audience is between the character of Jesus and the audience as groups of Jews who are struggling with whether or not to believe in him.

When heard in the context of the history of Johannine interpretation, the first striking dimension of the audience address is that all of these characters are identified explicitly as Jews. The only characters who are not explicitly named as Jews are "the crowd," "the disciples," the Samaritans, and the Greeks (John 12:20). But "the crowd" is clearly identified as Jews who were fed (John 6:24, 41) or were in Jerusalem (e.g., John 11: 35). "The disciples" are likewise identified as Jews (John 1:47). The Samaritans would be Jews except for the hostility that separates the two groups. And the Greeks are never addressed. That is, there are no non-Jews who are addressed in the interactions of the storyteller and the audience. The audience is never addressed as a character other than various groups of Jews. Throughout the story, the storyteller as Jesus always addresses the audience as Jews. The structure of Jesus' speeches moves from speeches to various groups of Jews who are interested in him, to Jews who are conflicted about believing in him or being hostile toward him, to his long talk with the audience as his Jewish disciples. Furthermore, the audience is never addressed as believing members of churches. Thus, in order to participate fully in the hearing of the story, the audiences of the Gospel, regardless of their actual ethnic or religious identity, must imaginatively become Jews. The audience is most frequently addressed as Jews who are torn between believing and not believing in Jesus.

The treatment of non-Jews in the Gospel is also significant. Other than Pilate and the Roman soldiers who divide Jesus' garments, the only non-Jews in the Gospel are the Samaritans and perhaps the Greeks who come to Philip. The audience is addressed as Samaritans in the story of the Samaritan woman. The Samaritans are treated in the Gospel as "separated" Israelites whose conversion to belief in Jesus is presented as a kind of re-conversion and reconciliation with the Jewish religious tradition. A sign of this is Jesus' address to the audience as Samaritans (John 4:21–24) in which Jesus states that a time is coming when the ethnic divisions between Jews and Samaritans will be transcended into a new religious community based on a common spirit. The Greeks, on the other hand, remain anonymous, make only one request to Philip, and disappear from the story. Jesus never talks to them in the story and the audience is never addressed as Greeks. Furthermore, the Greeks' request to see Jesus is the implicit cause of Jesus' recognition that the hour of his death has come. If anything, the story of the Greeks reinforces the ethnic identification of the audience as Jews.

The inevitable question that arises from the structures of audience address is whether there is any relationship between this structure and the actual historical audiences of the Fourth Gospel. In order to understand the Gospel of John in its original medium, we need to imagine a series of performance events in which audiences gathered to hear the story told by a storyteller or read from a manuscript. We have only indirect evidence about the identity of those audiences. But we have direct evidence from the script of the performances about how the audiences were addressed by the storyteller. The audiences of the Gospel of John were always spoken to as Jews who are drawn to Jesus, but conflicted about believing that he was the Messiah. The structure of the addresses to the audience also has an unambiguous structure in which the audience is addressed first as Jews (followers of John the Baptist, common folk, Pharisees, and Samaritans) who are drawn to him, and many of whom (Andrew, Simon Peter, Philip, Nathanael, many in Jerusalem, the Samaritan woman and many in her village, the father and household of the sick son in Capernaum) believe in him. Subsequently the audience is addressed as Jews who are torn between believing in him and wanting to kill him. Lastly, the audience is addressed as his disciples. *The most natural conclusion from this data is, first of all, that the Gospel was structured for performances to audiences of Jews. Second, this data would indicate that the primary Jewish audiences of the Fourth Gospel were persons who were conflicted about belief in Jesus rather than being members of believing communities.*

When heard in the context of current conclusions about the audience of the Gospel, the structure of audience address does not correspond with or support the conclusion that the Gospel was addressed to John's church or to the wider circle of churches in the eastern Mediterranean as envisioned, for example, by Richard Bauckham and his collaborators (Bauckham, 1998). The central section of John's story is addressed to Jews who are profoundly conflicted about Jesus and many of whom are initially strongly opposed to him. The structure of the storyteller's addresses to the audience invites the listeners to move *from* identification with those who want to kill Jesus *to* identification with those who abide in his love. This structure indicates that the audiences needed to go through a process of confrontation and change in order to hear the speeches of Jesus to his disciples at the last supper

sympathetically. The audiences of the Gospel in its final form are not addressed as persons who already believe that Jesus is the Messiah. They are
addressed as Jews who *may* come to believe that Jesus is the Messiah and
become his followers.

This dynamic of internal conflict in the audiences of the Gospel is reflected at several points in the Gospel by the storyteller's description of the
responses of Jesus' audiences. One of the techniques of audience inclusion
in storytelling is to name the responses that members of the audience are
having to the story as it is being told. This happens first in Jesus' speech after
the feeding of the 5000. After Jesus' statements about being the bread of life,
the storyteller describes the response of the Jews:

> Then the Jews began to complain about him because he said, "I
> am the bread that came down from heaven." They were saying,
> "Is not this Jesus, the son of Joseph, whose father and mother we
> know? How can he now say, 'I have come down from heaven?'"
> (John 6:41–42)

A little later in the story, the storyteller reports another audience response:
"The Jews then disputed among themselves, saying, 'How can this man give
us his flesh to eat?'" (John 6:52). The storytelling function of these statements is to name the responses that people *in the audience* are having to
Jesus' words.

This technique of naming the audience's response happens even more
explicitly later in the story:

> When they heard these words, some in the crowd said, "This is
> really the prophet." Others said, "This is the Messiah." But some
> asked, "Surely the Messiah does not come from Galilee, does
> he? Has not the Scripture said the Messiah is descended from
> David and comes from Bethlehem, the village where David
> lived?" So there was a division in the crowd because of him."
> (John 7:40–44)

This naming of the divisions that were happening in the audience
explicitly addresses the underlying question that the audience is asking
throughout the story, namely, is Jesus the Messiah? And some *in the storyteller's audience* were saying "Yes" and others were saying "No." The Johannine storyteller does this again when he names the varied responses of his
audience to the story of the man born blind and of Jesus' speech to them as
the Pharisees:

> Again the Jews were divided because of these words. Many of
> them were saying, "He has a demon and is out of his mind. Why

listen to him?" Others were saying, "These are not the words of
one who has a demon. Can a demon open the eyes of the blind?"
(10:19–21)

These statements are in effect quotations of the divided responses of segments of John's audiences to the dynamics of the story as it progresses.

The addresses to the audience of the fourth Gospel indicate, therefore,
that we can most appropriately imagine this story as having been performed
for diaspora Jewish communities in the cities and towns of the Hellenistic
world of the Roman empire. That diaspora Jews may have been open to listening to the Evangelist perform his gospel accords well with recent studies
that point not to a decisive "parting of the ways" towards the end of the first
century but to continued intermingling of Jewish Jesus-believers and other
Jews as well as of Jews with pagans at least into the fourth century.[23] Paula
Fredriksen writes, "As with contemporary Mediterranean paganism, much
of ancient Jewish religious activity (dancing, singing, communal eating,
processing, and—as Chrysostom mentions with some irritation—building
and feasting in *sukkot*) occurred out-of-doors, inviting and accommodat-
ing the participation of interested outsiders."[24] This kind of religious activity
provided ample opportunities for the performance of a story such as the
fourth Gospel.

The Medium of John and Martyn's Two-Level Drama

In this context, it may be possible to reconceive the implications of Martyn's two-level drama for understanding the impact of the Fourth Gospel.
If the Gospel was a story performed for audiences in the late first century
rather than an imagined drama, the two levels of the story's meaning were
equally present. In fact, Martyn's "two-level" hypothesis makes the interactions of the audiences and the performers of the Gospel more explicit.
The dynamics Martyn defines are descriptive at two levels, the responses
of Jesus' audiences in the early 30s and the responses of John's audiences
in the 90s. However, this is not a "two-level drama" in which characters in
the Jesus story *represent* the people in John's setting. Instead the responses
of the audiences in the stories of Jesus *are* the responses of John's audiences.
To state this more specifically, as John composed his story, he anticipated
that his audiences and the audiences of the others who told his story would
respond in these complex ways. And the probability is that he was right

23. Becker and Reed, eds. *The Ways That Never Parted*, 4–5, 23.
24. Fredriksen, "What Parting of the Ways?," 51.

about his projections. At the very least, the script of the story indicates that this was what he anticipated and built into his story. Furthermore, to return to the question of the identity of the Johannine audiences, the responses of extreme conflict about whether or not Jesus is the Messiah are not the audience responses that a storyteller would build into a story that is directed to a community of believers. These responses resonated with audiences that were wrestling with the question of Jesus' messianic identity, not those who had already answered the question affirmatively.

However, Martyn's description of the dynamics of the "two-level drama" also enables us to identify even more specifically the people who were present in the audiences of John's story. All of the elements of John's context and the discussions that John was having with Jews in his context that Martyn has identified are descriptive of the interactions that are implicit in the performance of John's Gospel. The probability is that the participants in those discussions or their representatives were present in the audiences for whom John's Gospel was performed. Thus, at any one performance of the Gospel in a diaspora city such as Alexandria, the audience might have included common people of the Jewish community, representatives of the Jamnia Academy, experts in midrash who wanted midrashic proofs of Jesus' identity as Messiah, Jewish followers who believed that Jesus was the Mosaic Prophet-Messiah but not the Son of Man/Son of God, secret believers in Jesus as Messiah/Son of God who were still part of the synagogue community, believers who had been expelled from the Jewish community and were part of the local Christian community, members of the Baptist and Samaritan communities, and Jewish Christians of John's community.

The identification of John's medium as performances of the story for a wide range of Jewish communities in the great cities of the Diaspora—Rome, Ephesus, Antioch, and Alexandria—as well as the Jews of the reconquered Palestine, does require a significant change in our perception of the meaning of the Gospel from the imagined two-level drama in the minds of a small, sectarian community of already believing readers. But it also gives greater vitality to our understanding of the dynamic power of the Gospel when it was performed for ancient audiences. Furthermore, it provides clues for understanding the phenomenal growth of the early Christian community.[25]

Another dimension of the two-level drama that appears in a different light when the Fourth Gospel is conceived as a performed story is the role of the Johannine community. Rather than being the primary intended

---

25. Rodney Stark's sociological analysis of the growth of early Christianity identifies the late first-century Jewish diaspora community as the most probable source of the initial growth of the nascent Christian movement (Stark, *Rise of Christianity*, 49–71).

audience of the story, the community is an implied dimension of the identity and role of the storyteller/performer. In four places in the story, the performer speaks in the first person plural—"we"—in explicit reference to the community for whom he/she speaks (1:14, 16; 3:11; 4:22; 21:24). Not surprisingly, two of those instances are in the prologue and epilogue of the story. In the prologue, the storyteller says, "And the Word became flesh and dwelt among us and we have seen his glory . . . From his fullness we have all received." The referent of "we" is ambiguous here and can be taken to refer to humankind as well as to the community of believers. While the most natural referent is humankind, it is also clearly a reference to the community that is bearing witness to its experience and belief. In the epilogue, "we" refers unambiguously to the Johannine community: "This is the disciple who is testifying to these things and has written them, and we know that his testimony is true" (21:24). Here the storyteller presents him/herself as speaking for the community who is bearing witness to the truth of the original disciple's story.

The other usage of "we" in reference to the community occurs in Jesus' conversation with Nicodemus: "We speak of what we know and we bear witness to what we have seen, but you do not receive our testimony" (3:11). In this instance Jesus speaks for the believing community and addresses the community represented by Nicodemus. In each of these instances, the storyteller uses "we" to refer to the community who is speaking through this story. A further dimension of this pronoun is Jesus' use of "we" in his conversation with the Samaritan woman: "You worship what you do not know; we worship what we know, for salvation is from the Jews." In this instance, the storyteller as Jesus speaks for the community of the Jews in relation to the Samaritans. In the Gospel as a whole, therefore, the storyteller addresses the audience as a representative of wider communities, thrice as a representative of the Johannine community and once as a representative of the community of Jews.

Furthermore, this definition of the audience of the Gospel in no way excludes the Johannine community that Martyn identifies as the primary location of the Gospel's readers. It is highly probable that members of the Johannine community were present in the audiences of performances of the fourth Gospel to the wider Jewish community and that there were occasions when the story was told to communities of believers. The structure of audience address indicates, however, that the audiences of the Johannine communities were addressed as Jews who were conflicted about belief in Jesus as the Messiah. The members of the believing community were invited to enter again into the process of being drawn to Jesus while struggling with the meaning of his identity and his statements. Thus, believers were undoubtedly among the hearers of the Fourth Gospel but they were addressed as Jews who were wrestling with Jesus and the God he embodies, not as Christians who were already confirmed in their beliefs.

What then is the message of the Fourth Gospel? At the first level, the message of the Gospel is that Jesus is the Christ, the Son of God. This message is addressed directly to each listener by the storyteller at the end of the first resurrection appearance stories as the purpose of the Gospel: "But these are written so that you may believe that Jesus is the Christ, the Son of God, and that believing you may have life in his name" (John 20:31). Implicit in the story is a redefinition of what the Messiah will do and be.

There are also several subsidiary messages. First, there is the message that the chief priests have no authority because of their forfeiture of legitimacy in their statement: "We have no king but Caesar!" And it is worthy of note that they have lost their legitimacy according to Jewish norms of judgment. Their collaboration with the Romans is also directly connected with the denial of Jesus' legitimacy as King. Another subsidiary message implicit in the Pilate trial and the inscription on the cross (also present in Nathanael's first confession, John 1:49) is that Jesus is the King of the Jews (Israel) who died for the nation and the dispersed children of God (John 11:50–52). A related message is that all of the Jews are one community in Christ. This includes those in Palestine and those in the Diaspora—Baptists, Pharisees, Christian Jews, and Samaritans (John 17:21–23).

But at another level, the message of the Gospel is directly related to the medium of the Gospel. In the telling and hearing of the story, a relationship is formed between the storyteller and the audience. That relationship in turn becomes the means by which a relationship is established between Jesus and the listener. This relationship is established in the series of long speeches that are addressed to the audience by the storyteller as Jesus. Martyn's description of the role of the Paraclete suggests a still further dimension to this relationship:

> The paradox presented by Jesus' promise that his work on earth will be continued because he is going to the Father is "solved" by his return in the person of the Paraclete. *It is, therefore, precisely the Paraclete who creates the two-level drama.* One cannot fail to be impressed by the boldness with which John re-interprets the traditional motif of the coming of the Spirit. That is especially true when we recognize that in order for the Paraclete to create the two-level drama, he must look not only like Jesus, but also

like the Christian witness who is Jesus' "double" in that drama
. . ."[26]

Rephrased as a description of storytelling, when the story is told by the Christian witness, the Paraclete is known in and through the presence of the witness who tells the story. That is, the Gospel is *a two-level story* in which the presence of both Jesus and the Paraclete are experienced in the telling of the story. Rather than happening in the imagination of the reader, the encounter of the members of the audience with the character of Jesus and the Paraclete happens in the experience of engaged listening to the story. Martyn's account of the Paraclete implies that John would state this more boldly. John would testify that in the telling of the story, it is the Paraclete who speaks in and through the Christian witness.

The two levels of the story, the "once upon a time" level of the early 30s and the present time of the early performances of the Gospel in the 90s, are integral dimensions of the story's meaning. As Martyn writes, "These events to which John bears witness transpire on both the *einmalig* and the contemporary levels of the drama, or they do not transpire at all."[27] If we substitute "story" for "drama," we have an accurate description of the multifaceted character of the impact of John in its original medium. For the audiences of the Gospel, the performance of John's story of Jesus was an experience of the "real presence" of Christ in their time and place.

The central meaning of the Gospel was then the relationship that the Gospel created between the members of the audience and the character of Jesus. The various conceptual dimensions of Jesus' identity as the Son of God, as the Son of Man, and as a messianic prophet-Messiah like Moses rather than as a Messiah like David added to the richness of the audience's experience of the character of Jesus. But these are dimensions of the relationship of the members of the audience with Jesus who is embodied by the teller of the story. It is hoped, therefore, that the richness of Martyn's insights into the dynamics of the Fourth Gospel in its original context will be deepened and enhanced by the reconception of the Gospel as a story performed for audiences.

The Reconception of the Gospel of John

This reconception of the medium of John requires, however, a sharp distinction between the meaning of the Gospel as it has been defined by the

26. Martyn, *History and Theology,* 140.
27. Martyn, *History and Theology,* 151.

exegesis of John's story as experienced by individual readers of the Gospel manuscript and the exegesis of the story as experienced by audiences of performances of the Gospel. Three specific dimensions of this reconception can be identified here: 1) the framework of the Gospel's meaning for audiences rather than readers; 2) the centrality of relationship as well as belief in the Gospel's message; and 3) the impossibility of the meaning of the story being anti-Jewish.

When analyzed as a text read by silent readers, the primary framework of meaning is the theological ideas that happen in the minds of readers who are looking at the manuscript with their eyes. In this medium, the dominant meaning is conceptual. In the medium of print read in silence the characters of John's story tend to be perceived as standing for or representing ideas and beliefs. That is, in addition to representing the groups of persons on the contemporary level of John's community—the Jamnia loyalists, the secret believers, the believing Jews who have been expelled from the synagogue—they also represent beliefs. The Jews represent unbelief, Nicodemus and his cohorts represent belief compromised by fear of excommunication. The Samaritan woman, the man born blind, Mary and Martha, and the disciples represent belief in various stages of formation. That is, the characters represent various dimensions of the theological beliefs that are interacting within the story. The history of exegesis of John's text has been primarily occupied with the identification of the interplay of those theological dynamics.

However, when the text is analyzed as a composition performed for audiences, the primary framework of meaning is the relationship that is established between the performer as a believing witness, Jesus as the main character and primary speaker, and the audience. The performer's goal is to establish a relationship between the audience as individual listeners and Jesus. The performer's story creates and invites the listener into a multi-faceted relationship between Jesus and the audience. A central facet of this relationship is a long and sustained intellectual engagement in a complex, evolving argument about Jesus' actions and their significance in relation to his identity, his relationship to God, and his role in the salvation of the world. For the listeners who became engaged in this argument, part of the fascination of the Gospel was this long and complex dialogue.

Following the moves of this argument was like the demands for an ancient listener who engaged the dialogues of Plato. As with listening to Socrates, listening to Jesus required a facile and perceptive mind in order to perceive and understand what is going on in his interactions with his various Jewish dialogue partners. Thus, a dimension of the meaning of the Gospel for a sympathetic listener was the recognition that Jesus is a major thinker, a Rabbi of substance, who invites at the very least intellectual respect and at most intellectual consent. Thus, the theological complexity of the Fourth Gospel was experienced by the audiences of the story as an encounter with the mind of Jesus.

Second, the story creates a relationship with the character of Jesus that invites each listener to experience growing intimacy with him. If entered into fully, that relationship ends in a profound bond of love. The emotional flow of John's story begins with the initial attraction to Jesus that is established with the storyteller's opening poem celebrating the coming of the *logos*. The *logos* is given a more human face in the exuberant responses to his presence by first John the Baptist, and then Andrew, Simon, Philip and Nathanael. The wild and instant enthusiasm of the disciples reaches its pinnacle of delightful confession in Nathanael's explosion of joy: "Rabbi, you are the Son of God! You are the King of Israel!" (John 1:49). These initial responses of surprising delight are deepened in the stories of his initial "signs" at the wedding in Cana, in the cleansing of the Temple, in his dialogues with Nicodemus and the Samaritan woman, and in the healing of the royal official's son. This opening section of the story has a dynamic not unlike the initial fascination of a new love relationship. Jesus is a wonderfully fascinating character who both fulfills the long-held hopes of the listeners and utterly confounds them by his unprecedented freedom.

This relationship is tested and deepened further in Jesus' long and highly conflictual debates with Jews who are torn between believing in him and being completely alienated from him. In these stories and long speeches (John 5–12) the dynamics of emotional distance in relation to the character of Jesus swing wildly from a high degree of sympathetic identification to total alienation in response to Jesus' incredibly provocative statements and actions. This section culminates in the raising of Lazarus and Jesus' direct invitation to the listener to believe in him (John 12:44–50). The relational dynamic of this section is analogous to an engagement in which a relationship is both tested and deepened by conflict.

The culmination of this growing relationship of love between the listener and the character of Jesus happens in the listener's inclusion as an actual participant in Jesus' last evening with his beloved disciples. In this dialogue (John 13–17) the intimacy of a loving relationship is firmly established. The dynamics of distance in this section are consistently positive in relation to Jesus. While he continues to make enigmatic statements, the speech ends with Jesus' prayer for the audience as his disciples. This section of the story is unambiguously intimate and is analogous to the relational dynamic of a happy and fulfilling marriage. That intimate relationship is the emotional context for the vicarious engagement in the story of Jesus' suffering, death and resurrection.

The centrality of this relationship of love for the dynamic structure of the Gospel is confirmed by the concluding dialogue of Jesus with Peter by the Sea of Tiberias (John 21:15–19). The final composer of the Gospel as we have received it probably added this story to the earlier ending of Thomas' climactic wrestling between unbelief and belief and the storyteller's statement to the audience that the purpose of the story has been that "you" would come to believe. The three-fold question to Simon Peter—"Do you love me?"—is addressed to the listener who identifies with Peter. Ending the story with Jesus' dialogue with Peter refocuses the central issue of the Gospel from belief to love. In the end, the story's long-term meaning for many listeners will be determined to a greater degree by the listener's response to Jesus' questions about love rather than about issues of belief.

Finally, in the context of hearing the Gospel as a performance, the Fourth Gospel was *not* anti-Jewish.[28] It is simply impossible that a story addressed to Jewish audiences would have been anti-Jewish. The Gospel of John, like the entire corpus of the Hebrew Scriptures, reflects a broad range of Jewish belief and practice as well as major conflicts between various Jewish groups. It is engaged in a major conflict with the Pharisees of the Jamnia Academy who were radically narrowing the definition of what it meant to be Jewish and were expelling those who accepted Jesus as Messiah from the Jewish community. But this conflict, while resulting in a catastrophic division in the house of Israel that remains in place, was an intra-Jewish conflict in which both contestants appealed to widely accepted Israelite norms and practices, specifically authentic succession to the Mosaic tradition. Such conflict is present throughout Israel's history prior to the first century of the coexistence of what later became Judaism and Christianity.

Audience Address and the Anti-Jewish Reading of the Fourth Gospel

The dynamics of audience address may provide a window through which light may shine on a dark corner of history. If the Gospel of John was originally addressed to late first-century Jews and was structured to appeal for

---

28. For the dominant position that the Fourth Gospel was anti-Jewish in its original context, see, for example, the collection of papers for the Leuven Colloquium in 2000, *Anti-Judaism and the Fourth Gospel.* Among these papers, the position of Martinus De Boer is most congruent with the conclusions here: "the peculiar Johannine use of the term 'the Jews' probably emerged in a debate *not with* but *within* the synagogue (between Jews who embraced Jesus as the expected Jewish Messiah and those who did not) about Jewish identity, i.e., about whether Christian Jews could properly be regarded as genuine 'disciples of Moses'" (DeBoer, "*Depiction*," 279).

belief in Jesus as the Messiah, how is it possible that it has come to be read as an anti-Jewish document? Several changes in the relationship of this story to its audiences have taken place that may shed light on this question. The first development has been that the actual audiences of the Gospel have changed in their self-definition. The audiences who hear the performances of the fourth Gospel have become predominantly Christian. Rather than being performed for audiences of Jews in the diaspora communities of the Roman empire, the Gospel has been read in the liturgies of Christian churches for congregations who do not think of themselves as Jews. As a result, the references to the Jews in the Gospel have changed in their meaning from being addressed to "us" to being descriptions of "them." Rather than hearing Jesus' speeches as being addressed to the various factions in "our" community, Jesus' speeches have been heard as addressed to "their" community. The only part of the Gospel that has been heard as addressed to "us" is Jesus' final speech to the disciples (John 13–17). Thus, later audiences of the Fourth Gospel have thought of themselves not as Jews, but as Christians.

The character of the performances has also changed. Rather than being performed as a long story, the Gospel has been read in short fragments. As a result, the dynamic structure of audience address has been interrupted and has been no longer experienced. No longer did audiences experience an intense and deepening relationship with Jesus as the main character of the story that moved from initial interest through intense conflict to intimacy and commitment. In fact, the Gospel has rarely, if ever, been heard as a whole. Other dimensions of the performances have also changed. The story came to be performed in cathedrals for large audiences rather than in small, more intimate settings. In that context, it has been virtually impossible to experience the character of Jesus as speaking directly to the audience in a manner that invites response and interaction. Jesus' words have been increasingly experienced as theological pronouncements rather than elements of a passionate conversation.

Furthermore, in the course of the centuries of the Christian church, the stories of the Gospel have come to be interpreted as encoded theology. In the aftermath of Origen's systematic reinterpretation of the Bible, allegorical interpretation became the dominant hermeneutical system. As a result, the characters of the Fourth Gospel were interpreted as allegorical representatives of doctrinal positions. It was in this context that "the Jews" came to be experienced as an allegorical character representing disbelief. As a result, the dynamics of distance in the audience's experience of the Jewish characters with whom Jesus interacted shifted from identification to alienation.

Especially in the aftermath of the mass printing of the Gospel, a primary audience of the Gospel has become readers rather than listeners. In private reading, the audience of the Gospel has shifted from communal audiences to individual readers. One result of that shift is that the Gospel text has become the object of study in which all of the parts of the document have been seen as equally indicative of the theology of the evangelist without regard for their place in the dynamic structure of the Gospel as a whole. In this context, the Gospel was rarely read as a diachronic whole but primarily as synchronic fragments of text.

Finally, the most radical change in the medium of the Fourth Gospel has been that it moved from the world of sound into the textual world of silence. In that world, the audiences of the Gospel have no longer heard the story with their ears but have read it only with their eyes. As a result of this development, the Gospel has been deconstructed as a story told to audiences by committed performers into a series of documentary fragments read either by silent readers or by lectors who perform these short episodes for Christian congregations in an emotionally detached manner. An additional dimension of this deconstruction of the original medium is that the Gospel of John has become a source document for scientific examination of its theological and historical data by an audience of objective readers who actively resist the invitations of the story to identify with the characters and to respond to the implicit addresses to the listeners.

All of these changes in the dynamics of audience address in the experience of the fourth Gospel have been factors in the reading of the Gospel as anti-Jewish. Thus, the radical change in the meaning and message of the Gospel that has happened over the last two thousand years is connected with radical changes in the medium of the Gospel. In as far as our goal is to understand and interpret the Fourth Gospel in its original historical context, it is essential to hear the story as performed for audiences that were predominantly composed of late first-century Hellenistic Jews.

Bibliography

Achtemeier, Paul J. "*Omne verbum sonat*: The New Testament and the Oral Environment of Late Western Antiquity." *JBL* 109 (1990) 3–27.

Ackerman, Diane. *A Natural History of the Senses*. New York: Random House, 1990.

Aland, Kurt. "Bemerkungen zum Schluss des Markusevangeliums." In *Neotestamentica et Semitica: Studies in Honour of Matthew Black*, 157–80. Edinburgh: T. & T. Clark, 1969.

———. "Der wiedergefundene Markusschluss? Eine methodologische Bemerkung zur textkritischen Arbeit." *ZTK* 67 (1970) 3–13.

Alexander, Loveday. "The Living Voice: Scepticism Towards the Written Word in Early Christian and in Graeco-Roman Texts." In *The Bible in Three Dimensions: Essays in Celebration of Forty Years of Biblical Studies in the University of Sheffield*, edited by David J. A. Clines et al., 221–47. JSOTSup 87. Sheffield: JSOT Press, 1987.

Allen, W. C. "St. Mark 16:8. 'They were afraid.' Why?" *JTS* 47 (1946) 46–49.

———. "Fear in St. Mark." *JTS* 48 (1947) 201–3.

Argyle, Aubrey W. "Did Jesus Speak Greek?" *Expository Times* 67 (1955) 91–93.

Aristotle. *The Poetic*. Cambridge: Harvard University Press, 1953.

Augustine. *The Confessions of Saint Augustine*. Translated by E. B. Pusey. Gutenberg Project. https://www.gutenberg.org/files/3296/3296-h/3296-h.htm#link2H_4_0006.

Baines, John. "Literacy (ANE)." In *ABD*, 4:333–37.

Balogh, Josef. "*Voces Paginarum*: Beiträge zur Geschichte des lauten Lesens und Schreibens." *Philologus* 82 (1926) 84–109, 202–40.

Balz, H. "φοβέω." In *Theological Dictionary of the New Testament* 9 (1974) 211.

Barbour, R. S. *Traditio-Historical Criticism of the Gospels*. London: SPCK, 1972.

Barrett, C. K. *The Gospel of John and Judaism*. Translated by D. M. Smith. Philadelphia: Fortress, 1975.

Bartholomew, Gilbert L. "Feed My Lambs: John 21:15–19 as Oral Gospel." *Semeia* 39 (1987) 69–96.

Bartsch, H. W. "Der Schluss Markusevangeliums: Ein überlieferungsgeschichtliches Problem." *Theologische Zeitschrift* 27 (1971) 241–54.

Batey, Richard. *Jesus and the Forgotten City: New Light on Sepphoris and the Urban World of Jesus*. Grand Rapids: Eerdmans, 1991.

Bauckham, Richard. "For Whom Were Gospels Written?" In *The Gospels for All Christians: Rethinking the Gospel Audiences*, edited by Richard Bauckham, 9–48. Grand Rapids: Eerdmans, 1998.

Bauckham, Richard, ed. *The Gospels for All Christians: Rethinking the Gospel Audiences.* Grand Rapids: Eerdmans, 1998.

Becker, Adam H., and Annette Yoshiko Reed, eds. *The Ways That Never Parted: Jews and Christians in Late Antiquity and the Early Middle Ages.* 2003. Reprint, Minneapolis: Fortress, 2007.

Best, Ernest. *Mark: The Gospel as Story.* Edinburgh: T. & T. Clark, 1983.

———. "Mark's Readers: A Profile." In *The Four Gospels 1992: Festschrift Frans Neirynck,* edited by F. Van Segbroeck et al., 2.839–58. Bibliotheca ephemeridum theologicarum lovaniensium 100. Leuven: Leuven University Press, 1992.

Birdsall, J. N. Review of W. R. Farmer, *The Last Twelve Verses of Mark. JTS* 26 (1975) 151–60.

Birk, Newman P., and Genevieve B. Birk. *Understanding and Using English.* 3rd ed. New York: Odyssey, 1958.

Blass, Friedrich Wilhelm, Albert Debrunner, and Robert W. Funk. *Greek Grammar of the New Testament.* Chicago: University of Chicago Press, 1961.

Bode, Edward Lynn. *The First Easter Morning: The Gospel Accounts of the Women's Visit to the Tomb of Jesus.* Analecta biblica 45. Rome: Pontifical Biblical Institute, 1970.

Boomershine, Thomas E. "Mark, the Storyteller. A Rhetorical-Critical Investigation of Mark's Passion and Resurrection Narrative." PhD diss., Union Theological Seminary, 1974.

———. *The Messiah of Peace: A Performance-Criticism Commentary on Mark's Passion-Resurrection Narrative.* BPCS 12. Eugene, OR: Cascade Books, 2015.

———. *Story Journey: An Invitation to the Gospels as Storytelling.* Nashville: Abingdon, 1988.

Booth, Wayne. *The Rhetoric of Fiction.* Chicago: University of Chicago Press, 1961.

Bousset, Wilhelm. *Kyrios Christos: A History of the Belief in Christ from the Beginnings of Christianity to Irenaeus.* Translated by John E. Steely. Nashville: Abingdon, 1970.

Braun, Herbert. *Jesus of Nazareth: The Man and His Time.* Translated by Everett R. Kalin. Philadelphia: Fortress, 1979.

Brown, Raymond E. *The Community of the Beloved Disciple.* New York: Paulist, 1979.

———. *The Gospel according to John.* Garden City, NY: Doubleday, 1966.

———. *Introduction to the New Testament.* Anchor Bible Reference Library. New York: Doubleday, 1997.

Brynie, Faith Hickman. *Brain Sense: The Science of the Senses and How We Process the World around Us.* New York: American Management Association, 2009.

Bultmann, Rudolf. *Theology of the New Testament.* 2 vols. Translated by Kendrick Grobel. New York: Scribner, 1951–1955.

———. *The History of the Synoptic Tradition.* Translated by John Marsh. New York: Harper & Row, 1968.

Carey, James W. *Communication as Culture: Essays on Media and Society.* Boston: Unwin Hyman, 1989.

Carr, David M. *Writing on the Tablet of the Heart: Origins of Scripture and Literature.* New York: Oxford University Press, 2005.

Carson, D. A. "The Purpose of the Fourth Gospel: John 20:31 Reconsidered." *JBL* 106 (1987) 639–651.

Charlesworth, James H., ed. *The Old Testament Pseudepigrapha.* 2 vols. Garden City, NY: Doubleday, 1983, 1985.

Chatman, Seymour. *Story and Discourse: Narrative Structure in Fiction and Film.* Ithaca, NY: Cornell University Press, 1978.

Collins, Adela Yarbro. *Mark: A Commentary.* Hermeneia. Minneapolis: Fortress, 2007.

Corbett, E. P. J., ed. *Rhetorical Analyses of Literary Works.* New York: Oxford University Press, 1969.

Creed, J. M. "The Conclusion of the Gospel according to Saint Mark." *JTS* 31 (1930) 175–80.

Crossan, John Dominic. "Empty Tomb and Absent Lord." In *The Passion in Mark: Studies on Mark 14–16,* edited by Werner H. Kelber, 135–52. Philadelphia: Fortress, 1976.

———. *The Historical Jesus: The Life of a Mediterranean Jewish Peasant.* San Francisco: Harper, 1991.

———. "Mark and the Relatives of Jesus." *Novum Testamentum* 15 (1973) 81–113.

Crowley, Daniel J. *I Could Tell Old-Story Good: Creativity in Bahamian Folklore.* Berkeley: University of California Press, 1966.

Croy, N. Clayton. *The Mutilation of Mark's Gospel.* Nashville: Abingdon, 2003.

Czitrom, Daniel J. *Media and the American Mind: From Morse to McLuhan.* Chapel Hill: University of North Carolina Press, 1982.

Daniélou, Jean. *The Theology of Jewish Christianity.* Translated and edited by John A. Baker. Philadelphia: Westminster, 1977.

Danker, Frederick W., ed. *A Greek–English Lexicon of the New Testament and Other Early Christian Literature.* 3rd ed. Chicago: University of Chicago Press, 2000.

Danove, Paul L. *The End of Mark's Story: A Methodological Study.* Biblical Interpretation Series 3. Leiden: Brill, 1993.

Davis, Henry Grady. *Design for Preaching.* Philadelphia: Fortress, 1958.

De Boer, Martinus C. "The Depiction of 'the Jews' in John's Gospel: Matters of Behavior and Identity." In *Anti-Judaism and the Fourth Gospel: Papers of the Leuven Colloquium, 2000,* edited by Riemund Bieringer et al., 260–80. Jewish and Christian Heritage Series 1. Assen: Royal Van Gorcum, 2001.

Degh, Linda. *Folktales of Hungary.* Translated by Judit Halasz. Folktales of the World. Chicago: University of Chicago Press, 1965.

Delia, J. "Communication Research: A History." In *Handbook of Communication Science,* edited by Charles R. Berger and Steven H. Chaffee, 20–98. Newbury Park, CA: Sage, 1987.

Dewey, Joanna. "The Gospel of Mark as an Oral-Aural Event: Implications for Interpretation." In *The New Literary Criticism and the New Testament,* edited by Elizabeth Struthers Malbon and Edgar McKnight, 145–61. Journal for the Study of the New Testament Supplements 109. Sheffield: Sheffield Academic Press, 1994.

———. *The Oral Ethos of the Early Church: Speaking, Writing, and the Gospel of Mark.* BPCS 8. Eugene, OR: Cascade Books, 2013.

———. "Oral Methods of Structuring Narrative in Mark." *Interpretation* 43 (1989) 32–44.

———, ed. *Semeia 65: Orality and Textuality in Early Christian Literature.* 1994.

Dormeyer, Detlev. *Die Passion Jesu als Verhaltensmodell: Literarische und theologische Analyse der Traditions und Redaktionsgeschichte der Markuspassion.* Neutestamentliche Abhandlungen n.F. 11. Münster: Aschendorff, 1974.

Downing, F. Gerald. *The Christ and the Cynics: Jesus and Other Radical Preachers in First-Century Tradition.* JSOT Manuals 4. Sheffield: JSOT Press, 1988.

———. *Jesus and the Threat of Freedom.* London: SCM, 1987.

Eco, Umberto. *Travels in Hyperreality*. Translated by William Weaver. New York: Harcourt Brace Jovanovich, 1986.

Edwards, James R. *The Gospel according to Mark*. Pillar New Testament Commentary. Grand Rapids: Eerdmans, 2002.

Elliott, J. K. "The Text and Language of the Endings to Mark's Gospel." *Theologische Zeitschrift* 27 (1971) 255–62.

Farmer, W. R. *The Last Twelve Verses of Mark*. Society for New Testament Studies Monograph Series 25. Cambridge: Cambridge University Press, 1974.

Farrell, Thomas J. "An Overview of Walter J. Ong's Work." In *Media, Consciousness, and Culture: Explorations of Walter Ong's Thought*, edited by Bruce E. Gronbeck et al., 25–43. Newbury Park, CA: Sage, 1991.

Fielding, Henry. *Tom Jones*. www.gutenberg.org/ebooks/6593.

Finnegan, Ruth. *Limba Stories and Story-Telling*. Oxford Library of African Literature. Oxford: Clarendon, 1967.

Fiske, John. *Introduction to Communications Studies*. New York: Methuen, 1982.

Fitzmyer, Joseph A. *A Wandering Aramean: Collected Aramaic Essays*. SBL Monograph Series 25. Missoula, MT: Scholars, 1979.

————. *The Gospel according to Luke I–IX*. AB 28. Garden City, NY: Doubleday, 1981.

Fowler, Robert M. *Let The Reader Understand: Reader Response Criticism and the Gospel of Mark*. Minneapolis: Fortress, 1991.

————. "Who Is "the Reader" in Reader Response Criticism?" *Semeia* 31 (1985) 5–26.

Francis, Frank C. "Library." In *Encyclopaedia Britannica*, 10:856–67. London: Helen Hemingway Benton, 1980.

Fredricksen, Paula. "What 'Parting of the Ways'? Jews, Gentiles, and the Ancient Mediterranean City." In *The Ways That Never Parted: Jews And Christians in Late Antiquity and the Early Middle Ages,* edited by Adam H. Becker and Annette Yoshiko Reed, 35–64. 2003. Reprint, Minneapolis: Fortress, 2007.

Freedman, David Noel. "Pottery, Poetry and Prophecy: An Essay on Biblical Poetry." *JBL* 96 (1977) 5–26.

Frei, Hans. *The Eclipse of Biblical Narrative: A Study in Eighteenth and Nineteenth Century Hermeneutics*. New Haven: Yale University Press, 1974.

Fuller, Reginald H. *The Formation of the Resurrection Narratives*. New York: Macmillan, 1971.

Gamble, Harry Y. *Books and Readers in the Early Church: A History of Early Christian Texts*. New Haven: Yale University Press, 1995.

————. "Literacy and Book Culture." In *Dictionary of New Testament Background*, edited by Craig A. Evans and Stanley E. Porter, 644–48. Downers Grove, IL: InterVarsity Press, 2000.

Geldard, Frank A. *The Human Senses*. 2nd ed. New York: Wiley, 1972.

Gerhardsson, Birger. *Memory and Manuscript: Oral Tradition and Written Transmission in Rabbinic Judaism and Early Christianity*. Acta Seminarii Neotestamentici Upsaliensis 22. Lund: Gleerup, 1961.

Hadas, Moses. *Ancilla to Classical Reading*. New York: Columbia University Press, 1954.

————. *Hellenistic Culture: Fusion and Diffusion*. New York: Norton, 1972.

Hahn, Ferdinand. "Methodische Overlegungen zur Rückfrage nach Jesus." In *Rückfrage nach Jesus*, edited by K. Kertelge, 11–77. Munich: Kaiser, 1974.

————. *Mission in the New Testament*. Translated by Frank Clarke. Studies in Biblical Theology 1/47. Naperville, IL: Allenson, 1965.

Harnack, Adolf von. *Die Briefsammlung des Apostel Paulus*. Leipzig: Hinrichs, 1926

———. *Die Mission und Ausbreitung des Christentums in den ersten drei Jahrhunderten*. 4th ed. Leipzig: Hinrichs, 1924.

Harris, William V. *Ancient Literacy*. Cambridge: Harvard University Press, 1989.

Hartman, Lars. "On Reading Others' Letters." In *Christians Among Jews and Gentiles: Essays in Honor of Krister Stendahl*, edited by G. W. E. Nickelsburg and G. W. MacRae, 137–46. Philadelphia: Fortress, 1986.

Harvey, F. D. "Literacy in the Athenian Democracy." *Revue des etudes Greques* 79 (1966) 585–635.

Havelock, Eric A. *The Literate Revolution in Greece and Its Cultural Consequences*. Princeton: Princeton University Press, 1982.

———. *Preface to Plato*. Cambridge: Harvard University Press, 1963.

Hays, Richard B. *Echoes of Scripture in the Gospels*. Waco, TX: Baylor University Press, 2016.

Hearon, Holly E., and Philip Ruge-Jones, eds. *The Bible in Ancient and Modern Media: Story and Performance*. BPCS 1. Eugene, OR: Cascade Books, 2009.

Heitmüller, Wilhelm. "Züm Problem Paulus und Jesus." *ZNW* 13 (1912) 320–27.

———. "Hellenistic Christianity before Paul." In *The Writings of St. Paul*, edited by Wayne Meeks, 308–19. New York: Norton, 1972.

Hengel, Martin. "Hellenisierung als literarisches, philosophisches, sprachliches und religioses Problem" and "Die Obernahme griechischer Sprache und Bildung durch die jüdische Diaspora im ptolemaischen Agypten." In *Juden, Griechen und Barbaren: Aspekte der Hellenisierung des Judentums in vorchristlicher Zeit*, 94–115 and 126–44. Stuttgrader Bibelstudien 76. Stuttgart: Katholisches Bibelwerk, 1976.

———. *Judaism and Hellenism: Studies in Their Encounter in Palestine during the Hellenistic Period*. Translated by John Bowden. Philadelphia: Fortress, 1974.

———. "Mc 7, 3 πυγμη." *ZNW* 60 (1969) 192.

Horsley, Richard A. *Jesus and the Spiral of Violence: Popular Jewish Resistance in Roman Palestine*. New York: Harper & Row, 1987.

———. "A Prophet Like Moses and Elijah: Popular Memory and Cultural Patterns in Mark." In *Performing the Gospel: Orality, Memory, and Mark*, eds. Richard A. Horsley et al., 166–90. Minneapolis: Fortress, 2006.

Humphrey, J. H., ed. *Literacy in the Roman World*. Journal of Roman Archaeology Supplementary Series 3. Ann Arbor: University of Michigan Press, 1991.

Hurtado, Larry W. *Destroyer of the Gods: Early Christian Distinctiveness in the Roman World*. Waco, TX: Baylor University Press, 2016.

———. "Oral Fixation and New Testament Studies? 'Orality,' 'Performance' and Reading Texts in Early Christianity." *NTS* 60 (2014) 321–40.

Incigneri, Brian J. *The Gospel to the Romans: The Setting and Rhetoric of Mark's Gospel*. Biblical Interpretation Series 65. Leiden: Brill, 2003.

Innis, Harold. *The Bias of Communication*. Toronto: University of Toronto Press, 1951.

———. *Empire and Communications*. Toronto: University of Toronto Press, 1972.

Iser, Wolfgang. *The Implied Reader*. Baltimore: Johns Hopkins University Press, 1974.

Iverson, Kelly R., and Christopher W. Skinner, eds. *Mark as Story: Retrospect and Prospect*. Atlanta, SBL Press, 2011.

Jones, A. H. M. *The Greek City from Alexander to Justinian*. Oxford: Clarendon, 1940.

Jüthner, Julius. *Hellenen und Barbaren*. Leipzig: Teubner, 1923.

Kähler, Martin. *The So-Called Historical Jesus and the Biblical Christ of Faith.* Philadelphia: Fortress, 1964.

Käsemann, Ernst. *New Testament Questions of Today.* Translated by W. J. Montague. Philadelphia: Fortress, 1969.

Kee, Howard Clark. "Early Christianity in the Galilee: Reassessing the Evidence from the Gospels." In *The Galilee in Late Antiquity,* edited by Lee Levine, 3–22. New York: Jewish Theological Seminary, 1992.

Kelber, Werner H. *The Kingdom in Mark: A New Place and a New Time.* Philadelphia: Fortress, 1974.

———. *The Oral and the Written Gospel: The Hermeneutics of Speaking and Writing in the Synoptic Tradition, Mark, Paul and Q.* Philadelphia: Fortress, 1983.

———. *The Passion in Mark: Studies on Mark 14–16,* edited by Werner H. Kelber. Philadelphia: Fortress, 1976.

Klatzky, Roberta L. *Human Memory.* San Francisco: Freeman, 1975.

Klein, Ralph W. "Books of Ezra-Nehemiah." In *ABD,* 2:731–42.

Knox, W. L. "The Ending of St. Mark's Gospel." *Harvard Theological Review* 35 (1942) 13–23.

Kuby, A. "Zur Konzeption des Markus Evangeliums." *ZNW* 49 (1958) 52–64.

Kuhn, Thomas. *The Structure of Scientific Revolutions.* Chicago: University of Chicago Press, 1962.

Kümmel, Werner Georg. *The New Testament: The History of the Investigation of Its Problems.* Translated by S. McLean Gilmour and Howard Clark Kee. Nashville: Abingdon, 1972.

Lee, Margaret Ellen, and Bernard Brandon Scott. *Sound Mapping the New Testament.* Salem, OR: Polebridge, 2009.

Lee, Margaret Ellen, ed. *Sound Matters: New Testament Studies in Sound Mapping.* BPCS 16. Eugene, OR: Cascade Books, 2018.

Lévi-Strauss, Claude. *Tristes Tropiques.* Translated by John and Doreen Weightman. New York: Atheneum, 1973.

Lightfoot, R. H. *The Gospel Message of St. Mark.* London: Oxford University Press, 1962.

Lincoln, Andrew T. "The Promise and the Failure: Mark 16:7, 8." *JBL* 108 (1989) 283–300.

Linnemann, E. "Die Verleugnung des Petrus." *ZTK* 63 (1966) 1–32.

———. "Der (wiedergefundene) Markusschluss." *ZTK* 66 (1969) 255–87.

Lipman, Doug. *Improving Your Storytelling: Beyond the Basics for All Who Tell Stories in Work or Play.* Atlanta: August House, 1999.

———. *The Storytelling Coach: How to Listen, Praise, and Bring Out People's Best.* Atlanta: August House, 2006.

Lord, Albert Bates. *The Singer of Tales.* Cambridge: Harvard University Press, 1960.

Lowery, Shearon A., and Melvin L. DeFleur. *Milestones in Mass Communications Research: Media Effects.* New York: Longman, 1983.

Ludel, Jacqueline. *Introduction to Sensory Processes.* San Francisco: Freeman, 1978.

Lüdemann, Gerd. "The Successors of Pre-70 Jerusalem Christianity." In *Jewish and Christian Self-Definition,* vol. 1: *The Shaping of Christianity in the Second and Third Centuries,* edited by E. P. Sanders, 161–73, 245–54. Jewish and Christian Self-Definition. Philadelphia: Fortress, 1980.

Lubbock, Percy. *The Craft of Fiction.* London: Cape, 1921.

Maccoby, Hyam. *The Myth-maker: Paul and the Invention of Christianity.* New York: Harper & Row, 1986.

Macdonald, Dennis R. *The Homeric Epics and the Gospel of Mark.* New Haven: Yale University Press, 2000.

Mack, Burton L. *A Myth of Innocence: Mark and Christian Origins.* Philadelphia: Fortress, 1988.

MacMullen, Ramsay. *Roman Social Relations 50 B.C.–A.D. 284.* New Haven: Yale University Press, 1974.

Marcus, Joel. "The Jewish War and the *Sitz im Leben* of Mark." *JBL* 111 (1992) 441–62.

———. *Mark 1–8: A New Translation with Introduction and Commentary.* AB 27. Doubleday: New York, 2000.

———. *Mark 9–16: A New Translation with Introduction and Commentary.* AB 27A. New York: Doubleday, 2009.

Marrou, Henri Irenee. *A History of Education in Antiquity.* Madison: University of Wisconsin Press, 1982.

Martyn, J. Louis. *History and Theology in the Fourth Gospel.* New York: Harper & Row, 1968.

Marxsen, Willi. *Mark the Evangelist.* Translated by James Boyce et al. Nashville: Abingdon, 1969.

Maxey, James A. *From Orality to Orality: A New Paradigm for Contextual Translation of the Bible.* BPCS 2. Eugene, OR: Cascade Books, 2009.

Maxey, James A., and Ernst R. Wendland, eds. *Translating Scripture for Sound and Performance: New Directions in Biblical Studies.* BPCS 6. Eugene, OR: Cascade Books, 2012.

McLuhan, Marshall. *Understanding Media: The Extensions of Man.* New York: McGraw-Hill, 1964.

Meeks, Wayne. "The Man from Heaven." *JBL* 91 (1972) 44–72.

Meier, John P. *A Marginal Jew: Rethinking the Historical Jesus.* Vol. 1, *The Roots of the Problem and the Person.* Anchor Bible Reference Library. New York: Doubleday, 1991.

Meyers, Eric M., and James F. Strange. *Archeology, the Rabbis, and Early Christianity.* Nashville: Abingdon, 1981.

Millard, A. R. "Literacy (Israel)." In *ABD*, 4:337–40.

Momigliano, Arnaldo. *Alien Wisdom: The Limits of Hellenization.* Cambridge: Cambridge University Press, 1975.

Moulton, J. H., and W. F. Howard. *A Grammar of New Testament Greek.* Edinburgh: T. & T. Clark, 1968.

Mowinckel, Sigmund. *He That Cometh: The Messiah Concept in the Old Testament and Later Judaism.* Translated by G. W. Anderson. 1954. Reprint, Biblical Resource Series. Grand Rapids: Eerdmans, 2005

Muilenburg, James. "Form Criticism and Beyond." *JBL* 88 (1969) 1–18.

Nelson, William. "From 'Listen, Lordings' to 'Dear Reader.'" *University of Toronto Quarterly* 46 (1977) 110–24.

Neusner, Jacob. "Comparing Judaisms: Essay-Review of *Paul and Palestinian Judaism* by E. P. Sanders." *History of Religions* 18 (1978) 177–91.

———. *The Formation of the Jewish Intellect: Making Connections and Drawing Conclusions in the Traditional System of Judaism.* Brown Judaic Studies 151 Atlanta: Scholars, 1988.

————. *Invitation to the Talmud*. 2nd ed. San Francisco: Harper and Row, 1984.

————. *The Making of the Mind of Judaism: The Formative Age*. Brown Judaic Studies 133. Atlanta: Scholars, 1987.

————. *The Memorized Torah: The Mnemonic System of the Mishnah*. Brown Judaic Studies 96. Chico, CA: Scholars, 1985.

————. "Types and Forms in Ancient Jewish Literature: Some Comparisons." *History of Religions* 11 (1972) 354–90.

Niditch, Susan. *Oral World and Written Word*. Library of Ancient Israel. Louisville: Westminster John Knox,1996.

Nineham, D. E. *The Gospel of St. Mark*. Baltimore: Penguin, 1963.

Ong, Walter J. *Orality and Literacy: The Technologizing of the Word*. New Accents. New York: Methuen, 1982.

————. *The Presence of the Word: Some Prolegomena for Cultural and Religious History*. New Haven: Yale University Press, 1967.

————. "Text as Interpretation: Mark and After." In *Oral Tradition in Literature: Interpretation in Context*, edited by John Miles Foley, 147–69. Columbia: University of Missouri Press, 1986.

Overbeck, Franz. "Über die Anfänge der patristischen Literatur." *Historische Zeitschrift* 12 (1882) 417–72.

Pattison, Robert. *On Literacy: The Politics of the Word from Homer to the Age of Rock*. Oxford: Oxford University Press, 1982.

Petersen, Norman R. "When Is the End not the End? Literary Reflections on the Ending of Mark's Narrative." *Interpretation* 34 (1980) 151–66.

Quesnell, Quentin. *The Mind of Mark: Interpretation and Method through the Exegesis of Mark 6, 52*. Analecta biblica 38. Rome: Pontifical Biblical Institute Press, 1969.

Reinhartz, Adele. "John and Judaism: A Response to Burton Visotsky." In *Life in Abundance: Studies of John's Gospel in Tribute to Raymond E. Brown*, edited by John R. Donahue, 108–16. Collegeville, MN: Liturgical, 2005.

Rhoads, David. "Performance Criticism: An Emerging Methodology in Second Testament Studies—Part I." *Biblical Theology Bulletin* 36 (2006) 118–33.

————. "Performance Criticism: An Emerging Methodology in Second Testament Studies—Part II." *Biblical Theology Bulletin* 36 (2006) 164–84.

————. *Reading Mark, Engaging the Gospel*. Minneapolis: Fortress, 2004.

————. "What Is Performance Criticism?" In *The Bible in Ancient and Modern Media*, edited by Holly E. Hearon and Philip Ruge-Jones, 83–100. BPCS 1. Eugene, OR: Cascade Books, 2009.

Rhoads, David, and Joanna Dewey. "Performance Criticism: A Paradigm Shift in New Testament Studies." In *From Text to Performance: Narrative and Performance Criticisms in Dialogue and Debate*, edited by Kelly R. Iverson, 1–26. BPCS 10. Eugene, OR: Cascade Books, 2014.

Rhoads, David, Joanna Dewey, and Donald Michie. *Mark as Story: An Introduction to the Narrative of a Gospel*. 2nd ed. Minneapolis: Fortress, 1999.

————. *Mark as Story: An Introduction to the Narrative of a Gospel*. 3rd ed. Minneapolis: Fortress, 2012.

Roberts, Colin Henderson. *Manuscript, Society and Belief in Early Christian Egypt*. Oxford: Oxford University Press, 1979.

Rostovtzeff, M. *The Social and Economic History of the Roman Empire*. Revised by P. M. Fraser. 2nd ed. Oxford: Oxford University Press, 1957.

Ruge-Jones, Philip. "The Word Heard: How Hearing a Text Differs from Reading One." In *The Bible in Ancient and Modern Media: Story and Performance*, edited by Holly E. Hearon and Philip Ruge-Jones, 101–13. BPCS 1. Eugene, OR: Cascade Books, 2009.

Rutherford, William G. *A Chapter in the History of Annotation*. Scholia Aristophanica 3. New York: Macmillan, 1905.

Sanders, E. P. *Jesus and Judaism*. Philadelphia: Fortress, 1985.

———. "Jesus in Historical Context." *Theology Today* 50 (1993) 429–48.

———. *Judaism: Practice and Belief, 63 BCE–66 CE*. Philadelphia: Trinity, 1992.

Sandmel, Samuel. "Foreword for Jews." In *The Pseudepigrapha of the Old Testament*, edited by James H. Charlesworth, 1:xi–xiii. Garden City, NY: Doubleday, 1983.

Schenke, Ludger. *Auferstehungsverkündigung und leeres Grab: eine traditionsgeschichtliche Untersuchung von Markus 16:1–8*. Stuttgarter Bibelstudien 33. Stuttgart: Katholisches Bibelwerk, 1969.

Scheppers, Frank. *The Colon Hypothesis: Word Order, Discourse Segmentation and Discourse Coherence in Ancient Greek*. Brussels: Brussels University Press, 2011.

———. "Discourse Segmentation, Discourse Structure and Sound Mapping (Including an Analysis of Mark 15)." In *Sound Matters: New Testament Studies in Sound Mapping*, edited by Margaret E. Lee, 133–78. BPCS 16. Eugene, OR: Cascade Books, 2018.

Scheub, Harold. "The Ntsomi: *A Xhosa* Performing Art." PhD diss., University of Wisconsin, 1969.

———. "Body and Image in Oral Narrative Performance." *New Literary History* 8 (1977) 34–37.

Schlesinger, Arthur. "Marshall McLuhan: The Man and His Message." PBS, Feb. 11, 1985.

Schmithals, W. "Der Markusschluss, die Verklärungsgeschichte und die Aussendung der Zwölf." *ZTK* 69 (1972) 379–411.

Schoeps, Hans-Joachim. *Paul: The Theology of the Apostle in the Light of Jewish Religious History*. Translated by Harold Knight. Philadelphia: Westminster, 1961.

———. *Theologie und Geschichte des Judenchristentums*. Tübingen: Mohr/Siebeck, 1949.

Schreiber, Johannes. *Theologie des Vertrauens: Eine redaktionsgeschichtliche Untersuchung des Markusevangeliums*. Hamburg: Furche, 1967.

———. "Die Christologie des Markusevangeliums." *ZTK* 58 (1961) 154–83.

Schürer, Emil. *The History of the Jewish People in the Age of Jesus Christ*. Vol. 2. Edited by G. Vermes, F. Millar, and M. Goodman. Edinburgh: T. & T. Clark, 1979.

Schwabe, M. "Greek Inscriptions Found at Beth Shearim in the Fifth Excavation Season." edited by G. Vermes, et al. *Israel Exploration Journal* 4:249–261. Edinburgh: T. & T. Clark, 1953.

Scott, Bernard Brandon. *Hear Then the Parable: A Commentary on the Parables of Jesus*. Minneapolis: Fortress, 1989.

Senior, Donald, and Carroll Stuhlmueller. *The Biblical Foundations for Mission*. Maryknoll, NY: Orbis, 1983.

Sevenster, J. N. *"Do You Know Greek? How Much Greek Could the First Jewish Christians Have Known?"* Novum Testamentum Supplements 19. Leiden: Brill, 1968.

Shiner, Whitney. *Proclaiming the Gospel: First-Century Performance of Mark*. Harrisburg, PA: Trinity, 2003.

Silberman, Lou H. "'*Habent Sua Fata Libelli*': The Role of Wandering Themes in Some Hellenistic Jewish and Rabbinic Literature." In *The Relationships among the Gospels: An Interdisciplinary Dialogue*, edited by William O. Walker Jr., 195–218. Trinity University Monograph Series in Religion 5. San Antonio: Trinity University Press, 1978.

Simon, Marcel. "La Migration à Pella: Légende ou réalité?" In *Judéo–Christianisme: Volume offert au Cardinal Jean Daniélou. Recherches de science religieuse* 60 (1972) 37–54.

———. *Verus Israel: Étude sur les relations entre chrétiens et juifs dans l'empire romain.* Paris: Boccard, 1948.

———. *Verus Israel: A Study of the Relations between Christians and Jews in the Roman Empire (135–425).* Translated by H. McKeating. Littman Library of Jewish Civilization. New York: Oxford University Press, 1986.

Slusser, Michael. "Reading Silently in Antiquity." *JBL* 111 (1992) 499.

Stark, Rodney. *The Rise of Christianity: How the Obscure, Marginal Jesus Movement Became the Dominant Religious Force in the Western World in a Few Centuries.* San Francisco: HarperCollins, 1997.

Stein, Robert H. "The Ending of Mark." *Bulletin for Biblical Research* 18.1 (2008) 79–98.

———. "Is Our Reading the Bible the Same as the Original Audience's Hearing It? A Case Study of the Gospel of Mark." *Journal of the Evangelical Theological Society* 46 (2003) 63–78.

Strecker, Georg. "On the Problem of Jewish Christianity." In Walter Bauer, *Orthodoxy and Heresy in Earliest Christianity*, edited by Robert A. Kraft and Gerhard Krodel, 241–85. Translated by the Philadelphia Seminar on Christian Origins. Philadelphia: Fortress, 1971.

Szlezák, Thomas Alexander. *Platon und die Schriftlichkeit der Philosophie.* Berlin: de Gruyter, 1985.

Tannehill, Robert C. "The Disciples in Mark: The Function of a Narrative Role." *Journal of Religion* 57 (1977) 386–405.

Taylor, Vincent. *The Gospel according to St. Mark.* London: St. Martin's, 1952.

Thatcher, Tom, ed. *The Dictionary of the Bible and Ancient Media.* London: Bloomsbury T. & T. Clark, 2017.

Theissen, Gerd. *The Miracle Stories of the Early Christian Tradition.* Translated by Francis McDonagh. Edited by John Riches. Edinburgh: T. & T. Clark, 1983.

———. *Urchristliche Wundergeschichten: Ein Beitrag zur formgeschichtlichen Erforschung der synoptischen Evangelien.* Studien zum Neuen Testament 8. Gütersloh: Mohn, 1974.

Thomas, Rosalind. *Literacy and Orality in Ancient Greece.* Cambridge: Cambridge University Press, 1992.

———. *Oral Tradition and Written Record in Classical Athens.* Cambridge: Cambridge University Press, 1989.

Tolbert, Mary Ann. *Sowing the Gospel: Mark's World in Literary-Historical Perspective.* Minneapolis: Fortress, 1989.

Trompf, G. W. "The First Resurrection Appearance and the Ending of Mark's Gospel." *NTS* 18 (1972) 308–30.

———. "The Markusschluss in Recent Research." *Australian Biblical Review* 21 (1973) 15–26.

Tyson, J. B. "The Blindness of the Disciples in Mark." *JBL* 80 (1961) 261–68.

Vermes, Geza. "Scripture and Oral Tradition in Judaism: Written and Oral Torah." In *The Written Word: Literacy in Transition*, edited by G. Baumann, 79–95. Oxford: Oxford University Press, 1986.

Vielhauer, Philipp. *Geschichte der urchristlichen Literatur: Einleitung in das Neue Testament, die Apokryphen und die Apostolischen Väter*. De Gruyter Lehrbuch. Berlin: de Gruyter, 1975.

Visotzky, Burton L. "Methodological Considerations in the Study of John's Interaction with First-Century Judaism." In *Life in Abundance: Studies of John's Gospel in Tribute to Raymond E. Brown*, edited by John R. Donahue, 91–107. Collegeville, MN: Liturgical, 2005.

Weeden, Theodore J. *Mark: Traditions in Conflict*. Philadelphia: Fortress, 1971.

Wellek, René, and Austin Warren. *Theory of Literature*. New York: Harcourt, Brace, 1942.

Wilentz, Joan Steen. *The Senses of Man*. New York: Crowell, 1968.

Woodthrope, William. *Alexander the Great*. Boston: Beacon, 1956.

Wrede, William. *The Messianic Secret*. Library of Theological Translations. Cambridge: James Clarke, 1971 (orig. 1901).

———. *Paul*. Translated by Edward Lummis. Boston: American Unitarian Association, 1908.

———. *Paulus*. Religionsgeschichtliche Volksbücher für die deutsche christliche Gegenwart 1. 5/6. Göttingen: Vandenhoeck & Ruprecht, 1907.

Yadin, Yigael. *Bar-Kokhba*. London: Weidenfeld & Nicolson, 1971.

Youtie, H. C. "*Agrammatos*: An Aspect of Greek Society in Egypt." *Harvard Studies in Classical Philology* 75 (1971) 161–76.

———. "*Bradeos graphoth*: Between Literacy and Illiteracy." *Greek, Roman, and Byzantine Studies* 12 (1971) 239–61.

———. "*Hypographeus*: The Social Impact of Illiteracy in Graeco-Roman Egypt." *Zeitschrift für Papyrologie und Epigraphik* 17 (1975) 201–21.

———. "Pétaus, fils de Pétaus, ou le scribe qui ne savait pas écrire." *Chronique d' Egypte* 41 (1966) 127–43.

Author Index

Subject Index

academic biblical courses, pedagogy of performance in, 11

Academy at Jamnia, 209, 210, 234

accent systems, development of, 26

actors, in drama, 12

Acts 2, devout Jews from every nation, 15

adversaries of Jesus, Mark engaging his audience as, 179

age of the Enlightenment, paradigm of biblical interpretation in, 28, 198

Alexander and Rufus
father of, 190, 192, 200, 204
Luke and Matthew not naming, 204
as a narrative comment, 203

Alexander the Great, literate culture and, 47

alienation effect, of a parable, 64

allegorical and theological methods, 40

allegorical interpretation, 26, 235

Ambrose, reading in silence, 103, 122–23, 214n20

anachronistic character, of biblical interpretation, 198

anagnostes, or professional reader, 197

ancient communication culture, as an early literate culture, 148

ancient education, trained memory as the goal of, 148

ancient literacy, William Harris's comprehensive study of, 213n14

ancient literate culture, place of the Gospel in, 213

ancient literature, 148, 214n17

ancient world
media cultures of, 1, 168–69
most people as illiterate, 9, 121
orality and literacy in, 122
reading aloud in, 103

ancient writers, as more like composers, 207

ancient writing, with no division of words, punctuation of sentences, or arrangement in paragraphs, 214

annotation, history of, 103–4

antiquity
communication culture of, 194n9
orality and literacy in, 46–55

apocalyptic, as cosmic, holistic thinking, 65

apocalyptic discourse, 179, 205

apostolic commission, Mark 16:8 and, 83–97

apostolic mission, Mark's concern about, 92

appositives, comments in the form of, 73

Aramaic, 45, 199–200

archives, transition from to libraries, 47

Aristotle, 48, 100

arrest and flight, short endings in, 134

King Artaxerxes, Ezra and, 51

Ashurbanipal, collection of, 48

Athens, literate culture in, 47